IEE DIGITAL ELECTRONICS AND COMPUTING SERIES 3

Series Editors: S.L. Hurst
M.W. Sage

Software engineering for microprocessor systems

Previous volumes in this series

Volume 1 Stochastic and determinist averaging processes
P. Mars and W.J. Poppelbaum

Volume 2 Semi-Custom IC design and VLSI
P.J. Hicks (Editor)

Software engineering for microprocessor systems

Edited by

P. Depledge

Peter Peregrinus Ltd
on behalf of the Institution of Electrical Engineers

Published by: Peter Peregrinus Ltd., London, UK.

ISBN 0 86341 016 2

Printed in England by Short Run Press Ltd., Exeter

Contents

List of contributors

Chapter 1
I. SOMMERVILLE
Dept. of Computer Science
University of Strathclyde
George Street
Glasgow

Chapter 2
P.G. DEPLEDGE
Dept. of Electrical and Electronic Engineering
UMIST
P.O. Box 88
Manchester M60 1QD

Chapter 3
R.D. DOWSING
School of Computing and Accountancy
University of East Anglia
Norwich NR4 7TJ

Chapter 4
M.T. FERGUSON
Dept. of Electrical and Electronic Engineering
UMIST
P.O. Box 88
Manchester M60 1QD

Chapter 5
A.C. DAVIES
Centre for Information Engineering
The City University
Northampton Square
London EC1V 0HB

Chapters 6 & 13
D.G. JENKINS, M.K. CROWE
Dept. of Mathematics and Computing
Paisley College of Technology
High Street
Paisley
Renfrew P1 2BE

Chapter 7
S.J. YOUNG
Dept. of Computation
UMIST
P.O. Box 88
Manchester M60 1QD

Chapter 8
H.W. THOMAS
University of Manchester
Oxford Road
Manchester

Chapter 9
R.H. PIERCE
Software Sciences
London and Manchester House
Park Lane
Macclesfield
Cheshire

Chapter 10
J. SHEMELD
Electronics Laboratory
University of Kent
Canterbury
Kent

Chapter 11
R. SPENCER, P. van der LINDEN
High Integrity Systems
41 Bell Street
Sawbridgeworth
Herts CM23 9AR

Chapter 12
N.C. SEDGEWICK
CAP Microsoft Ltd
233 High Holborn
London

Chapter 14
B.A. CARRÉ
Dept. of Electronics
The University
Southampton
SO9 5NH

Chapter 15
D.A. STUART
Marconi Avionics Ltd
Elstree Way
Borehamwood
Herts

Chapters 16 & 18
J. GALLACHER
Craigavon
Boltachan
Aberfeldy
PH15 2LB

Chapter 17
J.M. PORTEOUS
British Telecom
Room 260
207 Old Street
London EC1V 9PS

Preface

In several respects the development of the microcomputer has followed the same evolutionary path as the mainframe computer. Some of the lessons learnt in the development of computers have been remembered, others forgotten or ignored. One particular aspect of the utilisation of microcomputers that has too often been neglected is the employment of good engineering practice in the specification, design, implementation and validation of software. As the complexity of microcomputer-based systems has grown, it has become increasingly apparent that the ad-hoc software production techniques employed by many microcomputer engineers are inadequate. This situation has arisen for many reasons. These include the commercial pressures on engineers to develop products quickly in a very competitive market, the lack of good software tools and a poor understanding by engineering management of the problems of controlling software production. Another significant factor is that the electronic engineering community, which has been responsible for the development of most microcomputer products, has had only a limited education in software engineering. Within the constraints of an electrical engineering degree course, the learning of a programming language is typically as close to software engineering as the student is taken.

In an attempt to introduce some of the more important aspects of software engineering to electrical engineers, the IEE Computing and Control Division Professional Group C6 organised a Vacation School at the University of Kent in Canterbury in September 1983. This book consists of the notes produced by lecturers in giving this course.

Whilst it should be appreciated that in a text of this size, many aspects of this broad and expanding subject cannot be covered adequately, it is hoped that this book will serve as a useful introduction and stimulate further investigation of the techniques described.

I wish to express my sincere thanks to all those who contributed to the organisation of the School and to the lecturers whose efforts made this enterprise such a success.

Peter G. Depledge,
UMIST.

Chapter 1

Why software engineering?

I. Sommerville

1. INTRODUCTION

Like many other terms associated with information technology, the term 'software engineering' has been subject to a number of different interpretations. In some cases, it is applied to the construction of systems which require knowledge of both computer hardware and software. In other instances, it is simply another name for computer programming, and in yet others it is applied exclusively to the production of very large software systems.

However, if we take a dictionary definition of engineering and apply that to the term 'software engineering' we get a definition as follows:

> The profession of applying scientific principles to the design, construction, and maintenance of computer software systems.

This definition emphasises that software engineering is not just computer programming - the implementation of software systems - but includes all aspects of software production from initial conception through to maintenance after delivery of the completed software system.

The problems of developing software systems are akin to the problems which arise in other engineering disciplines - costs and complexity must be controlled and people must be managed and motivated. Software engineering embraces such non-technical considerations as documentation, user psychology, and software project management as well as the technical aspects of software design and production.

Software engineering is becoming of increasing importance as programmable microelectronic systems are used in more and more applications. Before such systems, the electronic systems engineer may have used computers to help him in his work but had no real need to develop well-engineered software systems. He may have been an amateur programmer writing 'cheap and nasty' programs but it was not cost effective for him to spend a lot of time developing professional quality software systems.

Now, software and hardware are so closely interlinked that it is essential that the electronic engineer has an understanding of the principles of software engineering and an appreciation of the true costs associated with software development. In the remainder of these notes, the stages of development of a software system, their associated costs, and the characteristics of well-engineered software are described.

2. THE SOFTWARE LIFE CYCLE

In the development and use of a software system, a number of distinct, interacting phases can be identified. These can be compared with the phases passed through by an insect or an animal as it is born, reaches maturity and ultimately dies. Hence, the term 'software life cycle' has been coined to describe these phases of a software system.

The stages of the software life cycle are:

(1) Specification
Before any software is actually produced, the functions of the software must be established and the operational constraints on that software defined.

(2) Design
The software specification must be analysed and a software design established. A software design is a machine independent statement of how individual programs units must interact to implement the software specification.

(3) Implementation
The software design is realised in a computer programming language which can be executed by the target computer destined to run the software system.

(4) Validation
This phase of the software life cycle is intended to validate that the implemented software meets the needs of the user. Sometimes, this stage is called 'testing and debugging' but this implies that it is concerned solely with validating the implementation phase of the life cycle. In fact, during this validation phase, it is common to detect errors and oversights in all preceding life cycle stages.

(5) Operation and Maintenance
The software system is put into use. As it is used, errors which have been missed by the validation phases are often detected and must be corrected. Furthermore, as the software system becomes an essential feature of the user's environment, the user's perception of what the software ought to do for him will change and the software must be modified to meet these changing user needs. Lehman (2) has called this process 'software evolution'.

As set out above, the software life cycle seems to be a straightforward linear progression from phase to phase. In fact, it is a cyclic rather than a linear process where each phase interacts with preceeding and succeeding phases. Usually, work done in early stages of the life cycle must be redone as problems arise in the later life cycle stages. As the design progresses, specification errors will be discovered requiring the specification to be changed. Some parts of the design may place constraints on the implementors, others may be unimplementable in the programming language used for the project. Thus, the design and possibly even the specification may have to be changed after the implementation phase has begun. Changes occur throughout the software development process and many software problems have come about because the complexity of the life cycle model has not been recognised.

Because of the interacting nature of the life cycle stages, it is difficult to establish an accurate costing for individual phases of the life cycle. Most estimators, such as Boehm (1), have made the simplification that the software life cycle is a linear process. Taking this simplification into account, there is a gross imbalance between the costs of software development, that is, producing the software in the first place, and the costs of software maintenance. Maintenance costs, the costs of modifying the software to correct errors and to adapt it to changing requirements are orders of magnitude greater than software development costs.

Specification, design, and implementation each account for about 20% of the total software development costs with the remainder taken up by validation costs. Therefore, if a system costs $1 000 000 to develop, the most expensive stage of that development will be software validation which might cost about $400 000. Maintaining that software after it has gone into operation, however, is likely to cost at least $5 000 000.

Typically, software maintenance costs are about 5 times development costs. However, for some types of system such as complex real-time systems reliant on state-of-the art hardware and subject to tight efficiency constraints, the system maintenance costs may be several hundred times the development costs. An example of this, cited in (1), estimated that for one USAF avionics system, the development cost was $30 per instruction and the maintenance cost was $4000 per instruction.

3. THE CHARACTERISTICS OF WELL-ENGINEERED SOFTWARE

Whilst it is all very well to talk in glib terms of software engineering, the software life cycle, etc. the working software engineer is faced with the problem of recognising well-engineered as distinct from poorly-engineered software. There are a number of criteria which can be used to assess software - space and time efficiency, speed of implementation, readability, etc. not all of which should be given equal importance in deciding if the software is well-engineered or not.

Bearing in mind the distribution of costs over the

software life cycle and the professional responsibility of the engineer, well-engineered software should exhibit three dominant characteristics:

(1) It should provide the facilities and operate within the constraints set out in the software specification.

(2) It should be reliable.

(3) It should be readily modifiable.

The first of these characteristics is, of course, a very general characteristic and places a great responsibility on the individuals responsible for drawing up the software specification. It is very common indeed for software systems to fail to meet the intentions of customers because of inadequate and ambiguous specifications and it is arguable whether such software should be considered well-engineered ot not. Our present notations for specifying software functions and constraints are grossly inadequate and until new notations are developed, it will remain very difficult to measure how well a software system meets its specifications.

As software systems become more diverse and are used in more and more application areas, it is becoming clear that reliability is the most important dynamic characteristic of a software system. This is partly due to the fact that software systems are now used as control systems in many larger systems whose failure could endanger life and partly due to cost considerations - unreliable software is very expensive indeed.

The immense costs of unreliable software can be illustrated by examples of situations where software system failure result in very high costs to the software customer.

Say a software system controls the drilling of an off-shore oil well. The cost of running an oil rig runs into thousands of dollars per hour and a software failure causing drilling to be suspended can result in costs which far exceed the original software costs.

Another type of situation where the costs of software failure may exceed the software development costs could arise in a situation where ROM based software controls the braking system in a car. Errors in the software, discovered after the car has gone into production, would result in all cars sold being recalled and the ROMs replaced. So far, this situation has not arisen but as ROM-based software is used in more and more products, it is likely that such a situation will eventually come about.

The third characteristic of well-engineered software - that it should be readily modifiable - arises directly from a consideration of life cycle costs. Because software maintenance, that is, the modification of existing software, is far and away the most expensive aspect of the software life cycle, the software development stage should be geared towards producing a readily maintained software system. This means that readability should take place over writeability - programs are read more often than they are written, documentation should be clear, concise, and complete, and program and data structuring techniques should be used so that the software is built as a loosely interacting system of independent components rather than a closely interlinked monolithic system.

Notice that a software characteristic which is not an explicit feature of well-engineered software is efficiency. This does not mean that efficiency is unimportant - in some cases efficiency in terms of operational execution speed or the size of the object software system is of paramount importance. However, this is not universally true and, as hardware becomes cheaper and single chips become more complex and powerful, software efficiency considerations are likely to become less and less important in the majority of software systems.

In those cases where software efficiency must take precedence over considerations such as modifiability, this ought to be clearly stated in the software specifications. The efficiency specifications are of particular importance to the microprocessor software engineer who must fit his system into as few chips as possible or who may have to construct a control system with a given response time. It is his responsibility to ensure that the software specifications are clear on this point and that the trade-off between efficiency and other software characteristics is made clear to the software customer.

To conclude, the production of well-engineered, professional software must be based on an appreciation of the real costs of software systems, an understanding of user problems, and on the individual professional integrity of the software engineer. The software engineer must be aware of and be able to apply developments in software technology which allow him to improve the quality of the systems he develops and maintains.

The answer to the question 'why software engineering?' is straightforward. Future economic progress depends on the production of reliable, maintainable software systems. We cannot afford to adopt any less professional approach to a subject area which will consume an increasing proportion of our intellectual and economic resources.

REFERENCES

1. Boehm, B.W.. 1975. The High Cost of Software. In 'Practical Strategies for Developing Large Software Systems'. ed. Horowitz, E, Reading, Mass. : Addison Wesley.

2. Lehman, M.M. 1980. Programs, Life Cycles and the Laws of Software Evolution. Proc. IEEE. 68(9), 1060-1076

Chapter 2

Software engineering terms and concepts

P.G. Depledge

2.1 INTRODUCTION

The purpose of this chapter is to introduce many of the terms and concepts that will be expanded upon later in the text and to outline the contents of the remainder of the book. As we have already observed, the overall life of a software system can, like any properly executed piece of engineering, be broken down into five major stages, i.e. specification, design, implementation, testing and operation. It is implicit that over the operational life of the system some maintenance will have to carried out, typically by staff not involved in the original design. It is this aspect of software production that is frequently neglected and a significant portion of this text is dedicated to addressing this problem either directly or indirectly.

The treatment of software engineering in the following chapters is biased towards the use of microprocessors or, more correctly, microcomputers in embedded systems. An embedded system involves the application of a computer as a component within a product rather than the computer being a product itself. Thus from an external viewpoint it may not be apparent that a computer forms any part of the system. By their very nature such systems are normally employed in real-time applications. These are situations in which a system must respond to a stimulus from a physical event within a time-critical period. Thus we are relating time to actual hours, minutes and seconds rather than computer clock cycles since the stimulus generating system will have its own "cycle time" that is asynchronous to the computer's machine cycles. Although from the software engineering point of view this distinction between real- and non-real-time applications may be largely irrelevant, it does affect, for the present at least, the kind of aids that are available to the programmer and is important to our consideration of the implementation and testing stages of a software-based system.

In our attempt to introduce software engineering to electrical engineers, we have chosen not to describe the elements of the five stages strictly in order and have occasionally diverted our attention to certain points prematurely in order to clarify the discussion.

2.2 SPECIFICATION

It is obvious that the first stage in producing a software system must be the generation of a requirements specification which defines the functions to be performed. The resulting requirements document is not concerned with the internal operation of the system but rather with its external characteristics. However, certain constraints on its implemenatation may be included, for example programming language or run-time environment to be employed. Ideally the specification should be unambiguous, complete and consistent. This goal is unfortunately difficult to achieve particularly in applications where the original specifier or purchaser of the system is not experienced in software engineering. This is very relevant to many microcomputer applications in industry where the specification may be drawn up by, for example, chemical engineers who are not aware of the capabilities of a computer-based system and are unfamiliar with computing terminology. This causes an immediate communication problem that is difficult to overcome. A common approach is for each party to become partially educated in the other's field but this is far from satisfactory. A more satisfactory solution is to produce a conceptual model of the system, Heninger(1), which indicates the main functions to be performed in a form that is clear to the non-specialist. The model will generally consist of arrows, boxes and circles which show the data flowing from one function to another without implying a particular solution.

Having agreed a model for the system, the next stage in the specification process would be to translate this into a more formalised software requirements document. This must include the functional requirements shown by the conceptual model and non-functional requirements such as input scan rates, response times etc. The traditional method of expressing the requirements is to combine the functional and non-functional aspects into a natural language (e.g. English) description typically in some hierarchical format. There are numerous drawbacks to this approach including problems of interpretation, the ambiguity of natural language and inadequate partitioning of the requirements. In addition requirements specified in this way do not lend themselves to computer analysis for consistency or completeness. To overcome this problem, several attempts have been made at defining structured languages tailored to requirements specification, Bell et al.(2). These bear similarities to modern programming languages, although they are less formally defined, and are most appropriate for the functional part of the specification. The non-functional requirements would still have to be specified in natural language.

In addition to these aspects of the system specification, the requirements document must also include assumptions made about the hardware implementation and maintenance operations. A glossary defining the software engineering and process specific terms used in the document is also essential.

Any ambiguities or other defects in the requirements specification will propagate through the design and the systems operational life. It is therefore essential that, as far as possible, errors are removed from this document. A validation process must be included as part of the specification to show consistency, completeness, realism and that the specification adequately meets the needs of the user. The last aspect can sometimes usefully be demonstrated by the construction of a prototype although this has to be approached with some care otherwise, at the two extremes, an inadequately representative model will be produced or the protoype will be unjustifiably expensive. The availabilty of a good development environment such as the Unix system described in Chapter 10 can be of particular help in the construction of a prototype software system.

2.3 DESIGN

The quality of the of the design of a piece of software affects not only the implmentation of the design but also the life-cycle costs of the resulting product. A well designed program will not only be more reliable than a program developed in an ad hoc manner and require less maintenance, but it will also be more easily maintained as the product requirements change during its lifetime. Poor program design has been a characteristic of many microcomputer systems over the past years. This is due to a variety of reasons. Firstly, many of the implementors of microcomputer software have had no formal training in software design techniques or even programming in some cases. Often such people have been "taught" programming by learning the rules of a language such as BASIC or FORTRAN with little consideration being given to the principles of program design. Secondly, it is only relatively recently that appropriate high-level language compilers have become available for many microprocessors. This has led to the development of much microcomputer software in assembly langauge and in extreme cases hexadecimal code! Whilst it is quite possible to implement high-quality software in assembly language particularly if macro features are used to provide high-level language features, it is much too easy to develop poorly structured programs based on a scribbled flow chart. Thus there is often little encouragement to use good design techniques and the result is usually that the design and implementation stages become indistinct and "spaghetti code" is generated. Thirdly, the development environments provided for the production of microcomputer software have generally been inadequate with little support for software engineering design methodologies. Even today many microcomputer development systems provide inadequate help in the production of good quality software and documentation. Finally, the development of the microprocessor has taken place at the same time as the development of the subject of software engineering. The term software engineering itself was first used in 1968, only three years before the first commercial microprocessor was available. It is perhaps not surprising that semiconductor manufacturers, bearing in mind the competiveness of their industry, have often not provided adequate software aids for their products. Today it should be possible to find an appropriate development environment for a microprocessor. If one cannot be found the only sensible solution is to look for another processor!

A common design methodology used in the production of a software system is the top down approach. In this methodology the design is developed in a series of stages with each successive stage being a more refined version of the last until, finally, excutable code is produced. As an example, a system to control a piece of industrial plant might initially be broken down into three components, input reading, control algorithm and control outputs. Notice that no mention of how these components is to be implemented has been made. The next stage would be to refine these components further, for example, elaborating on how the input reading is to be organised, outlining the control law etc. The details of the implementation are thus developed at an appropriate point rather than clouding more important structural decisions at an early stage.

In order for the top down methodology to be employed effectively, we must have a suitable notation for expressing our ideas. Ideally this notation should reinforce the concepts of good program design and discourage the generation of spaghetti code. Additionally it would be highly desirable for the notation used in the design process to serve two other roles. Firstly if the notation could be used to validate or formally prove the correctness of the design before coding then a significant reduction in development costs would occur and the resulting code would be more reliable. This is not yet feasible for the majority of programmers because of the mathematical background required, but significant progress is being made in this area, Jones(3), Bjorner and Jones(4). Secondly, if the design notation can be used to document the program, then a seperate exercise in producing maintenance documentation may not be required. Apart fron the obvious time saving, we are also ensured that the maintenance information corresponds to the actual software. The use of the design notation in this manner should be perfectly feasible.

Several notations have been developed for use in the design of a software system. These are typically based on either a structured high-level programming language or on a graphical repesentation. The notations that are based on programming languages include the three basic activities of sequence, choice and iteration described in Chapters 3,4 and 5 and have the advantage that it should be relatively straightforward to check the consistency of the design and translate it into the target programming language. The notations that are based on a graphical notation include flowcharts, data flow diagrams, Warnier Orr diagrams, syntax diagrams, structure diagrams and HIPO charts. These are described in more detail in Chapter 4 and in Sommerville(5).

Once the design has been completed using one of the notations described, the result should be validated in an attempt to verify that the software design is correct (i.e. it complies with the designers' perception of the solution) and that it meets the requirements specification. These objectives can be achieved, as alluded to earlier, using mathematical proofs although this currently a difficult process. In addition other techniques which use control-,data- and information-flow analysis to check for inconsistencies, bad programming practice and to analyse the program structure can be employed. These flow analysis techniques are largely mechanical in nature and, like the mathematical proofs, require considerable discipline on the part of the programmer. Both these techniques are discussed in detail in Chapter 14. A less rigorous approach to showing that a design meets its specification and that it is correct, is to carry out a design review. This normally involves using a team of programmers or an individual not involved in the project, to check the design and its verification procedures.

2.4 IMPLEMENTATION

Consideration of the implementation of a software system must include two important aspects, the programming language and the development environment to be employed. The programming language is the medium through which the implementor builds his system and its features are of obvious importance. The development environment is the equivalent of a craftsmans workshop and it describes the hardware and software tools available to the programmer. We shall now consider the features that are of importance to the programmer in these two areas.

2.4.1 Programming Languages

Although several thousand programming languages have been developed over the last 25 years, there are only a relatively small number in common usage today. However in spite of the small number, there is significant controversy about the quality of existing programming languages and about the features desirable in a language. In the application of microcomputers to solving real-time problems, the number of languages available is very limited and some features we might regard as mandatory. The desirable features of a high-level programming language are discussed in detail in Chapter 5 whilst chapter 7 outlines the particular requirements for handling real-time events. For the present we shall consider how programming languages can be classified and the broader aspects of choosing a language.

The lowest-level of programming language is assembly language. Assembly languages are essentially concerned with the manipulation of the processor registers and memory rather than problem solving. In general there is a one-to-one correspondence between an assembly language statement and a machine instruction although many of the better assembly languages allow macros which enable some higher-level features to be included. Although some attempts have, and still are, being made at defining standard assembly languages, most assembly languages are particular to a given processor or its relatives and all require an intimate understanding of the processors operation. Because it is so closely linked with machine operation, there is a large gulf between assembly language and the design notations discussed earlier. The translation from design to implmentation is thus a difficult and error-prone operation. For this reason, it is difficult to justify the use of assembly language except in rare circumstances. In normal programming these might include limited areas where very efficient execution is required and applications where a special-purpose processor is being employed that has an architecture that is unsuitable for high-level language compilers.

The other major class of programming language are the high-level languages. These languages are usually related to particular applications rather than to the processor itself. Their statements allow meaningful names for the entities to be manipulated, allow relatively complex decision making and generally are easier to read and understand than assembly language (although there are one or two notable exceptions to this). Furthermore each high-level language statement may generate a large number of machine instructions. A common criticism of high-level language compilers, particularly those for microcomputers, is that they generate inefficient code. Even if this is true, and it is certainly less so nowadays, the other advantages of high-level implementation far outweigh the potential losses in code efficiency. The ease of development and maintenance are of greater importance in almost every application.

Falling between high-level and assembly languages come what are often called systems implementation languages. These languages share many of the features of higher level languages whilst still allowing easy access to the underlying machine hardware. Typical applications for such languages are in writing operating systems and their associated utilities. The programming language C, developed at The Bell Laboratories, is perhaps the most commonly used of this class of language and is becoming increasingly popular as an alternative to assembly language for microprocessors, Ritchie et al(6). C provides support for structured programming and with some care can be used to produce reliable software. However because of its terse style and its low-level features programs written in C can be difficult to decipher.

We now come to the true high-level languages. These are sometimes classed according to the way in which they allocate storage to a program. The older high-level languages such as FORTRAN use a static storage allocation scheme which enables the compiler to evaluate the memory requirements for the program and its variables before execution. The use of static storage allocation is a limitation on the programmer although it makes life simpler for the compiler designer. At the other extreme are languages like LISP and APL in which all storage allocation is performed dynamically as a program is executed. There are no general-purpose languages that use full dynamic storage allocation and those languages that exist are tailored to specific applications such as list processing. Between these two extremes come the increasingly popular block-structured languages that have largely evolved from ALGOL. Perhaps the most commonly used block-structured language is Pascal. In such languages the program is naturally made up of a set of blocks. As each block of program is entered or left the store required for the block to be executed is automatically allocated or de-allocated respectively. This scheme has one significant advantage and that is that variables have a limited scope, i.e. they are only accessible within the block in which they are declared. This means that variables have some protection against inadvertent interference from another part of the program. Some languages, for example MODULA-2 and Ada, extend this concept further and permit the definition of modules (or packages) to provide even better security. Both MODULA-2 and Ada are significant in the context of this book in that they provide support for real-time applications and they are described in some detail in Chapters 8 and 9 respectively. It is apparent that these two languages and any others that are available which share their features, should be the first choice for a real-time application.

2.4.2 Development Environments

The environment in which a software system is developed is of crucial importance to the success of a project since it has a great impact upon programmer efficiency, documentation quality, project management and product quality. In this book we are primarily concerned with the software aspects of microcomputer-based product development and so we will assume that appropriate aids are available for hardware development and testing although, given the availabilty of a good software development environment, hardware engineers would find some of the facilities useful particularly in the production of documentation. As a first requirement of a software development environment we need a computer. Most early microcomputer development systems were based on 8-bit microprocessors with a fairly limited amount of store and a pair of floppy disks. These, largely because of the primitive design of the microprocessors employed, had a poor performance and were unable to provide adequate software support. The general weakness of this approach has more recently been recognised and with the availabilty of more powerful 16-bit microcomputers, better systems are emerging. These typically have a large amount of working store, hard disk(s) and a powerful operating system such as Unix. The development computer is often quite distinct from the target machine and must therefore support some mechanism for transferring programs to the target machine. During the testing phase this is most coveniently achieved using a hardware link rather than PROM.

The software development environment must obviously provide the language translators (i.e. compilers and assemblers), module linkers and libraries to allow a program to be converted into machine code. An extremely important feature of the translators is the quality of the error reporting provided. Although it is a difficult task for the compiler designer to generate helpful error reports it is essential that these are provided. The libraries provided may include standard I/O drivers, special-function routines and some of the algorithms described in Chapter 6. More comprehensive systems may also provide code for real-time operating systems including the features outlined in Chapter 13. The programmer also needs an editor program to create and modify files. The most suitable type is the screen editor, which allows the programmer to view a VDU screenful of text at a time and, typically via a cursor, insert, delete, and replace characters, lines and blocks of text. In addition a good screen editor should provide character-string searching and replacement and command repetition. Some language translators are intimately linked with a screen editor and upon detection of an error automatically invoke the editor and position the cursor at the predicted point of mistake. Another increasingly important feature of program development environments is some means of controlling the way in which code is modified. Two such aids are SCCS and MAKE which run under Unix and are described briefly in Chapter 10.

As well as aids to program translation, a software development environment should also provide support for:-

(i) requirements specification and validation,
(ii) text processing for documentation production,
(iii) testing,debugging and validation and
(iv) project management software for estimation, planning and progress monitoring.

Probably the most well known development environment that approaches these requirements is the Unix Programmers Work Bench. The Ada language project also includes the specification for such a system called APSE (Ada programming support environment) the main features of which are described in Chapter 11.

2.5 TESTING

The major emphasis of software engineering is to produce high-quality programs that are reliable and easy to maintain. Throughout the discussion so far, stress has been placed on those aspects of software system production which will assist in the development of error-free code. However, even with meticulous care, it is likely that some errors will occur in the design or implementation. In order to increase overall confidence in the software it is necessary to perform tests in order to identify the existence of errors and to follow this with a debugging procedure in order to correct the error-generating fault. It is important to realise that testing alone cannot prove the correctness of a program simply because of the number of permutations of states in the system. VLSI circuit designers are now faced with a similar problem of complexity.

It has already been suggested that verification methods be employed at both the specification and design stages and it could be reasonable to assume that formal verification should also take place after the implementation since more errors can be generated at this stage. Unfortunately this is even more difficult to achieve than at the earlier stages and hence even more expensive. It is usually far more cost-effective and beneficial to validate the system at the earlier stages and rely on less rigorous testing at implementation time.

Testing usually takes place at several levels of implementation since the testing of the complete software system as a single unit is unlikely to be very productive initially. Starting at the lowest level, the basic building block of the system is a "function" which has a single role. Functions can normally be tested in isolation as they are usually designed to operate without dependence on other functions at the same level. The next level in the hierarchy is the module which comprises several co-operating functions. Again it is normally possible to test modules individually. Modules are combined to form sub-systems and since we should be reasonably confident in the behaviour of the constituent modules, the testing effort at this stage is directed at detecting errors in the interfaces between modules. There are two main philosophies employed in testing functions, modules and sub-systems. These are top-down and bottom-up strategies. In the former, untested modules or functions are replaced by "stubs" which present the same interface as the original function or module, in the function or module under test. In bottom-up testing all the functions and modules are tested before being used in conjunction with each other. These two techniques are discussed further in Chapter 15.

We now come to the software integration stage when the various sub-systems are combined into a single entity. At this level we are concerned with checking the system operation against the requirements document and in particular that real-time performance is achieved. Real-time testing involves activating each process individually and testing its operation and then gradually observing the response to actively co-operating processes for a single stimulus and so on until stimulii of several types are active, representing a complete system. The MASCOT system, Jackson(7), is designed to help in the testing of real-time systems by permitting processes to be activated and removed without affecting others in the system. Finally acceptance tests must be carried out using real input and output data. These final tests can often show up inadequacies in the requirements specification.

2.6 MANAGEMENT ASPECTS

The production of large software systems has a poor reputation for meeting deadlines and cost estimates. An interesting book, amusingly entitled "The Mythical Man-Month", Brooks(8), describes a project that has led to this often justified reputation. Many of the projects that have failed in this way have suffered from bad management due to a general lack of understanding of appropriate techniques for controlling software projects. Although there are still many inadequacies, the availability of specification, design and implementation methodologies has led to a better general approach to software projects and experience has resulted in a more satisfactory management approach. The use of the kinds of procedures described in Chapter 16 are typical of modern industrial practice.

One aspect of software project management that has made some progress is in the estimation of programmer productivity and project timescales. This usually relies on historical data on previous projects within the company but general guidelines based on a large set of empirical data can be useful. These guidelines and their justification are considered in detail in Chapter 18.

REFERENCES

1. Heninger, K.L., 1980, 'Specifying Software Requirements for Complex Systems. New Techniques and their Applications.' IEEE Trans. Software Engineering, SE-6, 1, 2-13.

2. Bell, T.E., Bixler, D.C., and Dyer, M.E., 1977, 'An Extendible Approach To Computer Aided Software Requirements Engineering.' IEEE Trans. Software Engineering, SE-3, 1, 49-60.

3. Jones, C.B. , 1980, 'Software Development - A Rigorous Approach', Prentice-Hall International, London.

4. Bjorner, D., and Jones, C.B., 1982, 'Formal Specification and Software Development', Prentice-Hall International, London.

5. Sommerville, I., 1982, 'Software Engineering', Addison-Wesley, London.

6. Ritchie, D.M., Johnson, S.C., Lesk, M.E. and Kernighan, B.W., 1978, 'The C Programming Language', The Bell System Technical Journal, 57, 6, 1991-2020.

7. Jackson, K., 1977, 'Language Design for Modular Software Construction', Information Processing 77, 577-582, North-Holland, Amsterdam.

8. Brooks, F.P., 1975, 'The Mythical Man-Month', Addison-Wesley, Reading, Mass.

Chapter 3

Stepwise refinement

R.D. Dowsing

3.1 INTRODUCTION

In the general context of problem solving the major difficulty is one of understanding and containing complexity. A human being is not very efficient at dealing with large quantities of complex information as a single entity (1). The normal method by which humans contain complexity is to subdivide a problem into a number of subproblems and to deal with each of these subproblems independently.

There are a number of different ways of partitioning a problem into a set of subproblems. One of the best known methods is functional decomposition whereby a problem is broken down into a set of subproblems, the partitioning of which is based on the designers view of what subfunctions have to be solved to solve the original problem. For example, the functional decomposition of the problem of sorting a set of numbers might be

input the numbers
sort them
output the sorted numbers,

where the functions involved are input, sort and output. A different decomposition method is based on the structure of the data. For example, if the problem involved sorting a large amount of data the decomposition might be based on structuring the ordering of sorting subsets of the data. Which type of decomposition is used will vary with the type of problem under consideration. For microcomputers in engineering, it is the former method, based on decomposing the control flow, which is normally applicable, and the method which is described in this chapter (2). For applications which involve handling large quantities of data, for example, business applications, different techniques are applicable (3).

3.2 DESIGN METHODOLOGY

In order to understand a problem and produce a correct solution to it a number of different steps have to be taken by the problem solver

- Step 1 An understanding of the problem and the production of an unambiguous, correct, well defined statement of the problem to be solved
- Step 2 An analysis of the problem and an outline algorithm to solve the problem
- Step 3 Detailed design and implementation of the outline algorithm

Step 4 Testing of the implementation
Step 5 Maintenance of the product

Traditionally Steps 1 and 2 were performed by the system analyst and Steps 3 and 4 by the programmer with Step 5 being shared between them.

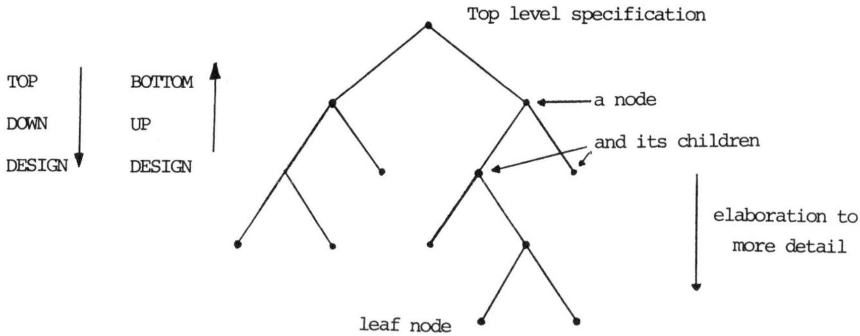

Fig.1.1 The elaboration tree structure showing stepwise refinement

There are a number of different ways of viewing this design process, for example, each stage may be viewed as a transformation of the previous stage, but the method adopted here is to view the process of gradually defining more and more detail as design and implementation proceeds, or stepwise refinement (Fig.1.1). At each level of the design there are a set of subproblems to be solved and implemented and these will be independent of each other. In Fig.1.1 the nodes of the tree structure represent stages in the gradual evolution of the problem statement to its solution. At each node design decisions are taken on how to further decompose the problem into more detail and this results in one or more child nodes. By only considering small steps of elaboration and only considering details as they become important the overall complexity can by managed. It is this management of complexity which is the challenge to the designer and implementor.

3.2.1 The benefits

If a structured method is adopted for problem solution then a number of benefits accrue to the user (see Fig.1.1)

a) the elaborations are independent of one another at the same level
b) any errors can be systematically traced back to the elaborations at higher levels
c) testing can be carried out of subsolutions separately from other subsolutions
d) at any stage of design only a small amount of information has to be manipulated
e) a design performed in this way is suitable for the application of formal mathematical techniques of analysis

3.2.2 The relationship to programming

Taking the tree structure shown in Fig.1.1, how is this

represented in program text? Bearing in mind that what is being done is that text is being expanded, section by section, in a modular fashion the program structure corresponding to Fig.3.1 is a "boxes-within-boxes" structure where an elaboration means replacing a statement by a set of statements, the process of stepwise refinement.

This structure looks, at first sight, to be a flowchart which it is but it has a particular property. The control flow into and out of any section of code which is a representation of a node , in the tree structure of Fig.3.1, is guaranteed to be a single entry point and a single exit point. In terms of normal programming practice this means that the scope of transfer-of-control instructions for example jumps is restricted. This restriction on transfer of control is imposed so that the flow of execution can be seen, in a relatively simple manner, from the structure of the code. Since debugging programs implies tracing back from where they failed to see how they arrived at the failure point the closer the structure of the program text follows the execution sequence the easier it is to reason about the execution sequence. Another reason for insisting on single entry-single exit control structures is that all structures then have identical control interfaces and so stepwise refinement, the process of replacing a simple control structure by a more complex one, is much simpler.

3.2.3 Programming Constructs for single entry-single exit control structures

In programming terms what is required is a set of control structures which exhibit the single entry-single exit control.

a) sequence

```
        A;B
```

Each of these two statements is single entry-single exit so that sequences of statements are a well formed structure

b) repetition

A structure is required where one or more actions, a sequence of actions, is repeated a number of times

```
    repeat   statement(s)
    until    condition

or  while    condition
      do     statement(s)

for example,   while  count > 1
                 do   add next value to total
                      subtract 1 from count
```

It is interesting to note that both constructs involve internal transfer of control under some condition but that, as far as the external interface is concerned they are both single entry, single exit control structures. Although these constructs do not occur in all programming languages they may be decomposed into lower level statements, for example

```
repeat  s  is equivalent to   L1:s
until   c                        if not(c) go to L1
```

What is important is that the designer designs using the structured version and that the translation to the "go to" version only happens at the last stage of implementation so that the required structure is preserved.

c) selection
   A simple selection statement is:-

   if C then A else B

   Again this statement involves internal transfer of control but the external interface is single entry, single exit.

d) subprograms

   The various types of subprogram, routines, procedures, functions are also structured control constructs provided that they are single entry, single exit structures.

The structures given above are just some of the possible control structures which obey the single entry, single exit rule. Other structures may be used if required, such as case, parbegin and for.

3.2.4 The use of these control constructs

The task of design and coding using these control structures is simply the elaboration of the outline design by replacing a simple statement by a more complex one, such as a series of statements or a repetition statement. Since the repetition and selection structures internally contain a statement or set of statements these in turn may be elaborated further by the substitution of a statement by some other more complex statement and hence nested control structures can result. Elaboration is complete when the complete problem solution is described in the required language.

At each stage of elaboration the designer has to make some choices about how the elaboration should be done. These decisions concern how to map objects in the problem domain onto components of the programming language such as data structures. Associated with these decisions will be implementation constraints such as the size of memory available, the speed of the processor and the input-output mechanisms. The decisions taken will also be influenced by the level of the programming language to be used. This means that the detailed algorithm chosen for a high level language implementation may be different from that chosen for an assembly code implementation because design tradeoffs will differ for the different languages.

To comprehend the benefits of using this technique is difficult, if not impossible, unless the reader tries some design for himself. It is strongly suggested, therefore, that the reader attempts to solve the problem outlined in the following section before reading the author's solution. It is only through much practice that the application of these techniques leads to better design approaches.

3.3 AN EXAMPLE OF THE USE OF STEPWISE REFINEMENT

3.3.1 Problem

A ten turn potentiometer is connected to an analog-digital (A-D) converter which is in turn interfaced to an Intel SDK-85 microcomputer system. Write a program which will display the potentiometer dial reading on the display of the SDK-85.

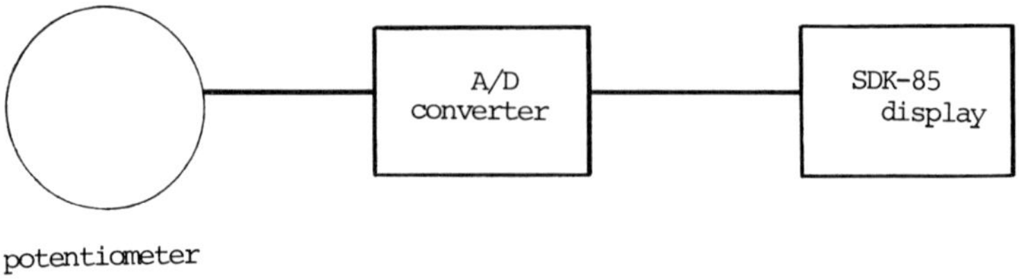

3.3.2 Initial considerations

The Intel SDK-85 is a simple microcomputer board including an 8085 processor, PROM monitor, RAM-I/O chip and display/keyboard. For this exercise two 8 bit I/O ports are required to interface the A/D converter, assuming 8 bits for data and 3 bits for control and status.

Assume port 0 = data from A/D converter
port 1 = bit 0 = convert signal
bit 1 = select signal (logic 1 for A-D conversion)
bit 2 = status signal
data valid = 0
data invalid = 1

To start A-D conversion a pulse 1-0-1 with a delay of $>$ 5mS in the 0 state must be given.

A monitor routine OUTPT, address 2B7H, is available to display information on the seven segment display. On calling the routine registers A and B must contain zero and H and L the starting address in memory of the characters to be sent. This routine automatically displays four characters. Another monitor routine READKB is available at address 2E7H to read a character from the keyboard.

3.3.3 An outline design

Before detailed design of the algorithm to solve this problem can proceed some general exploration of the problem is required. The nature of this exploration will obviously depend on the general approach of the designer, his experience and problem solving ability. There is no "correct" way to solve the problem; several different approaches may lead to equally good solutions. The solution given here is not the "best", it is simply the one which was produced using the author's experience and general perception of the problem.

The problem of using A-D converters lies in their accuracy and stability. For the problem under consideration a question arises as to how accurately the potentiometer position can be measured. For an 8 bit A-D converter the maximum resolution is 1 in 256. Assuming the potentiometer can be wired to give maximum swing on the input to the A-D converter for maximum and minimum potentiometer readings then ten turns of the potentiometer is equivalent to 256 values or a difference of one on the output of the A-D converter is equivalent to about 1/25th of a turn on the potentiometer. On the assumption that the A-D converter is accurate to $\pm$ 1 then a reasonable estimate of the accuracy to which a value can be displayed is one tenth of a turn.

The basic algorithm required to solve this problem is a read of the A-D input, a conversion to dial reading and an output to the display. Or is it? How can the conversion be performed? Should it be assumed that a reading of zero on the potentiometer produces zero input to the microcomputer? It probably does not, therefore we need some scaling. Secondly, is the output from the A-D converter linear with dial reading? Again, probably not, so we may have to use different scaling for different input values. To answer these questions some initial investigations of the equipment is required. After this initial investigation a decision can be taken and for this exercise it was decided that if readings were taken at potentiometer reading 1 turn and 9 turns linear scaling across the range would give a reasonably accurate value.

The result of this initial investigation, therefore, was an outline of the design with some simple experimental evidence that a solution based on these ideas was feasible.

3.3.4 The design

As shown above, preliminary thoughts and tests have suggested an outline design

```
L0      « initialise»
        « read 1 turn value of potentiometer»
        « read 9 turn value of potentiometer»
        « while TRUE do»
        « read unknown value»
        « convert to display value»
        « display value»
        endwhile;
```

The phrases in brackets « » represent actions which have to be elaborated further to produce statements in the desired language.

Assuming that the aim is to produce a design in a Pascal like language then each of the phrases in brackets has to be elaborated into one or more PASCAL like statements. If the decomposition has been performed correctly the elaboration of each bracketed phrase should be independent of any other.

Since the object of this example is to illustrate stepwise refinement and not to discuss input/output programming the input from the A-D converter will be assumed to be read via IN function calls which take the port number as a parameter. It will be assumed that the low level control of the A-D converter is contained within this function call. Similarly it will be assumed that the direction registers are set up automatically by the PASCAL runtime system. Again for ease of programming, it will be assumed that a procedure OUTPT is available which takes an integer argument and displays that value on the seven segment display, and a function KEYBD is available which waits until a key is depressed on the keyboard and then returns its value.

The next level of elaboration then becomes

```
L1      « initialise »
          dummy:=keybd;
          turn 1:=in(0);
          dummy:=keyboard;
          turn 9:=in(0);
```

```
while true do
  begin
    unknown:=in(0);
    « convert to display value»
    outpt (display value)
  end;
```

Because Pascal is a high level language and because the input-output programming is assumed to be via system routines elaboration of most of the phrases is trivial. The only one which is not obvious is how to convert an unknown reading into the corresponding dial reading. The basic calculation is to interpolate between the values for the ends of the potentiometer scale.

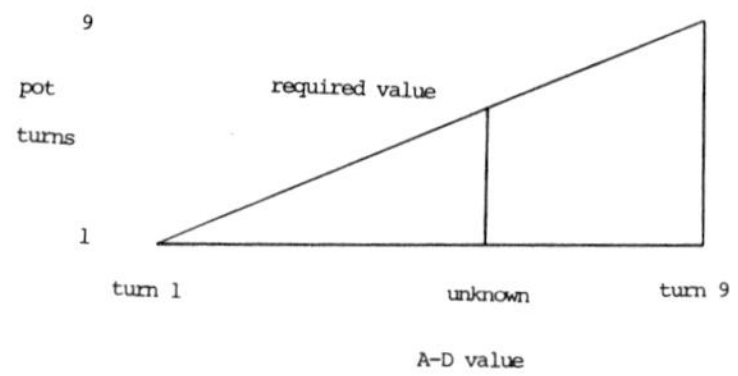

$$\text{Hence required value} = \frac{(\text{unknown} - \text{turn } 1)*8}{\text{turn } 9 - \text{turn } 1} + 1$$

for whole number of turns or ten times that for the display value. Rewriting in Pascal this becomes

```
displayvalue:=round(80* (unknown - turn 1)/(turn 9 - turn 1)+10);
```

Adding the standard structure to the Pascal program this becomes

```
program  potentiometer (input,output);
var  dummy: char;
     turn 1, turn 9, unknown, display value:integer;

begin
     dummy:=keybd;
     turn 1:=in(0);
     dummy:=keybd;
     turn 9:=in(0);
     while true do
       begin
         unknown:=in(0);
         display value:=round(80*(unknown - turn 1)/
                        (turn 9 - turn 1)+10);
         output (display value)
         end
end.
```

Note that no initialisation was required for this program.

The design of this program has been relatively simple since it is a short program and, in a high level language, it is almost possible to design in a single stage. The benefits and the method of stepwise refinement are not at all obvious in this program so the same problem is tackled but the target code is Intel 8080 assembly code.

To the unwary it may seem that, since a Pascal compiler translates the above solution to machine code before execution, the method to adopt to produce an assembly code solution is to take the design above and elaborate it stage by stage until the desired level of detail is reached. Before attempting this, however, the design should be examined to detect any differences in approach which might be simpler or more efficient in a low level language. In the low level language input-output routines will probably not be provided so the input-output will be considerably more complicated, but the overall structure will be made similar to that above. The major problem with this example concerns the calculation of displayvalue. Any calculation involving multiplication or division on the Intel 8085 processor will be difficult and slow due to the lack of a hardware multiply or divide operation. The alternative method is to store a set of values and look up the required one from the table. This is a case of the classic space-time tradeoff. In terms of design what has been done is that the design has been reconsidered and at some level elaboration will proceed in a different manner due to a changed design decision. This also illustrates another design facet; design is never solely a top-down or bottom up approach, the designer needs to be aware of constraints at all levels and to use them to design in an order which is "natural" for that problem. In many cases the design is mainly top down but it is not a universal solution.

Taking these points into consideration the outline design to start with here is

```
LO      « initialise»
        « turn 1:=readval»
        « turn 9:=readval»
        « call setup to set up table»
          while true do
           « unknown:=getval»
           « call tablelookup»
           « call output»
          endwhile
```

Here it is assumed that a function called readval will be required to read the A-D value on a key depression, a function called getval will be required to read an A-D value and routines setup and tablelookup will be required to manipulate the required tables. Before proceeding any further with design a decision has to be taken on how to deal with communication between subprograms. There are three possible alternatives - communicate via specified registers, communicate via named variable, communicate via a stack. For more complicated examples the latter two techniques are best but for simple examples the first method suffices. The main problem with this first method is in identifying the contents of registers and specifying their usage by a subprogram. This is normally done by the use of comments in the program.

Turning to the problem of what to store in the tables and how to store it it has already been pointed out that the A-D accuracy and range limits the output to a two digit integer. One method would be to store the expected A-D value for each potentiometer value and simply to look up the unknown value against this table. However, this requires 101 bytes of storage whereas if each whole turn value is stored in one table and the additions for each partturn in another table then only two tables each of length 11 bytes are required. The latter technique requires some extra calculation to find the value to display; the space-time tradeoff again. Because of the saving in storage the latter technique is used here.

The next stage of design is to decide how to organise the memory. For this a simple map suffices (note: the memory on the SDK-85 starts at 2000H).

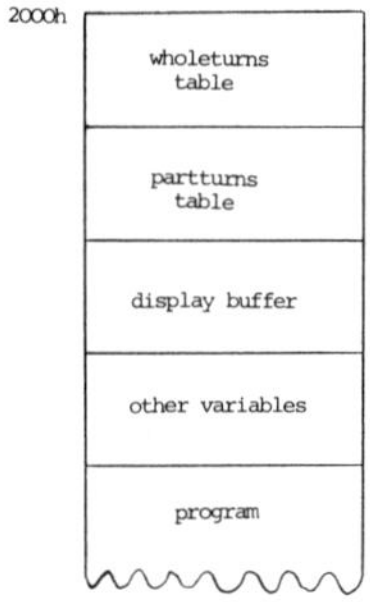

Returning to the design of the program.

```
L1    «readval»   is a function which returns a value in register A
                  ≡ «wait until a key is depressed»
                    «read A-D converter»
                     ret

L2    «wait until key is depressed» ≡ call rdkbd   ; given in
                                                     problem spec
      «read A-D converter»          ≡ call getval  ; as proposed at LO
   so«readval»    ≡   readval:        call rdkbd   ; wait for key dep
                                      call getval  ; get A-D value
                                      ret
```

Note the use of comments to summarise design aims in English.

To complete the design of this routine the values of registers required on input and produced on output should be specified together with the registers used, that is, destroyed, within the routine. An alternative approach to the latter problem is for the routine to save and restore all the registers it uses internally.

The final design of the routine is

```
L3          ;  function readval
            ;      returns the A-D value when a key is depressed on the
            ;      keyboard
            ;  uses         all registers
            ;  inputs       none
            ;  outputs      A      - A-D value
            ;
            ;
               readval:     call rdkbd   ; wait for key depression
                            call getval  ; get A-D value
                            ret          ; return to caller
```

Note the uses of layout to improve the readability.

The design of getval is more interesting in that it involves the use of delays to produce the correct timing of the convert pulse.

```
L1    «getval»    is a function to activate the A-D converter,
                  wait until ready and return the data value in
                  register A
                  ≡   «send pulse of appropriate size to A-D»
                      «wait for status to indicate conversion finished»
                      «read A-D value into A»
                       ret
```

Assuming that the port has been initialised in « initialise » the reading of the A-D value is simple

```
L2      « read A-D value into A »   ≡ in 0
```

Also the waiting on the status signed in simple

```
L2      «wait for status» ≡  g1: in 1        ; input CSR
                                 ani 4        ; get status bit
                                 jnz g1       ; wait until 0
```

The production of the pulse, however, is more complex.

```
L2         send pulse       ≡  «set A-D to A-D conversion and convert=1»
                               «set A-D to A-D conversion and convert=0»
                               «wait 5mS»
                               «set A-D to A-D conversion and convert=1»

L3      «set A-D to A-D conversion and convert to 1» ≡ mvi a, 3
                                                       out    1
        «set A-D to A-D conversion and convert to 0» ≡ mvi a, 2
                                                       out    1
```

But the delay creates a problem. How is this done on the SDK-85? Some code needs to be written to do this but this involves calculations using the clock time ($3MH_Z$) and the number of cycles for an instruction sequence. Normally a good way to produce a long delay with a small amount of code is to use PUSH and POP instructions (these use 12 and 10 cycles respectively on the 8085). At $3MH_Z$ we need to delay about 15000 cycles for 5mS so with 2 PUSH and 2 POP instructions we take 44 cycles which, together with the decrement and test required takes a total of 59 cycles. So a count of 255 for a loop including 2 PUSH and 2 POP instructions will delay for about 5mS.

```
So      «wait 5mS»   mvi e, offh   ; set count to 255
                 g2: push h
                     pop  h
                     push h
                     pop  h        ; delay
                     dcr  e        ; end of loop
                     jnz  g2
```

The routine output is required to set up the parameters for the monitors outpt routine as stated in the problem. If it is assumed that the tablelookup routine puts its output directly into the display buffer the output only has to set up the values for registers A and B and call this routine.

```
L1       «output»  output: mvi a, 0
                           mvi b, 0
                           call outpt
                           ret
```

The only part of the design left is that of the table routines. To generate the wholeturns table the increment for each turn need to be calculated from the initial calibration and this used to generate the table by addition in a loop, and similarly for the partturns table.

```
L1       «setup»  ≡  «stepinc = (turn 9 - turn 1)/8»
                     «firstval = turn 1 - stepinc»
                     «for i:=1 to 10»
                       «nextval = lastval + stepinc»
                     «small step = stepinc/10»
                     «firstval = 0»
                     «for i:=1 to 10»
                       «nextval = lastval + smallstep»
```

A number of points arise from this design. Firstly, some of the stages in this design are almost identical. On consideration they may be extracted into a subroutine called, say, fill, which both shortens the code length and further modularises the design. The reader may wish to consider here the reasons why this common operation, filling the table, was not observed earlier. Did the designer take too large a step from L0 to L1 for setup? By abstracting the fill routine has the design effectively gone back to some level between L0 and L1? A point worthy of mention here is that the designer should never be afraid of rewriting or redesigning some or all of his code. Critical review of a design of code will almost certainly result in some improvements which necessitate some redesign or recoding; the design explained here is no exception!

A second problem with this design is that of accuracy. Those readers with some appreciation of numerical analysis will know that producing the table by continually adding the step value in integer form will lead to significant errors in the higher values due to rounding. This could be overcome by using floating point values, as the Pascal version does, or by using scaled integers. Since the program is already lengthy this complication has been ignored but the interested reader is invited to attempt this design. For similar reasons of length the partturns table is kept to length 9 because this can be produced by a simple shift instead of division. Again the interested reader is invited to try the decimal modification for himself.

The design of the rest of the program is straightforward using these techniques. Because of lack of space only the final code is shown.

3.3.5 The final program

```
                 org 2000h
               ; definition of data areas
wholeturns   :   ds 11              ; reserve 11 bytes for table
partturns    :   ds  9              ; reserve  9 bytes for table
displayarea  :   0,0,0,0            ; define area of zero's
unknown      :   db 0
turn 1       :   db 0
turn 9       :   db 0
               ; addresses of standard routines
readkb       equ   2e7h
outpt        equ   2b7h
               ; start of program
               ;
               ; function readval, reads an A-D value on key
                                                      depression
               ; uses    all registers
```

```
            ;  inputs   none
            ;  output   A    A-D value
            ;
readval :   call readkb    ; wait for key depression
            call getval    ; get A-D value
            ret
            ;
            ;  function getval, initiates and reads an A-D value
            ;  uses     registers A, E
            ;  inputs   none
            ;  outputs  A   A-D value
            ;
getval  :   mvi a,3            ;  set control = 1, convert = 1
            out 1
            mvi a,2            ;  set control = 1, convert = 0
            out 1
            mvi e, offh        ;  delay loop 5mS
  g2    :   push h
            pop h
            push h
            pop h
            dcr e
            jnz g2
            mvi a,3            ;  set control = 1, convert = 1
            out 1
  gl    :   in  1              ;  read status bit
            ani 4
            jnz gl             ;  wait until status = 0
            in  0              ;  read A-D value into A
            ret
            ;
            ;  output routine, set up params and calls outpt
            ;  uses     registers A and B
            ;  inputs   none
            ;  outputs  none
            ;
output  :   mvi a,0
            mvi b,0
            call outpt         ;  standard display routine
            ret
            ;
            ;  setup routine, sets up wholeturns and partturns
                                                        table
            ;  uses     registers A,B,C,H,L
            ;  inputs   none
            ;  outputs  none
            ;
setup   :   lda  turn 1
            mov b,a
            lda  turn 9
            sub  b             ;  a = turn 9 - turn 1
            rrc                ;  divide by 8
            rrc
            rrc
            ani lfh            ; mask unwanted bits
            mov c,a
```

```
                    mov  a,b
                    sub  c               ;  a = turn 1 - stepsize
                    mvi  d,11            ;  table size
                    lxi  h, wholeturns ;  table address
                    call fill            ;  fill table
                    mov  a,c             ;  retrieve stepsize
                    rrc
                    rrc
                    rrc                  ;  a = stepsize/8
                    ani  3h              ;  mask unwanted bits
                    mov  c,a
                    mvi  a,0
                    mvi  d,9             ;  table size
                    lxi  h, partturns  ;  table address
                    call fill            ;  fill table
                    ret
                    ;
                    ;  fill routine, to fill wholeturns or partturns table
                    ;  uses    A,D,H,L
                    ;  inputs  hl - address of start of table
                    ;               d - table size
                    ;               c - step size
                    ;               a - initial value
                    ;  outputs      none
                    ;
     fill     :     mov  m,a             ; store value in table
                    inx  h               ; increment table pointer
                    add  c               ; update table value
                    dcr  d               ; decrement count
                    jnz  fill            ; loop until zero
                    ret
                    ;
                    ;  table lookup routine, looks up value in tabel and
                    ;                            returns position ≤.
                    ;  uses    A,D,H,L
                    ;  inputs  none
                    ;  outputs none
  tablelookup :     lda  unknown         ; get value
                    lxi  h,wholeturns  ; table address
                    call lookup
                    sta  displayarea    ; store in most sig.pos.
                    mov  d,m             ; get tabel value
                    lda  unknown         ; get value
                    sub  d               ; get remainder
                    lxi  h,partturns    ; table address
                    call lookup
                    sta  displayarea +2; store in least sig.pos.
                    ret
                    ;
                    ;  lookup routine, gets position in tabel ≤ given val
                    ;  uses    A,C,E,H,L
                    ;  inputs  hl - table start address
                    ;          a  - value to be looked up
                    ;  outputs hl - table address containing value
                    ;          a  - position in table
                    ;
```

```
lookup  :  mov  c,a          ; save value
           mov  e,l          ; save initial table value
look 1  :  mov  a,m          ; get table value
           inx  h            ; increment table address
           cmp  c            ; compare values
           jm   look 1       ; go on
           dcx  h            ; restore pointer
look 2  :  mov  a,l          ; present addr
           sub  e            ; minus initial
           ret
           ;
           ;  main program
           ;
start   :  lxi  sp,20c2h     ; initialise stack pointer
           mvi  a, 0eh
           sim
           ei                ; enable keyboard
           mvi  a,0          ; initialise port 0 for input
           out  2
           mvi  a,0fbh       ; initialise port 1 for I/O
           out  3
           call readval
           sta  turn 1
           call readval
           sta  turn 9
           call setup        ; set up tables
L1      :  call getval       ; get val from A-D
           sta  unknown
           call tablelookup  ; convert to display value
           call output       ; output to display
           jmp  L1           ; loop forever
           end
```

There are a number of details in the final program which are worthy of mention. Firstly, some of the routines use parameters in registers and others use what are essentially parameters from memory locations. This is deliberate and is meant to show how much more readable the latter is. This highlights one of the major problems of design at this level; the conflict between readability and efficiency. For example, to clear the accumulator should the code used by mvi a,0 or xra a? The former is clearer in meaning whilst the latter is faster. On the basis of experience designers will almost always err on the side of readability and understandability and so the former would be used. When it comes to coding, however, there are a few cases where speed and memory usage are very important. In these cases the latter would be used but the necessity for it is very rare. This argument can also be applied to a large number of forms of "optimisation". The general principle should be - don't make things any more difficult or complex than necessary.

A second observation concerns the coding of tablelookup and lookup. Lookup return both the address of the current table position and its offset position. A question may be asked as to why both values are returned. The reason here is due to the function decomposition. On contemplation a better decomposition might have produced a cleaner interface. This is another example where re-examination of a design can show places where it may be improved. There are almost certainly other places in this design where improvement is possible.

3.4 CONCLUSION

The design of this problem solution should have illustrated the power of stepwise refinement and the necessity of using this technique or a similar one when tackling the design of complex programs. Exactly what constitutes a complex program will depend both on the problem to be solved and also the target language. The problem considered here was solved trivially using a Pascal like language but it was a far more demanding task to produce an assembly code program to do the same job. This should also have shown you that wherever possible high level languages should be used for program development rather than assembly code, since the former are very much easier to use. For very complex problems even current high level languages are inadequate and hence the search for even higher level languages.

REFERENCES

1. Miller, G.A., 1956, Psychol. Rev., 63, 81-97

2. Dahl, O.J., Dijkstra, E.W., and Hoare, C.A.R., 1972 'Structured Programming', Academic Press, New York.

3. Jackson, M.A., 1975, 'Principles of Program Design', Academic Press, New York.

Chapter 4

Some notations for structured software design

M.T. Ferguson

4.1. INTRODUCTION

4.1.1. Purpose of Notations

A notation is a set of symbols used to represent a class of objects. A notation may also represent concepts that have no physical existence. Notations were introduced to enable the description of some situation, so that the situation may be reproduced. We now also use notations to describe problems so that they may be analysed and solved.

Figure 4.1 A well known sound.

The marks in Fig. 4.1 are an example of a well known notation for musical sounds, that has been developed over many centuries. It contains all the information necessary to reproduce those sounds.

Figure 4.2 Seven sheep please.

Numbers are a notation probably introduced for commerce (Fig. 4.2), from which the concept of number, independent of any object has been derived.

Figure 4.3a The set of all men who are affluent sheep owners

$A = \{m \mid s(m) > 1\}$

Figure 4.3b How far have you come?

$d = \int_0^t v \, dt$

The notations of mathematics have been developed to express things concisely that are difficult to say, or have no relation to physical things (Fig. 4.3).

If you want to do more than just describe a situation with your notation - you want to do some analysis for example - the choice of notation is important. Consider the Roman numerals in Fig. 4.4. The numbers are a little unfamiliar and fairly long, but they describe the number of objects adequately. But how could you do the long division?

Figure 4.4 Long division in Rome

I II III

DCLXI

MCMLXXXIII

```
                ?
DCLXI ) MCMLXXXIII
```

Now consider the arabic numerals in Fig. 4.5. The division is possible by following a small set of rules. Note that the numbers haven't changed, only the way we draw them, and by implication, the way we think about them.

Figure 4.5 Long division in Baghdad

1 2 3

661

1983

```
         3
661 ) 1983
      1983
         0
```

So in general the notation you use influences the way you think about a problem and the ease with which you obtain a solution.

The notations we use should be descriptive, expressive, clear, concise, and readable. Sometimes there may be conflict between these features, for example, between conciseness and readability. Some experience is usually necessary before a notation can be read easily.

4.1.2. Concepts of Software Engineering

One of the most important concepts is that of hierarchical decomposition, the divide and rule approach that helps you design a program that will work. This should be readily indicated with the notation.

The three structured control constructs, sequence, iteration and alternation should be expressible.

There should be some way of showing how the data processed by the program is transformed. This can happen in any particular way depending on the application, so the notation for this must be open-ended. We usually use English or borrow some notation from programming languages.

The design that you end up with will be built by coding it into some language which the computer can execute. A notation that enabled you to design the program and formally prove that the design was correct before coding would be useful. This is a difficult area at present.

When the program is designed and enters service, some documentation will be needed so that bugs can be fixed and new features added. The notation that was used to describe the design should also serve the maintenance team.

4.2. NOTATIONS

We shall consider some notations that are or have been used for the design of programs.

4.2.1. Flowcharts

Figure 4.6 Flowcharts

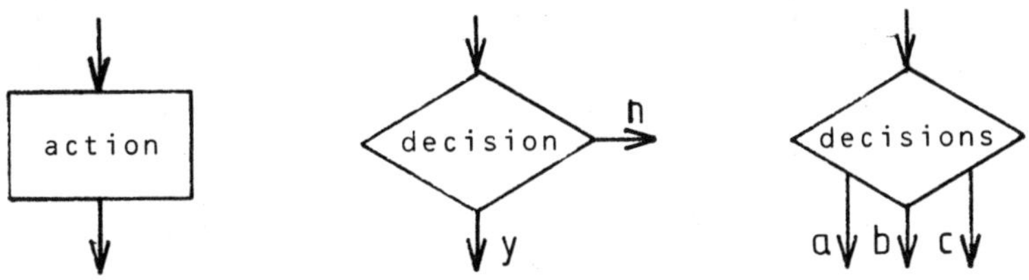

A flowchart is the oldest notation for representing a program. It consists of essentially two types of boxes - action boxes and decision boxes - joined together with arrows (Fig. 4.6). The control flow of the program is explicitly marked on the chart, being the way the boxes are joined up. The data transformations are found by inspecting the words in the action boxes. The data transformation, therefore, has to be designed in another way.

Figure 4.7 Sequence, alternation and iteration on a flowchart

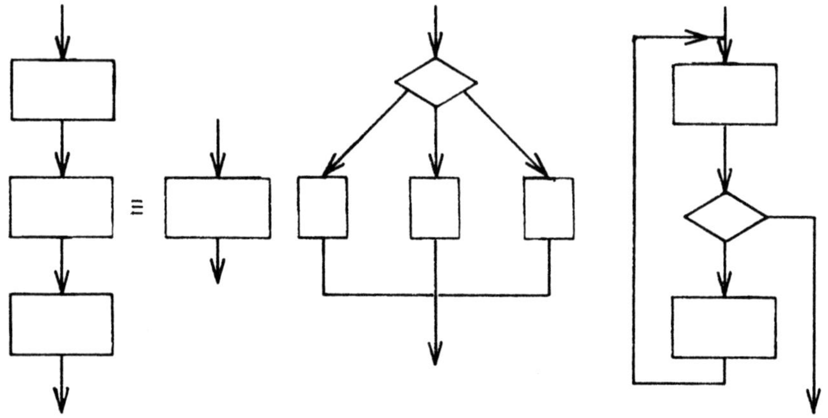

The structured programming concepts of hierarchical decomposition, sequence, iteration and alternation can be represented (Fig. 4.7). However it is all to easy to draw a flowchart that is not structured (Fig. 4.8). In addition, although decomposition and composition can be represented on a flow chart, the notation does not aid the process of decomposition. Furthermore, the control construct - a decision box with arrows - is too low level. You have to draw at least two or three boxes for a loop, two or three boxes for an if statement, and it is all too easy for the arrows to go in the wrong place.

Figure 4.8 Spaghetti

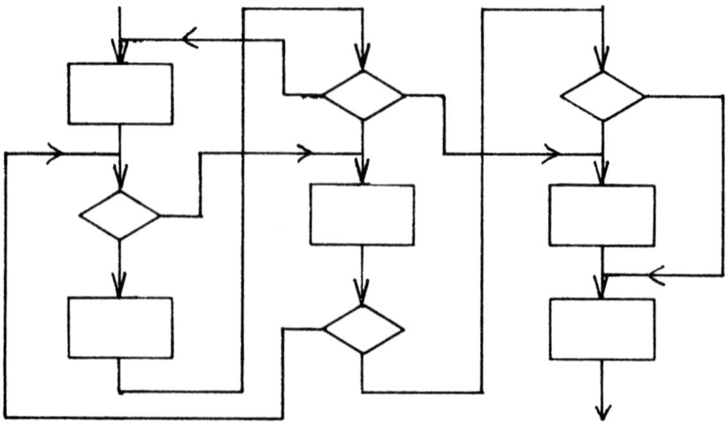

Finally flowcharts are not easy to draw. It takes too long to make them look nice. We've all heard stories about programmers producing flowcharts for documentation purposes from the code of the finished program. Perhaps this is because if they had used them as a design aid, they would have spent most of their time redrawing. In all, flowcharts are no good as a design aid.

4.2.2. Pseudo-Code

Figure 4.9a Pseudo-code

```
IF boolean              IF boolean              IF boolean
THEN statements         THEN statements         THEN statements
FI                      ELSE statements         ELIF boolean
                        FI                      THEN statements
                                                . . .
                                                ELSE statements
                                                FI

# comment #

CASE expression
IN val, val, . . . : statements
IN val, val, . . . : statements
OUT statements
ESAC

PROC procedurename parameters:
      statements
CORP

WHILE boolean           TO 10                   DO statements
DO statements           DO statements           # for ever #
OD                      OD                      OD

INT i; CHAR c;

TYPE STRING = SEQUENCE OF CHAR;
SEQUENCE OF STRING wordlist;

TYPE NODE = STRUCT (
                POINTER TO NODE left,
                STRING value,
                POINTER TO NODE right
            );
```

c.f. Algol68, Ada

Pseudo-code[1] resembles a very high level programming language. We do not use an existing high level language because:

i. we need flexibility to add new concepts or data types to the language

ii. we want to be able to use English descriptions to avoid excessive detail

iii. we want our design to be free of the idiosyncrasies of existing programming languages - our thoughts (and designs) are to be unconstrained by those things

iv. if the design is ever reimplemented we do not want to redesign it - just code it in the new language. For this reason the design has to be done at as high a level as possible.

Fig. 4.9 shows how the control structures may be indicated in a typical pseudo-code. You may also invent high level data types, such as sequences and stacks, and the operators to go with them.

Figure 4.9b ADC and Display Program

```
PROC read_adc_and_display_value:
    ADC_VALUE value; # whatever that may be #
    calibrate;
    DO
        read(value);
        scale_and_convert(value);
        display(value)
    OD
CORP;

MODULE calibration_and_scaling:
    ADC_VALUE nine_turns, one_turn;

    PROC calibrate:
        ok("nine turns");
        read(nine_turns);
        ok("one turn");
        read(one_turn)
    CORP;
    PROC scale_and_convert(VAR ADC_VALUE value):
        value := (value - one_turn) * 80
                / (nine_turns - one_turn) + 10
    CORP
ELUDOM
```

When using pseudo-code it may be difficult to avoid excessive detail. You may get bogged down in its syntax. Inventing features is one of pseudo-code's strengths. However, if other people have to read your design, you will have to document your pseudo-code features as well. Hierarchical decomposition can be represented by means of the procedure. That is not particularly concise, but has the advantage of being able to represent functions with parameters. Data types are represented particularly clearly and concisely.

Pseudo-code is generally used at the later stages of the design process. If you were producing a program in assembler, for example, you would typically code it into pseudo-code first.

Good programming style is the way of writing programs (in any design notation, in this context) so that they are readable[2]. A brief introduction, by means of some suitably pithy axioms, is appropriate here.

> "Use variable names that mean something."

Imagine the ADC program above if the variables were called x, y and z. The slight increase in verbosity is more than compensated for by the increase in readability.

> "Format a program to help a reader understand it. Indent to show the logical structure."

Imagine the ADC program if it were compressed in to as few lines as possible.

> "Make sure comments and code agree. Make every comment count, don't repeat the code. Document the data. Don't over comment."

Erroneous comments make it difficult to debug the code - you believe the comments! Comments like

```
i := i + 1; # add one to i #
```

are useless. A comment describing the purposes of variables is often useful, especially when a meaningful name would be too long. If you put too many comments in, you will hide the code. How many is right depends on the language, you need more when writing assembler than when writing Pascal.

> "Say what you mean simply and directly. Write clearly - don't be too clever."

Even you might not be able to read it next year.

> "Make your program right before you make it faster. Make it clear before you make it faster. Measure your program before you make efficiency changes. Keep it simple to make it faster. Find a better algorithm to make it faster."

Many sins are committed in the name of efficiency. If you need a an order of magnitude increase in speed, you won't get it by code optimizations.

Figure 4.10 Data Flow Diagram

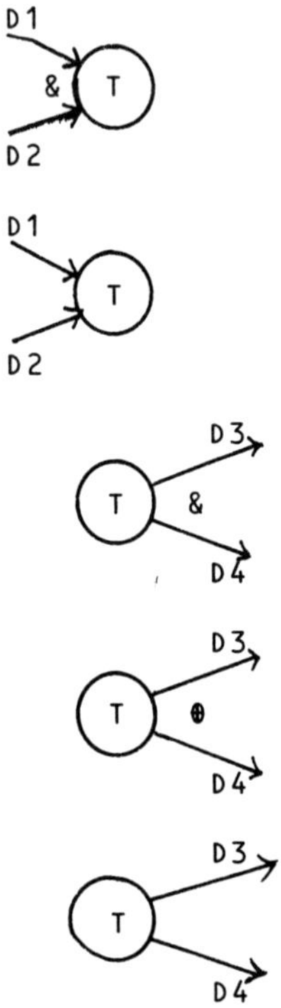

output produced when D1 and D2 present

output produced when any input present

outputs D3 and D4 produced

output D3 or output D4 but not both are produced

either D3, D4 or both are produced

4.2.3. Data Flow Diagrams

A data flow diagram[1] shows only how the data is transformed. No control flow at all is shown. The principle elements of a data flow diagram are labelled circles, which represent the data transforming processes, and labelled arrows, which represent the data (Fig. 4.10). Data availability is indicated by the & and ⊕ operators.

Some hierarchical decomposition is possible, as in the example of a spelling checking program, Fig. 4.11.

It is interesting to note that a subset of data flow diagrams may be implemented directly by the pipeline feature of Unix (see chapter 10) (Fig. 4.12). Fig. 4.13 shows another representation of the ADC and display program.

Data flow diagrams are useful mainly for the high level or overall view of a system.

Figure 4.11 Spelling Checker

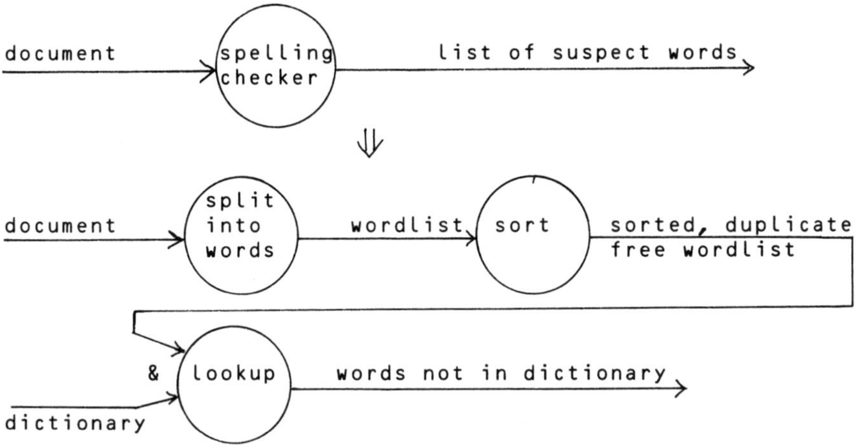

Figure 4.12 The Spelling Checker as a Unix pipeline

```
prep document | sort -u | comm -23 - /usr/dict/words
```

Figure 4.13 ADC and Display Data Flow

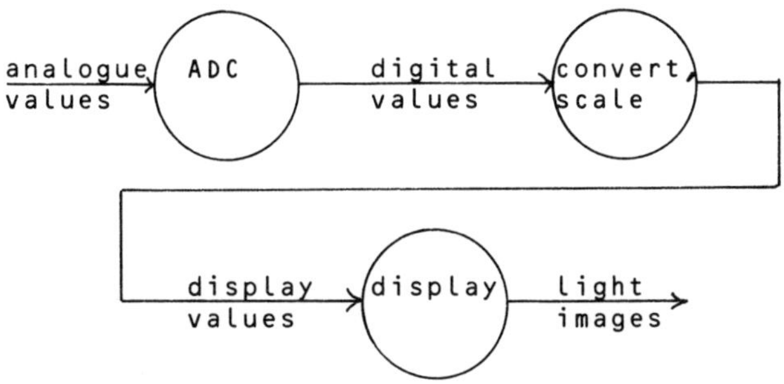

4.2.4. Warnier Orr Diagrams

4.2.4.1. Introduction - HIPO diagrams

So far we have not seen a notation that emphasises the hierarchical nature of the design process. We would like a notation that helps us decompose the problem and so enable us to design and implement a solution with reasonable chance of success. The same notation should act as machine independent documentation for the program[3].

The Hierarchical-Input-Process-Output diagram was devised by IBM in the late '60s as an attempt to formalize the steps of a top-down design in this way.

Figure 4.14 HIPO diagram - overview

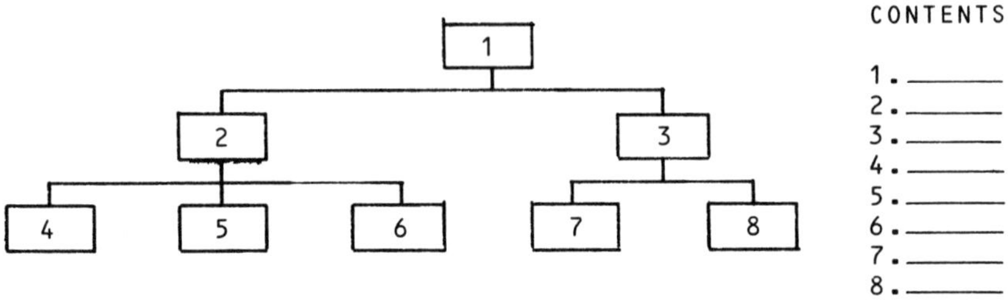

The overall system structure is shown in an overview diagram (Fig. 4.14). How the various modules relate to each other is easily seen. Each module is described further in a detail diagram (Fig. 4.15). Additional levels of detail diagrams may be drawn if needed.

Figure 4.15 HIPO diagram - detail

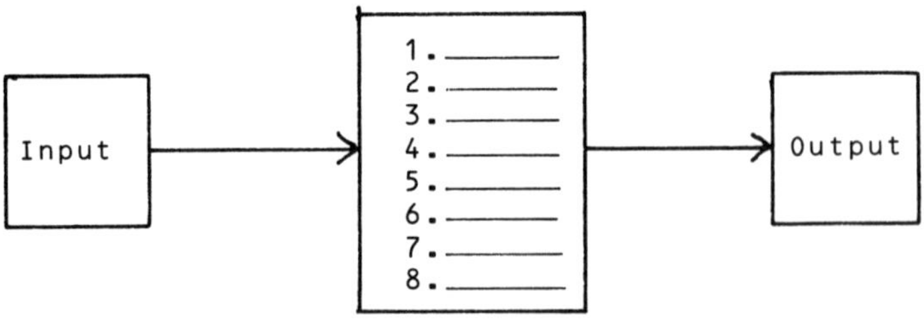

HIPO diagrams tend to be verbose and bulky. But the concepts they describe are useful. We shall see a more flexible notation in the Warnier Orr diagram.

4.2.4.2. Warnier Orr Diagrams

Warnier Orr Diagrams[4, 5] were invented by J D Warnier, of France, in the late '60s. They were developed by K T Orr in the USA.

They are based on the idea of ordered sets of objects. The order gives the sequence of objects. Hierarchical decomposition is based on the idea of subsets of objects. A big curly bracket is used to indicate the sets (Fig. 4.16).

The notation can also represent repetition (Fig. 4.17) and alternation (Fig. 4.18).

Figure 4.16   Warnier Orr Diagrams - sequence and hierarchy

```
          /
          |              / object 1.1
          |              |
          | object 1     < object 1.2    { and so on
          |              |
          |              \ object 1.3
          |
          |              / object 2.1
          |              |       .
object    < object 2    <       .
          |              |       .
          |     .        \ object 2.n
          |     .
          |     .        / object n.1
          |              |       .
          | object n     <       .
          |              |       .
          |              \       .
          \
```

Figure 4.17a Repetition

```
for each day   /
 of the week   <
     (7)       \


               /  start reading
               |
 read a book   <   read a leaf
     with      |       (60)
  120 pages    |
               \ finish reading
```

The repetition is indicated by putting the number of times an object is to be repeated underneath it in brackets. If you don't know how many times exactly, you can put a pair of numbers in the brackets for minimum and maximum values. If one of the numbers is represented by a name - (1, leaves) - it implies that the repetition occurs until sufficient. This is an abstract form of iteration. If necessary you can annotate the diagram to show what test is made to determine when to stop. The note is usually indicated with a question-mark.

Alternation is indicated by joining several objects with the exclusive-or (⊕) operator. Only one of the objects will occur, as appropriate. This is also indicated by a

Figure 4.17b Reading a real book

```
              /                    / take the book
              | start reading      < open it
              |                    \ turn to page 1
              |
read a book   <                    / read this side of the leaf
              | read a leaf        < turn the leaf
              | (1, leaves)        \ read the other side
              |
              | finish             / close the book
              | reading            < replace it
              \                    \
```

Figure 4.18 Alternation

```
             / Monday, Tuesday
             | or Wednesday         { watch TV
             | (0, 1)
             |     ⊕
             | Thursday
things to    | or Friday            { visit pub
do in the    < (0, 1)
evening      |     ⊕
             | Saturday             { visit cinema
             | (0, 1)
             |     ⊕
             | Sunday               { visit mother-in-law
             \ (0, 1)


             / its raining
             | (0, 1)
what to do   < ____⊕______
on Sunday    | its raining
             \ (0, 1)
```

repetition count of (0, 1) underneath the object. The names of these objects are usually interpretable as propositions, to aid the reader. A vertical bar over one indicates its negation.

Fig. 4.19 shows what is indicated on a Warnier Orr diagram. Moving down gives you the order or sequence of objects. Moving left tells you why you have an object, moving right tells you how you make an object.

The objects mentioned in the description above can be almost anything. Warnier developed his notation to describe data hierarchies. The objects would be data elements. We

Figure 4.19 What's what on a Warnier Orr Diagram

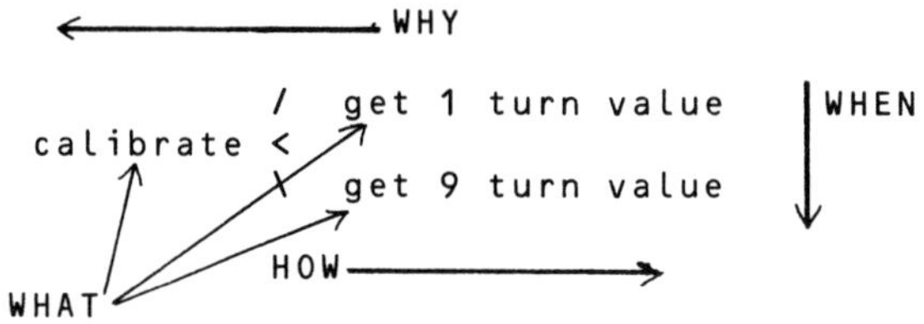

are more likely to decompose the control structure of a program, in which case the objects will be program actions. The notation is abstract enough to be able to decompose any system to any desired level.

Warnier Orr diagrams do not say anything about data types or variables. If it was necessary to declare these things we could perhaps borrow from a pseudo-code notation. But note that the Warnier Orr diagram can describe data structures easily. The actions are usually written in English. Again we could borrow from pseudo-code if required. The points made about style in the pseudo-code section apply equally well to the writings on Warnier Orr diagrams.

Warnier Orr diagrams effectively represent the hierarchical nature of a program, and clearly and concisely express the concepts of iteration and alternation. They are reasonably easy to draw. They are a good design aid.

Figure 4.20a Waveform

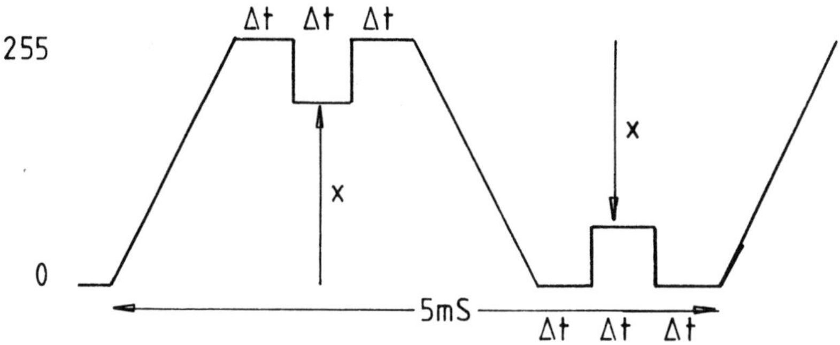

Lets consider some examples. Fig. 4.20b shows a design to generate the waveform of Fig. 4.20a. Fig. 4.21 shows a design for a program whose output is the same as its input, except that any tab characters have been replaced by the appropriate number of blanks. Fig. 4.22 shows how you could decompose the ADC and display program from Chapter 1.

```
Figure 4.20b  Outline of Waveform Generator


           / begin    {
           |
           |          /          / ramp up
           |          | first    | wait
           |          | half     < change
           |          | cycle    | wait
           |          |          | restore
           |          |          \ wait
waveform   < cycles   <
           | (0, n)   |          / ramp down
           |          | second   | wait
           |          | half     < change
           |          | cycle    | wait
           |          |          | restore
           |          \          \ wait
           |
           \ end      {
```

```
Figure 4.21   A program to remove tab characters


       /           / set tabstops
       | initialize<
       |           \ position on line := 1
       |
       |           /       / output blanks to
       |           | char  | next tab stop
       |           | is tab< (1, b)
       |           | (0, 1)| position on line
       |           |       \ := next tab stop
       |           |   ⊕
       |           |       / output
       |           |       | character
replace| for all   |       |
tabs by< characters<       | backspace char{ decrement
spaces | in input  |       | (0, 1)          position on line
       | (0, c)    | char  |   ⊕
       |           | is any< newline char  { position
       |           | other | (0, 1)          on line := 1
       |           | (0, 1)|   ⊕
       |           |       | printing char { increment
       |           |       | (0, 1)          position on line
       |           |       |   ⊕
       |           \       \ any other char{ skip
       |
       | finalize  {
       \
```

Warnier developed a design methodology to go with the diagrams, based on an analysis of the output. The structure of the output provided the framework of the program. Most commercial data processing programs can be designed in this way.

Analysis of the output is always a good idea as you can't specify a program until you know what it is to produce. However, in microprocessor work, this analysis may not provide enough structure to be the skeleton of the program.

The waveform generator can be analysed in this way. The program follows the structure of the output.

Figure 4.22 ADC and display

```
           /              / get 1 turn         { ok for 1 turn
           |              | value                read ADC
           | calibrate    <
           |              | get 9 turn         { ok for 9 turns
           |              \ value                read ADC
ADC        <
display    |              / read ADC
           | run          |
           | (0, n)       < scale and
           | ?until       | convert reading
           | reset        |
           \              \ display on leds
```

The output of the tab removing program has a structure, very similar to that of its input. This program was designed by decomposing the input into a file of characters, some of which are tabs and some of which are not tabs. You could also decompose the input into a file of lines of characters, some of which are tabs ... , to obtain an alternative solution. Decomposing the output led to a framework where it was difficult to see where the tabs had to be changed.

The ADC program is an example where neither the input or output has any hierarchical structure. Both are more or less the same, a sequence of numbers. This solution was designed by decomposing the control flow.

4.2.5. Backus Naur Form (BNF) and Syntax Diagrams

These notations were devised for describing the syntax of computer programming languages. They can be used to describe the structure of the input (or output) of any program. They can also be used as a design aid for a program that recognizes that input[6]. The meaning of the input is not defined by these notations. That must be done in another way.

A valid sequence of input symbols to a program is called a sentence.

A set of sentences is called a language. Many languages have an infinite number of sentences.

The rules which describe how sentences are composed are called a grammar. BNF is a notation for writing a grammar.

A terminal symbol is one that cannot be broken down any further. The sequence of input symbols fed to a program comprises only terminal symbols, for example letters and numbers. Terminal symbols are usually denoted by just writing them:

```
Mark
```

If ambiguity would arise the terminal symbols would be enclosed in quotes:

```
"+"     "*"     "|"     " "
```

A non-terminal symbol is one that is made up from a sequence of other symbols, both terminal and non-terminal. It is written as a word in angle brackets:

```
<identifier>
```

A brief notation, used where no ambiguity would arise, uses single capital letters for non-terminal symbols:

```
I
```

::= means 'is defined as'. It relates the non-terminal symbol on its left to the sequence of symbols on its right to form a grammar rule:

```
<non-terminal symbol> ::= <symbol-a> <symbol-b>
                          <symbol-c> <symbol-d>
```

-> means the same in the brief notation:

```
S -> AbCd
```

The left hand side of ::= is always a single non-terminal symbol. The right hand side may specify alternation and repetition of symbols, as well as sequence. White space may be introduced freely to aid readability.

| means or.

Figure 4.23   An identifier is a letter followed by any number of letters or numbers

<identifier> ::= <letter> {<letter> | <number>}*

identifier

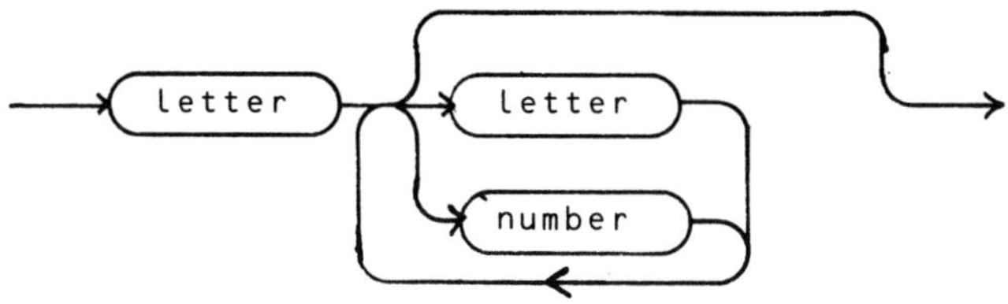


```
               / letter
               |                 / letter
identifier     < letter or       | (0, 1)
               | number          <    ⊕
               | (0, n)          | number
               \                 \ (0, 1)
```

{ <sequence> } means an optional occurrence of <sequence> (0 or 1 times repetition).

[<seq> | <seq> | <seq> ...] means one of the alternative sequences must occur. The brackets are being used to give precedence to the | sign.

An asterisk * to the right of a symbol or sequence of symbols inside { } or [ ] means repeat the sequence 0 or 1 or 2 or ... n times.

A plus + to the right of a symbol or sequence of symbols inside { } or [ ] means repeat the sequence 1 or 2 or ... n times.

EMPTY is a terminal symbol denoting replacement by nothing.

A set of syntax diagrams also describe a grammar.

A non-terminal symbol is described with a syntax diagram labelled with the symbol's name. The syntax diagram is composed of rounded boxes, which are terminal symbols, and square boxes, which are non-terminal symbols, joined together with arrows. The boxes are labelled so that you know which symbol they represent. You follow the arrows and the boxes that you come across are the input to be expected. Where the arrows diverge you have a choice.

Some examples are shown in Figs. 4.23, 4.24, and 4.25. Note that a Warnier Orr diagram can also express the structure of input, but perhaps not as concisely as BNF.

Figure 4.24 A personal name

```
<initial> ::= <letter> "."

<name> ::= <letter>+

<title> ::= Mr | Mrs | Miss

<personal name> ::= <title> {<initial> | <name>}* <name>
```

name

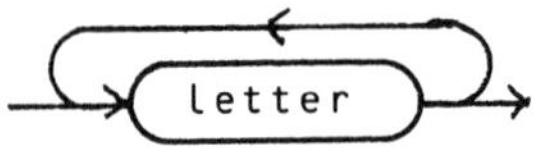

title

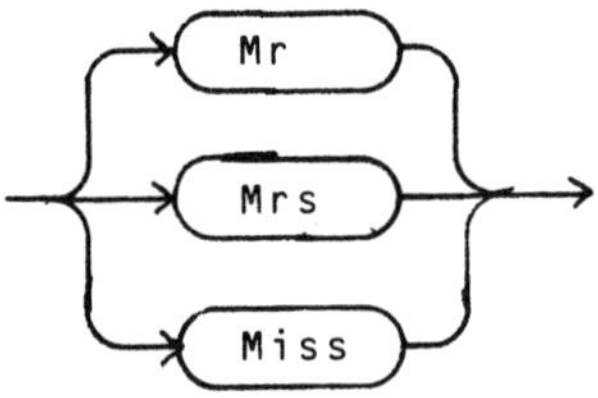

personal name

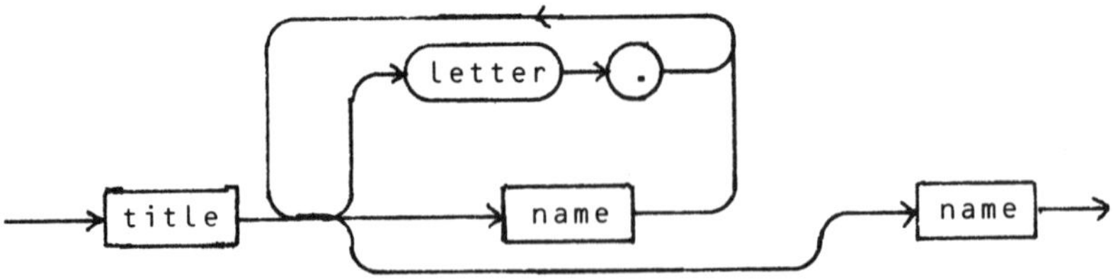

BNF is often used to describe the input to programs such as compilers or microprocessor monitors. BNF is very concise notation. Syntax diagrams have the same function. They are perhaps easier for the uninitiated to read, but are harder to draw.

4.2.6. Notations for Proving Program Correctness

4.2.6.1. Introduction

In all the notations we have seen so far, the meaning of the signs has been defined in an informal way. The fundamental point of all ways of proving program correctness is a formal way of specifying meaning[7, 8]. Three distinct

Figure 4.25 Microprocessor monitor commands

```
<input> ::= <command>+
<command> ::= <reset> | <substitute memory>
          | <examine registers> | <single step>

<reset> ::= Reset.
<substitute memory> ::= Subs. <address> [","  {<data>} ]+ "."
<examine registers> ::= Exam. <register> [","  {<data>} ]+ "."
<single step> ::= Step. {<address>} ","+ "."

<address> ::= <hex> <hex> <hex> <hex>
<data> ::= <hex> <hex>

<hex> ::= 0|1|2|3|4|5|6|7|8|9|A|B|C|D|E|F
<register> ::= A|B|C|D|E|F|I|H|L|SPH|SPL|PCH|PCL
```

areas of a notation can be identified.

> Syntax deals with the combination of signs without regard for their specific significations or their relation to the behaviour in which they occur.

> Semantics deals with the signification of signs.

> Pragmatics deals with the origin, uses and effects of signs within the behaviour in which they occur.

For example, a colleague observes that "The windows are wet" (or passes a note in some computer language asserting wet(windows)). The syntax is just the way the words are placed together, the semantics is the fact that the windows are wet, and you may take pragmatic actions like looking at the window, seeing drops, concluding that it is raining and preparing your raincoat.

Notations for syntax have been defined; BNF has widespread acceptance. There is no general agreement for a semantic description. We shall consider three techniques of describing semantics, plus the notion of abstract syntax, below.

4.2.6.2. Abstract Syntax

An abstract syntax is produced from the concrete syntax of a programming language (say) by removing all semantically irrelevant notational details. It reduces the syntax to define the essence of the linguistic forms. For example an assignment statement may be written:

```
v = e     v := e     e -> v
```

The construct has two linguistic components, the expression and the variable. The abstract syntax for an assignment would contain just those parts.

Abstract syntax has the advantage that the number of grammar rules is significantly reduced. Meaning is associated with the abstract syntax.

4.2.6.3. Mathematical or Denotational Semantics

The semantics of the language are formalized by associating a suitable mathematical object (set, function, or whatever) with each phrase of the language.

The phrase is said to denote the associated object. The object is called the denotation of the phrase. Denotations of composite phrases are to be described only in terms of the denotations of sub-phrases. We write M[f] for the denotation of the phrase f. For example:

    M[x := x+1]

is the denotation of the assignment statement x := x+1.

Consider an elementary language with only identifiers, expressions, assignments, and compound statements (S1; S2). To model the execution of the program we provide state vectors, $\tilde{s}$, which are functions from variable names ID into the set of values VAL:

    $\tilde{s}$: ID -> VAL

Let $\underline{S}$ be the set of all possible states. The kind of denotations that occur in the example language are as follows:

    M[e] : $\underline{S}$ -> VAL

    M[st] : $\underline{S}$ -> $\underline{S}$

that is denotations of expressions are functions from states into values, and denotations of statements are functions of states into states.

The denotation of a composite phrase is given in terms of the denotation of its immediate sub-phrases:

    M[[S1; S2] = M[S2] o M[S1]
    where o denotes functional composition

New language features may require revisions to the definitions of states, introduction of new ways to compose denotations, or even definition of new kinds of mathematical objects. Deep mathematical issues are raised in the treatment of a typical programming language. It is hoped that the mathematical issues can be resolved and a practical tool be made available.

4.2.6.4. Operational Semantics

The semantics of the programming language are defined using a hypothetical machine which interprets the programs of that language. The machine has a structure with a set of states with two subsets, the initial states and the end states, a state transition function, a function to map programs and data into initial states and a function that takes the end states and produces the program results (Fig. 4.26).

Figure 4.26 Operational Semantics Machine

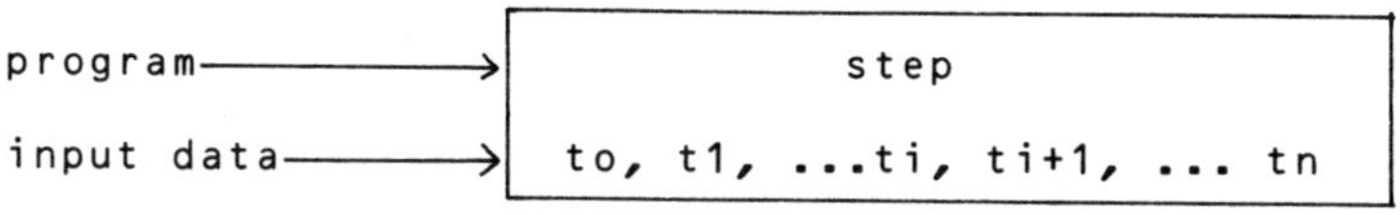

to -- initial state tn -- end state
step -- state transition function
to, ..., tn -- computation

The definition of the step function will reflect the syntactic structure of the language, so that we can relate sub-phrases of a program to sections of the computation, that is, we can tell what a specific sub-phrase means.

This method is the only one presently known which is capable of describing existing language constructs. It was used in the ANSI standard for PL/1.

4.2.6.5. Axiomatic Semantics

The semantics of a programming language are defined by a collection of axioms and rules of inference, which permit proof of properties of programs, for example, that they are correct. This system permits proofs using only the uninterpreted program text, without reference to denotations or program parts. The axioms and rules of inference can be regarded as theorems in mathematical semantics. Mathematical semantics is used to provide useful rules of inference and axioms.

The problem of proof of program correctness is usually split into two parts, first, proof of conditional correctness (that is, the program is correct if it terminates), and second, proof of termination.

A notation due to C A R Hoare is used:

p1 {st} p2

where p1 and p2 are propositions referring to variables of the program and st is a statement. The notation means if p1 is true before execution of the statement, and the statement terminates, then p2 is true after the statement terminates.

p1 is called the pre-condition, p2 is called the post-condition or consequence.

The axiom for the assignment is

p_e^x {x := e} p

where p_e^x means replace all free occurrences of x in p by e

For example:

0<x+1 {x := x+1} 0<x

It is not necessary to refer to the denotation of x := x+1 to use the axiom.

The compound statement is define by a rule of inference:

IF p1 {st1} p2 AND p2 {st2} p3 THEN p1 {st1; st2} p3

A full language description would typically have one axiom per primitive statement and one rule of inference per compound statement.

Axiom systems for programming languages are intimately connected with issues of programming style and development methodology. The essence of structured programming is to use only constructs that have simple axioms. This excludes the general form of goto statement. We can thus obtain guidance on program development, as well as a formal correctness proof.

4.3. CONCLUSIONS

A means of describing your design is essential. We have looked at some ways of doing this and seen what areas of description they cover and what advantages each has. Conciseness is important. We think quickly when designing, and don't want to be spending all our time drawing, for example.

The Warnier Orr diagram has many advantages. It is useful for all stages of design. Formal correctness proofs will be of increasing importance in future years.

4.4. BIBLIOGRAPHY

[1] I Somerville, "Software Engineering", Addison Wesley, 1982.

[2] B W Kernighan and P J Plauger, "The Elements of Programming Style", McGraw Hill, 2nd Edition, 1978.

[3] E Yourdon, "Techniques of Program Structure and Design", Prentice Hall, 1975.

[4] J D Warnier, "Logical Construction of Programs", Van Nostrand Reinholt Co., 1975.

[5] D A Higgins, "Program Design and Construction", Prentice Hall, 1979.

[6] R Bornat, "Understanding and Writing Compilers", The Macmillan Press, 1979.

[7] C B Jones, "Software Development", Prentice Hall, 1980.

[8] D Bjorner and C B Jones, "Formal Specification and Software Development", Prentice Hall, 1982.

Chapter 5

Programming language features which support software engineering design methods

A.C. Davies

5.1 INTRODUCTION

It is now widely accepted that software design should proceed in a top-down manner from a requirements-specification to a detailed implementation, and that the successive stages of stepwise refinement are best managed by using single-input single-output blocks (nested within one another as required), so that the program can be expressed in a well-structured form at all stages, avoiding the production of 'spaghetti-code' having a complex pattern of unconditional jumps.

Although the later stages of a design may be expressed directly in terms of the instruction-set of the processor to be used, clearly this is not possible for the earlier stages (except for a trivially-simple task), and a suitable language is needed in which to express the successive stages of design. It is common practice to use a stylised form of English language for the earlier stages, but this risks ambiguities of meaning and does not have a formal syntax to permit correctness to be easily demonstrated (either by humans or by machine). Various forms of pseudo-code ("pidgin" PASCAL, "structured English") are often used by designers to meet this need, although these suffer from non-standardization and the non-availablity of compilers to translate the pseudo-code into a machine-executable form. An ideal objective is to use one programming language throughout the design process so providing a unified notation for initial ideas and for the final detailed design. Features required for such a language are discussed in the following sections.

5.2 GENERAL FEATURES

Desirable features of any language are portability, to enable designs to be re-used, simplicity so that one can learn to use it properly, and to increase the likelihood of being able to obtain validated, or at least reasonably error-free, compilers, and standardization, to discourage the development of non-standard extensions. Simplicity is not intended to imply ease of writing programs (e.g. in the style of BASIC): ease of subsequent understanding and ability to make modifications without creating unexpected side-effects is generally far more important.

Interactions between portability, simplicity and standardization are of crucial importance. If the language is too simple, the argument that it does not support various essential requirements may carry so much weight that implementors of compilers will be unable to avoid the addition of non-standard extensions, resulting in non-portability. However, if the language is adequate for complex systems, subsets will be needed for simple systems that do not require or cannot afford the overheads of the full language. (The worst situation arises from adding non-standard extensions to a subset to produce a language which does not meet the standard for the full language).

In the case of software for serious applications, program correctness and readability are of overriding importance, and of the three features described, simplicity is likely to make the greatest contribution to this.

5.3 HIGH-LEVEL LANGUAGES VERSUS ASSEMBLY-LANGUAGE

It is generally understood that the use of a high-level language typically results in the compiled program-code occupying more memory than if assembly-language had been used, and that the execution-speed of the compiled program is also typically lower. If an interpreter rather than a compiler is used to translate the high-level language (as is often done for BASIC and for the UCSD version of PASCAL) the execution-speed penalty may be very serious indeed. However, there are major cost, time-scale and reliability penalties in using assembly-language for other than small programs or program modules. In applications where some assembly-language programming must be used software tools are needed which permit the main structure of the software to be developed using a suitable high-level language while allowing those parts for which high execution-speed is essential to be incorporated as assembly-language segments.

Although a skilled assembly-language programmer can often produce good results even for fairly large and complex programs, subsequent maintenance of the software may prove difficult because the program-structure is not easy to understand from an assembly-language listing or other documentation likely to accompany it, the "skill" of the programmer is likely to have been used to incorporate clever "tricks" into the program to "improve performance", and those doing the maintenance are unlikely to be as skilled as the original designer, who is typically no longer available. In any case, there is a shortage of sufficiently-good assembly-language programmers.

The argument that the programmer needs to be able to directly control the processor resources, which cannot be done in a high-level language, carries little weight against the need to protect the processor from the probable mistakes of the programmer. The language should positively prevent the writing of code that could undermine system integrity.

Programming in assembly-language is therefore best regarded as a rather dangerous practice, only to be adopted if it can be justified. Even if circumstances do seem to justify the use of assembly language, it is worth considering the alternative of a higher-performance microprocessor, perhaps with some functions distributed to simpler microprocessors operating in a slave mode to the main processor.

Individual high-level languages do, however, differ considerably in the extent to which they support engineering design methods.

5.4 SUPPORT FOR STRUCTURED PROGRAMMING

For a single task (process) running on a single processor, any language must provide for the three elementary operations of sequencing, choice and iteration.

To support structured programming, these should be available as single-input single-output control structures with no opportunity for uncontrolled 'jumps' into or out of the middle of the structures.

The fundamental idea of a n-way choice may be expressed as

```
if   C1    execute  S1
     |C2   execute  S2
             .
             .
     |Cn   execute  Sn
endif
```

where the C_i are Boolean conditions. The inclusive-OR of the conditions must satisfy C_1.OR.C_2.OR....C_n = **true** (e.g. some S_i must always be executed). If more than one C_i = **true** then any one of the corresponding S_i could be executed; as far as program correctness is concerned it is immaterial which one but this indeterminacy has to be resolved before coding in any specific language. A mutually-exclusive two-way choice (if-then-else) is the commonest form:

```
if   C̄     execute  S1
     |C    execute  S2
endif
```

The actual format in several languages is as follows:

```
BASIC:          IF C̄ THEN nn
                statements implementing S1
                GOTO mm
             nn statements implementing S2
             mm (continuation of program)
         (nn,mm denote statement numbers)
```

```
PASCAL:   if C then begin
                    statements implementing S1
                    end
               else begin
                    statements implementing S2
                    end

ADA:      if C then statements implementing S1;
               else statements implementing S2;
          endif;
```

Clearly the risk of errors is far less if the language contains the required construction than if it has to be built up (as in BASIC or most assembly languages) from a careful arrangement of conditional and unconditional jumps.

Some languages (PASCAL, ADA) also provide the CASE statement as a direct implementation of an n-way choice, while in others this must be constructed by nesting a hierarchy of two-way choices.

The fundamental idea of iteration may be expressed as:

dowhile C **execute** S **enddo**

which means that if C is true, S is executed and the process repeated. An inherent feature of such a loop is an invariant, P, such that if P is true on entry, P AND $\overline{C}$ is true on exit. Finding the invariant is an important aspect of designing a correct loop.

Iteration is implemented in a variety of ways in programming languages (while-do, perform-until, etc.). A few examples are:

```
BASIC:    nn IF C THEN mm
             statements implementing S
             GOTO nn
          mm (continuation of program)     ["perform-until"]

PASCAL:   repeat
            begin
              statements implementing S
            end
          until C                           ["perform-until"]

          while C do
            begin
              statements implementing S
            end                             ["do-while"]

ADA:      loop
            statements implementing S;
            exit when C;
          endloop                           ["perform-until"]

          while C loop
            statements implementing S;
          endloop                           ["do-while"]
```

```
BCPL:     statements implementing S
          REPEATWHILE C                    ["perform-until"]
```

Iterative loops are associated with a risk of non-termination. Obviously it is insufficient for the loop to give a correct result only if it terminates (partial correctness); it must be guaranteed to actually terminate (total correctness).

Many languages provide a construct for iterative loops where the number of iterations is pre-determined; for example, in PASCAL:

```
for i := 1 to n do
    begin
    statements to be repeated n times
    end
```

Correct behaviour (looping n times) is, however, bound up with the value of the index i. If the body of the loop is allowed to change the value of i, the number of iterations can be changed. This is an inherent insecurity in many languages. Under no circumstances should assignments to i be permitted, and an ideal language would forbid this (hence enabling a compiler to detect violations). Thus, the compiler should not permit the programmer to get away with the following:

```
for i = 1 to n    begin i := i-1  end
```

In PASCAL, the semicolon is used as a statement separator whereas in ADA it is a statement terminator. This difference and the explicit use of **endif**, **endloop**, etc. in ADA removes the need for the **begin ... end** words which are extensively required in PASCAL. The inadvertent omission of a semicolon can often have an unexpectedly serious impact on the syntax analysis performed by the compiler, and hence on the diagnostics the compiler provides.

5.5 SUPPORT FOR GOOD DOCUMENTATION

Flow diagrams are a primitive form of high-level language and were useful when nothing higher than assembly language was available and prior to the adoption of structured programming. A well-structured program can be expressed unambiguously by a linguistic description using indenting to denote the hierarchical status of the statements. Thus, the program segment:

```
if   P  then    if Q  then A
                      else B
                endif
        else    if R  then C
                      else D
                endif
endif
```

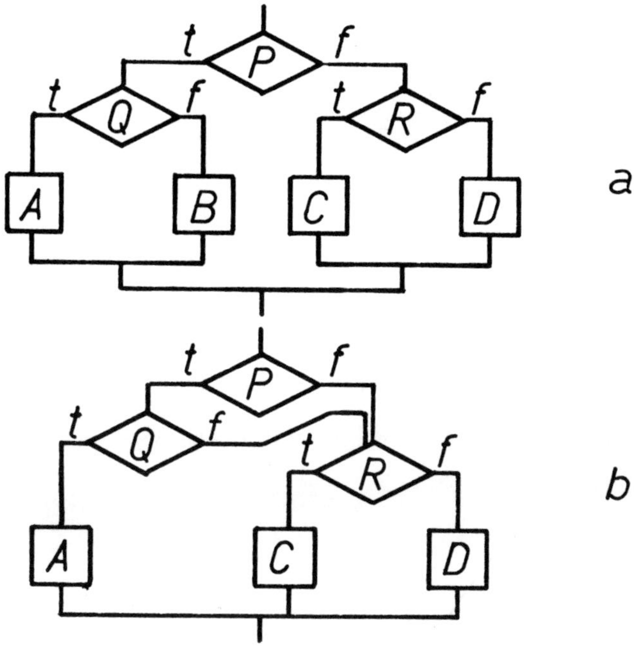

Fig. 5.1 Structured and unstructured flow-diagrams.

is in one-to-one correspondence with the flow-diagram shown in Fig. 5.1a. Fig. 5.1b on the other hand, cannot be so represented because of ambiguity about the level of the block containing R, C, D. Depending on whether it is reached from P or Q it is either one or two levels below P. Such difficulties do not arise in a properly-structured program, for which there is no reason to use flow-diagrams; they are not useful for design, of doubtful value for understanding, and because they are not machine readable, they typically do not get up-dated concurrently with the software being designed. Their use often detracts from good software design practice.

Brevity in choosing names for identifiers (variables, constants, etc.) is no longer regarded as a virtue. Two equivalent PASCAL programs are shown below to emphasize the advantages of choosing meaningful names and sensible layout. Careful choice of identifiers can have a major impact on the subsequent understanding and maintainability of a program, and languages which restrict the length or format of identifiers are very unsatisfactory. Perhaps even worse are those implementations which allow long identifiers to be used, but only use the first few characters. A compiler which allows the programmer to use long identifiers such as 'channelone' and 'channeltwo' and then only takes note of the first six characters (so rendering the two identifiers equivalent) is worse than one which allows only short identifiers.

```
program trianglegenerator;
const maximum = 80;
      minimum = -80;
var   level: integer;
begin
level:=0;
  while(TRUE)do
  begin
   while (level<maximum) do
   begin
    level:=level + 1;
    writeln (output,level)
   end;
   while (level>minimum) do
   begin
    level:=level - 1;
    writeln (output,level)
   end;
  end
end.
```

```
program myprogram;
const ml=80;
m2 = - 80;
var fred:integer;
begin
fred:=0;while(true)do
begin while(fred<ml)do begin
fred:=fred+1;
writeln(output,fred)
end;
while(fred>m2)do begin;
fred:=fred-1;
writeln (output,fred) end;
end
end.
```

5.6 SUPPORT FOR COMPILER-DETECTION OF ERRORS

In view of the overriding importance of correctness, and the inevitability that the software designers will make errors, the manner in which errors are detected is crucial. For real-time control applications in particular, running the program to see if it 'crashes' or produces bad results may be totally unacceptable in terms of cost or safety. A language that maximises the ability to detect errors at compile-time is therefore needed. This leads to a requirement for the programmer to be able to specify the 'type' of all identifiers that he uses, including the ability to create new data-types.

The instruction-sets and architectures of early microprocessors provide no support for distinguishing different types of data. An 8-bit word may represent an integer, a character, a mask, etc. and nothing prevents the addition of an integer to a character, even though such an operation is likely to be a design or coding error.

Most high-level languages provide some support for different data types. For example FORTRAN distinguishes real and integer variables. However, such older languages often allow mixed-type expressions which can be a source of ambiguity and elusive errors. For example, consider the following program segment:

```
a := 1
b := 4
c := 2.5
d := (a/b) * c
```

Since a, b are integers, (a/b) might be evaluated by integer arithmetic, so that d becomes zero. Alternatively, the compiler might be so written that a, b are converted to real prior to division, in which case d becomes 0.625. Although such uncertainities can usually be resolved by careful study of the small print in the programming manual, they do not help the production of reliable software.

The policy on mixed-type expressions varies from the PL/1 philosophy of always delivering some result ("if the mixed-type expression does not make sense, execute something, never mind if the results are rubbish") to the ADA philosophy of rigidly specifying what is permitted and informing the programmer of any deviations <u>prior</u> to execution. The latter is a sounder basis for developing reliable software.

If the following data-types are defined:

```
const m = 500;
var   x : integer;
      b : 0..255;               (sub-range type)
    y,z : character;
```

the assignments below are all compiler detectable errors.

```
z := x + y        (adding character to integer)
b := m            (out of range)
y := 2            (assigning integer to character)
```

The assignment y := '2' would be correct syntax (assuming quotes are used to indicate characters).

A mandatory requirement to declare all identifiers before use enables the compiler to detect many typical errors (including typographical mistakes) - and has an incidental benefit of encouraging more careful planning.

For example, a new data-type DAY might be defined:

```
DAY: (SUN, MON, TUE, WED, THU, FRI, SAT)
```

and variables TODAY, TOMORROW, of type DAY declared.

Then,

```
TODAY := MON
```

would be a valid assignment statement, whereas

```
TODAY := 3 * TUESDAY - 5
TODAY := MØN                          (Ø = zero)
```

would both be compiler-detectable errors.

As well as creating new data-types, it is often advantageous to be able to define operators to be used with them. For example, if a special interpretation can be given to '+' when it is used with the type DAY, the following assignment can be made meaningful:

```
TOMORROW := TODAY + 1
```

and would result in TOMORROW taking the value TUE if TODAY = MON.

This is not simply a matter of setting up a correspondence between the integers 1..7 and SUN..SAT, because if TODAY = SAT, the above statement needs to assign the value SUN to TOMORROW. Few programming languages provide a mechanism to define new operators in this way.

Further common errors can be detected if the compiler is able to identify statements which attempt to use the value of variables to which no value has been assigned.

This is not as easy to implement as it may seem. Even in the following simple example, the error in the last assignment statement would be difficult for a compiler to discover:

```
(i, j not initialised)
if (some condition) then i := 7;
                    else j := 8;
endif
k := i + j
```

Detection of such errors often has to take place at run-time, and therefore a safer strategy is to require the initial value of variables to be specified when they are declared.

5.7 SUPPORT FOR ABSTRACTION

A major need in software design is the management of complexity, and abstraction is the principal tool to achieve this. Software design is a hierarchical process, in which a correct high-level description is successively refined to produce more detailed, lower-level, descriptions. Errors arise from the inability of human designers to simultaneously comprehend the full complexity of the problem, and so it is essential that in going from one refinement to the next, the correctness property is maintained: without this, the whole basis for the design is compromised. Stepwise refinement does not mean taking a partially-complete and incorrect program and tinkering around with it until it seems to be correct! At each step of the refinement, every effort must be made to ensure that the program is strictly correct, otherwise errors will simply propagate through the refinements.

The 'block-structure' of languages such as ALGOL and PASCAL prevents outer blocks from accessing those identifiers defined within inner blocks, and goes some way to providing "information hiding", e.g. preventing the outer blocks from having more information (data) from inner blocks than they "need to know". This tends to reduce unintended interactions between different parts of the program, and modifications and corrections are less likely to have unforeseen side-effects.

In the example which follows, all three variables called index are unrelated. In 'first' size must take the value 100, since it is not defined within 'first'. In 'second' size takes the value 200 and size and start are both invisible from outside 'second'. Also, the outer size (=100) is invisible within 'second'.

```
Program scopeexample;
    const size = 100;
    var index: integer;
    procedure first;
        var index: integer;
        ---
        for index := 1 to size do
        ---
        end;
    procedure second;
    const start = 5;
          size = 200;
    var index : integer;
        begin
        ---
        for index := start to size do
        ---
        end;

    begin (* scopeexample *)
        first;
        second;
        ---
    end;
```

The identifiers of outer blocks are visible to inner blocks (unless hidden by a local declaration of an identifier with the same name), so that the information hiding is somewhat unidirectional and inadequate.

It is advantageous to be able to define software modules which have clearly defined interfaces but totally inaccessible internal structure ('software components'), though most widely-used programming languages at best only partially support this idea.

5.8 RUN TIME SUPPORT

Even the best possible language and the best possible compiler cannot detect all errors. For example, if a program contained the statements:

```
a := 1
b := 0
c := a/b
```

a simple compiler would probably not detect the error (division by zero), because individually the assignment statements all have the correct syntax (if a, b are constants, detection is more likely, since then c should be evaluated at compile-time).

If the second statement were replaced by

```
read(b)
```

it would be impossible for any compiler to object because an error would occur only if, during execution, a zero value were entered for b. Such errors can <u>only</u> be detected at run-time.

Controlled recovery from run-time errors is therefore important in real-time software. Detecting an execution-time error during the operation of an automatic-braking system or a missile-guidance system requires something other than displaying a message such as "Error 273 encountered at line 46701". (An increase in system reliability can be achieved by using multiple computers and a voting system for error correction but for software errors this is only an improvement if each computer uses a different software design: otherwise the same error will occur on each computer simultaneously, and will not even be detected.)

The language therefore needs an "exception handling mechanism" which enables the program designer to specify the action that should follow a run-time error. Thus, if an error occurs within a procedure which is, as a result, unable to continue meaningful execution, the error may be automatically notified to the calling procedure. Should this procedure not contain code to recover from the error, notification would be passed in turn to its calling procedure - and so on - until a procedure were eventually encountered which contained an error recovery routine provided by the designer. Of the generally available languages, only ADA supports this method of recovery from run-time errors.

5.9 SUPPORT FOR THE DEVELOPMENT ENVIRONMENT

Requirements of the program-development environment are somewhat distinct from language features. However, there is some interaction between the two, and the ability to compile modules separately and combine them to form an executable package is a convenient feature more easily provided in some languages than others.

To support top-down testing it must be possible to execute the software at all stages of development, by incorporating stubs for unwritten parts. This implies that pseudo-code cannot be used for the earlier stages of the design: a machine-translatable language is needed from the beginning. Top-down testing is not widely used, and is the subject of some controversy, but it does appear to be the best method of spreading the software validation process over the whole design cycle, and hence gaining early confidence about the progress of the design, as opposed to waiting until the first version of the design is complete before any system testing (as opposed to module testing) can begin.

5.10 MULTIPROCESSOR AND MULTITASKING SUPPORT

So far, all that has been said pertains to a single task (process) running sequentially on a single processor. If there are multiple tasks running on one or more processors, many additional sources of incorrect behaviour arise. A well-known example is 'deadlock', in which each task waits for another to proceed.

A key feature is communication between asynchronous tasks, and the essential requirement is to be able to synchronise these two tasks at the moment of information transfer. This may be assisted by hardware resources of the processor(s) being used, and newer designs of microprocessor typically cater for this. Inter-task communication usually involves providing a memory area accessible to each task. Mutual exclusion of access is essential to prevent corruption of data in the shared area. Although it is possible to write programs even at the assembly-language level which implement reliable communication between tasks, this is a source of serious programming errors and using a language which provides constructions to handle concurrency is much to be preferred.

Semaphores provide a basic construction to manage communication between tasks which share memory: two mutually-exclusive procedures **wait**(s) and **signal**(s) are used to control an otherwise-inaccessible shared variable s. A task calls **wait** to check if it is allowed to enter a critical section of program (one which must not be entered until the other task is ready for this) and it calls **signal** to indicate to the other task that it has left the critical section.

Even with semaphores, concurrency is difficult to handle correctly, and higher-level constructs are provided in some languages ("monitors" in concurrent PASCAL and the "rendezvous" mechanism of ADA).

5.11 CONCLUSIONS

Production of software which is correct, and sufficiently well-structured and understandable to encourage this correctness to be maintained throughout a life-cycle of revisions and extensions, is a difficult and challenging engineering task. The overview provided in this chapter is intended to form a basis for making a reasoned choice of a suitable programming language, and to give some guidance in its proper use.

It is often argued that rigorous methods of designing correct software will always be beyond the capability of most programmers, who are said not to have an adequate mathematical background to understand or to use such formal methods.

However, rather than just having more programmers, there may be a case for having fewer, better qualified, ones. An army of trained monkeys is not always an adequate substitute for the occasional Isaac Newton or Leonardo da Vinci.

Chapter 6

Practical real-time algorithms and data structures

D. Jenkins, M.K. Crowe

6.1 INTRODUCTION

In this chapter we begin with a brief examination of a problem requiring the use of data structures. The types of data structure used in real time work are then covered.

6.2 A SWITCHING PROBLEM

A fairly typical real-time problem arises in connection with route-switching for data communications. We wish to program a communications controller with one input channel and N output channels to handle 1024-byte packets, prefixed by an 8-byte destination identifier. The relationship between destinations and output channels is not fixed, and may change dynamically, but for simplicity we shall not concern ourselves with network management issues, or with transmission identification, retries, or other protocol issues. We are simply looking at the dispatching side of a network switching station.

Our problem is thus a very simple one in concept, but we shall see it is nevertheless fairly interesting. The constraints are that the data transmission rate is high, and there is no delay between the 8-byte destination prefix and the 1024-byte package. N is (say) 10, and there are thousands of possible eventual destinations coded in the 8-byte prefix.

6.3 SOME SIMPLE STRATEGIES

1. We could maintain a simple list of destinations and corresponding output channels:

Smith	1
Jenkins	5
Crowe	3
IEE-HQ	9
...	

and simply scan down the list when the prefix is received. Since there are a lot of possible destinations, we need to store the 1024-byte package in a buffer meantime for retransmission as soon as we find out which output channel to send it on.

Now this simple strategy in unsatisfactory for various

reasons. First, if input messages are coming in constantly, we may never get round to doing either the look-up of the table or the retransmission.

2. We could use an associative, content-addressable, memory for the table of destinations. This is expensive, but it has the advantage that no buffering is necessary. The disadvantage is that the cost of the equipment then becomes very sensitive to the number of destinations: and it presupposes that the communications system is not likely to grow very much.

3. We could try using three interlinked processes:

Processor A sends the prefix to Processor B and stores the packet in Memory;

Processor B looks up the table and advises Processor C of the output channel;

Processor C sends the packet stored in memory as advised by Processor B.

But even this fairly elaborate hardware probably will have a problem, since Processor B has to do on average say 2000 8-byte comparisons in the table lookup during the time it takes for 1032 bytes to be transmitted. Maybe we need several Processors B: and the hardware starts looking very expensive.

6.4 PRACTICAL IMPROVEMENTS TO SEARCHING STRATEGIES

Solution 3's hardware is not nearly as expensive as solution 2's, provided we have just one processor B. We can, however, improve our algorithm for looking up the destination in the table. If there are 4000 destination prefixes, an ordinary linear scan will take on average 2000 8-byte comparisons, and at most 4000. In real-time work, scanning an array is rarely possible.

A binary searching technique (and there are several) would cut this worst-case to 13 8-byte comparisons. What is even better is that doubling the number of destinations only alters the 13 into a 14, since the relationship is logarithmic. We will discuss these searching techniques in some detail in a moment.

Hashing techniques could help even more: most of the time, with a well-designed hashing system, we could manage with just one 8-byte comparison, together with a small overhead of (say) 7 shifts and 7 divides for computing the hash value. The problem with hashing is that the worst-case situation is very bad, and the system must be able to take advantage of the fact that searching for different destinations may take widely differing lengths of time.

6.4.1 Binary Chop Searching

The simplest binary search method works well when the list of destinations is not going to change very often, so that it can be kept in alphabetical order. A familiar example of this sort of list is given by the telphone directory:

```
var
   entry: array [1..15000] of string;
```

We suppose for simplicity that a parallel array contains the corresponding telephone numbers. (Pascal actually allows us to define a record-type containing both the subscriber's name of type string, and the telephone number, and then have an array of these records, but it is not faster.)

If we want to look up a name in a telephone directory, we do not start at the beginning, and compare each name in turn with the name we want. A better way would be to test against the middle name in the directory, to decide which half of the directory to look in, then try the middle of that half, and so on. This is called "binary searching" and the algorithm is quite famous:

```
              l:=1; r:=lastentry;
      repeat
        m:=(l+r) div 2;
        if name<=entry[m] then r:=m-1;
        if name>=entry[m] then l:=m+1
      until l>r;
      (* now if l=r+1 it isn't there,
         else it's the m-th entry *)
```

As a matter of fact, it appears that we need two 8-byte comparisons here. But obviously we will speed this up when we code into assembly language. One 8-byte compare operation yields a one-byte result which can then be tested as shown in the Pascal code.

6.4.2 Hashing

With hashing, we have a special array called a hash-table, preferably about three times as long as the directory, but each entry being an integer (the index of a directory entry). We need to concoct a way of calculating an arbitrary integer (a hash-value) from a given name, such as:

```
function hash(name:alfa):integer;
var h:integer;
begin
   h:=0;
   for j:=1 to 20 do
     h:=(h*7 + ord(name[j])) mod size;
   hash:=h
end;
```

(where size is the length of the hash-table, about 3 x lastnum). The idea is then that the hash-value we get from a name is simply looked up in the hash-table, which tells us where the name is in the directory! Unfortunately, it is almost certain that several names will have the same hash-value ("conflict"), so our code will need to allow for this possibility.

One way of dealing with this is called "open hash" where we move on by one in the hash-table until we find a blank entry. For the open hash algorithm, the hash-table is built from the directory as follows:

```
(* build hash table *)
for h:=0 to size-1 do table[h]:=0;
for k:=1 to lastnum do
  begin
    h:=hash(entry[k]);
    while table[h]<>0 do h:=(h+1) mod size;
    table[h]:=k
  end;
```

Now when we want to look up a name, we need

```
(* find entry equal to name *)
h:=hash(name); found:=false; k:=table[h];
while (k<>0) and not found do
  if name=entry[k] then
    found:=true
  else
    begin
      h:=(h+1) mod size;
      k:=table[h]
    end;
```

With a carefully selected hashing function, hashing always gives the fastest method of finding an entry in a list.

A slight refinement on hashing is "random hashing", where the hashing function also gives a step to use in the event of conflicts. With the open hash method presented above, this step is always 1. We must take care that step is not zero (or a multiple of size), and in order to avoid the situation where the step divides into size, size had better be a prime number.

6.5 ALIASING BY ROUTE

So much for straightforward implementations of the problem as stated. However, an important part of system design consists of building a logical model of the given problem and solving that. A very little thought suggests that the problem as stated already seems to contain some implementation details: the table of destinations and corresponding output channels. This is presumably part of a larger system which allows people to send packages to each other. Now it is entirely reasonable that I should wish to send a message to Angela, say, mentioning her by name in my request. It is really not very reasonable that I should actually insist that her name should be used internally at every stage by the message switching machinery. If the network system uses an "alias" for destination names, we can save a lot of money.

After all, if the sending station has up-to-date information about the network, it can compute what route will be taken by the message, and the prefix can contain a sequence of output channels. Our station would see a package prefix looking like

0 0 4 6 6 3 2 0

and would simply send the package to output channel 4, with a new prefix:

0 0 0 6 6 3 2 0

From this point of view it is extremely wasteful for the destination name to be looked up in tables at every switching station. An 8 byte prefix would allow for up to 16 switching stations en route, which should be sufficient for most systems. Only the sender of the message needs to look up the alias to use for the required destination.

This is an example of aliasing: as far as our station is concerned, the destination "Larry" has alias 46632, and no tables are necessary. This allows us to economise further on our hardware, as a single processor will suffice, no buffering of any kind being necessary. A special prefix such as F could be used for network information that is to be transmitted to every channel, to be used by the subscribers to update their alias tables.

Note that destinations have different aliases at each point in the network on this strategy. But the only sites that are interested in knowing the real names that correspond to the aliases are the sites at the edges of the network (i.e. not the switching stations).

At these edge sites, a fairly sophisticated set of algorithms is required for computing aliases. Typical network information messages would say things like "Station Fred has gone off line", or "Fred now reached on output 5 from Betty", and if Fred is a switching station, quite a few aliases would need to be recalculated. However, these calculations are not time-critical, as were the calculations required during switching operations, so we need not discuss them here.

As for the hardware implementation at the switching site, the most we ever need to buffer is 8 bytes. This can be done using a hardware FIFO, so no software buffering is required.

6.6 INVERSION

For a moment, let us stay with our earlier example, of a table which associated destination names with aliases. Probably, this table will be structured in some way (or just arranged in order) to make it easy to look up a particular destination to obtain its route key (called its "alias" previously).

Now suppose that we need to know what destination corresponds to a given route key. Maybe this question does not arise all that often, but it probably will need to be answered sometimes, for accounting or post-mortem purposes. At first sight we need to look through the whole list, since it has been constructed for fast look-up of destinations, but not of route keys.

Suddenly, we want a list which makes it easy for route-keys to be looked up. We want the table to be "inverted". It is a bit like the subject-index problem in a library, where we have an index by author, and want to invert it to get an index by subject.

It often happens that it is worth constructing and updating an inverse table at the same time as the main table. This will become especially necessary when we come to linked lists and trees, but for the moment, let us stay with simple arrays.

Suppose we want to know (for debugging or accounting purposes) which destination name corresponds to a given alias. At first sight, we are back to our array-scanning problem. So we need another array, ordered by alias number, so that we can use binary search: or we need a second hashing table so that we can look up the alias number. (The first idea perhaps better deserves the name of "inversion", which comes originally from mathematics: we should regard an array as a mapping from the domain of its subscript to its set of values, so that the inverse of the array

```
        a[0..5] = [ 4,5,3,6,8,2 ]
```

is

```
        ainv[2..8] = [ 5,2,0,1,3,-,4 ]
```

for example.) We will see more examples of inversion later on.

6.7 A REVIEW OF PRACTICAL DATA STRUCTURES

6.7.1 Queues (FIFO stores)

We are all familiar with queues, in supermarkets and the like. People get added to the tail of the queue, and get served at the head of the queue:

```
                T  x x ... x : H
             x /
                    ----->
```

FIFO stands for First In, First Out. Each time the person at the head of the queue is served, all the individuals in the queue move up one. (If this fails to happen, the body of the queue moves steadily backwards into the supermarket.)

Now this is rather expensive to implement directly using an array: although there are even hardware devices that move all the entries in the queue when the head entry is taken off the queue! Note also that providing an array for the queue means that we need to set an arbitrary maximum size for the queue.

Before we consider practical implementations for queues, let us look at their uses. We mentioned earlier that FIFOs could be used as buffers. The output stage of our switching station needs one. They are also used as actual queues, of course, when we scehdule processes. For example, suppose several jobs are waiting for some resource - a piece of memory, or a printer. They will need to be held in some sort of queue until the resource becomes available.

There are two alternatives to having the queue move. One is to use linked lists, which we will come to in a little while. The other is to have the head and tail of the queue move, using a "circular" array:

```
                    x x x x : H ......        T > x x x x
```

Removing the head of the queue gives

```
                    x x x : H .......         T > x x x x
```

and adding at the tail gives

```
                    x x x : H .......       T > x x x x x
```

We still have a maximum size for the queue, of course:

the queue is full when the head catches up with the tail, and empty when head and tail are same.

This gives the following Pascal implementation:

```
var
        queue: array[0..N] of person;
        head, tail: 0..N;
function AddToQueue (x: person):boolean;
  begin
    if (head+1)mod N = tail then
      AddToQueue:=false (* queue full *)
    else
      begin
        queue[head]:=x;
        head:=(head+1)mod N;
        AddToQueue:=true
      end
  end;
function TakeFromQueue (var x:person):boolean;
  begin
    if head=tail then
      TakeFromQueue:=false
    else
      begin
        x:=queue[tail];
        tail:=(tail+1)mod N;
        TakeFromQueue:=true
      end
  end;
procedure MakeQueue;
  begin
    head:=0;
    tail:=0
  end;
```

6.7.2 Stacks (LIFO stores)

LIFO stands for Last In, First out, of course. The entries in the stack are like plates in a canteen servery:

```
T -> x     Top Plate
     x
     x     Bottom Plate
     >     Spring
     <
```

Stacks are used in coping with interrupts and recursive operations: stacks are used to save the state of some low-priority activity while we go away and perform some high-priority activity. When the high-priority activity is complete, the top process is removed from the stack and reactivated.

Stacks are easier to implement than queues: assuming we can set an arbitrary maximum size for the stack, we can use a simple array. In Pascal we get

```
var
  stack: array[0..N] of object;
  top: 0..N;
```

```
function AddToStack(x:object):boolean;
  begin
    if top=N then
      AddToStack:=false (* stack full *)
    else
      begin
        top:=top+1;
        stack[top]:=x;
        AddToStack:=true
      end
  end;
function TakeFromStack (var x:object): boolean;
  begin
    if top=0 then
      TakeFromStack:=false (* stack empty *)
    else
      begin
        x:=stack[top];
        top:=top-1;
        TakeFromStack:=true
      end
  end;
procedure MakeStack;
  begin
    top:=0
  end;
```

(Some remarks about modularity and Pascal: assuming this is a separately compiled implementation of the three external procedures shown, the objects called "stack" and "top" are not visible from the main program. But separate compilation is not available in standard Pascal.)

We will see some applications of stacks when we walk around trees later on - but it should be noted that if a real-time application uses recursion, or tree-walking, in a time-critical environment, something has gone wrong with the design!

6.7.3 Lists

If it is inconvenient to specify maximum sizes for a queue or a stack, or if several such structures are competing for memory, it may be necessary to implement the queue or stack by a linked list. Another reason for preferring lists is that many 8-bit microprocessors do not provide sufficiently powerful address computation facilities for fast implementation of arrays.

A memory allocator is assumed to be available, which will make available a contiguous piece of memory or demand. There had better be some way of releasing memory thus allocated, and at least a way of coalescing adjacent freed areas of memory. For simplicity we ignore details of the memory allocator here: it is available in Pascal through the standard procedures "new" and "dispose". They take as parameter a pointer (access variable) to the object being allocated or freed.

With this apparatus, a linked list of people would

look like

```
    ---       ---       ---                 ---       ---
   : D :    ->: G :    ->: M :              ->: W :    ->: Z :
   :---:  :  :---:  :  :---:     : ...  :  :---:  :  :---:
   : .-+--   : .-+--   : .-+---            : .-+--   :   :
    ---       ---       ---                 ---       ---
```

A list of this form can be used to implement a stack or a queue. (But for double-ended queues or "deques" we need backward pointers as well if we are not to scan along the list.)

```
        type
           lptr = © link;
           (* this is the type of an access to a link *)
           link = record
                    content: person;
                    (* the person here in the list *)
                    next:    lptr
                    (* points to the next link     *)
                  end;
        var
           list: lptr;   (* the top of stack, or head of queue
           tail: lptr;   (* only needed for queues *)
        procedure AddToStack(x: person);
          var
            p: lptr;
          begin
            new(p);
            p©.content:= x; p©.next:= list;
        (*  if list=nil then tail:=p;
               only needed for queues *)
            list:=p
          end;
        procedure AddToQueue(x:person);
          var
            p: lptr;
          begin
            new(p);
            p©.content:= x; p©.next:= nil;
            if tail=nil then
              list:=p
            else
              tail©.next:= p;
            tail:= p;
          end;
```

```
function TakeFromList(var x:person);
  var
    p: lptr;
  begin
    p:=list;
    if p=nil then
      TakeFromList:=false (* list is empty *)
    else
      begin
        x:= p©.content;
        list:= p©.next;
        dispose(p);
        TakeFromList:=true
      end
  end;
procedure MakeList;
  begin
    list:=nil;
    tail:=nil   (* only needed for queues *)
  end;
```

Lists can be used for information maintained in some order that is subject to addition and deletion. But binary searching is impossible, so there seems little point in such lists. Rearranging an array would be more economical.

6.7.4 Trees

An alternative to binary search that is useful if the list is subject to addition (but not deletion), uses binary trees. An ordered binary tree looks like

```
      CAT
     /   \
  ANT    LION
         /   \
       DOG   MOUSE
```

where at any node, the left branch leads to smaller entries, while the right leads to larger entries. The number of comparisons required still depends logarithmically on N, but if the tree is unbalanced, the worst case gets even worse.

The strategy for adding and searching is exactly the same, and the Pascal implementation naturally uses recursion:

```
type
  nptr = © node;
  node = record
           content:    person;
           left, right: nptr
         end;
var
  tree: nptr;
```

```
function SearchTree (x: person): nptr;
  procedure Search (p: nptr);
    begin
      SearchTree:=p;
      if p<>nil then
        if p©.content>x then
          Search(p©.left)
        else if p©.content<x then
          Search(p©.right)
    end;
  begin  (* SearchTree *)
    Search(tree);
  end;
procedure AddToTree (x: person);
  procedure Add (var p: nptr);
    begin
      if p<>nil then
        if p©.content>x then
          Add(p©.left)
        else if p©.content<x then
          Add(p©.right)
        else
          begin
            new(p); p©.content:=x;
            p©.left:=nil; p©.right:=nil
          end
    end;
  begin  (* AddToTree *)
    Add(tree);
  end;
procedure MakeTree;
  begin
    tree:=nil
  end;
```

Of course, the nodes will usually contain information in addition to the key used for sorting. This is why we make the SearchTree function return the whole node, which may have other fields in it. AddTree would then have other parameters which would be copied into the new node.

Purists may object that non-local variables are used in the internal procedures: some may even object that internal procedures are used at all. There are arguments in favour of the above coding, but the principal disadvantage is inefficiency. For real time work, recursion is a luxury we can rarely afford, and it can always be eliminated with more or less effort. For the SearchTree function we get:

```
function SearchTree (x: person): nptr;
  var
    p: nptr;
    found: boolean;
  begin
    p:=tree;  found:=false;
    while (p<>nil) and not found do
      if p©.content>x then
        p:=p©.left
      else if p©.content<x then
        p:=p©.right
      else
        found:=true;
    SearchTree:=p
  end;
```

For completeness, let us observe that binary trees can be used very efficiently for sorting. Using the above procedures to build the tree, we can dump the nodes in order by tree-walking, as follows:

```
procedure DumpTree;
  procedure Dump (p: nptr);
    begin
      if p<>nil then
        begin
          Dump(p©.left);
          WritePerson(p©.content);
          Dump(p©.right);
        end
    end;
  begin
    Dump(tree)
  end;
```

A non-recursive version of this uses a stack:

```
procedure DumpTree;
  var
    p: nptr;
    more,junk: boolean;
  begin
    p:=tree; more:= p<>nil;
    while more do
      if p=nil then
        if TakeFromStack(p) then
          begin
            WritePerson(p©.content);
            p:=p©.right
          end
        else
          more:=false
      else
        begin
          junk:=AddToStack(p);
          p:=p©.left
        end
  end;
```

Chapter 7

Real-time features of a high-level language

S.J. Young

7.1 INTRODUCTION

In many respects the requirements of a language suitable for programming real time systems are identical to those for any other computer-based task. In order to support the production of reliable easily maintained software, it must provide a good data typing system, structured control statements, procedures and functions and some facility for data abstraction and program modularisation. Real time systems, however, have certain special characteristics which ideally require explicit language support. These special characteristics are exemplified by typical embedded-microprocessor systems such as digital controllers, intelligent instruments, communication switches, etc. In these systems the software must

(a) handle external asynchronous events within specified response times

(b) perform several tasks concurrently

(c) control special purpose input/output devices

(d) operate continuously even when errors occur

Curiously, perhaps, traditional real time languages such as CORAL 66 and RTL/2 have provided very little explicit support for these real time functions. In fact, the only difference between these older real time languages and general purpose languages is that they were designed to allow the production of very efficient object code. Access to device registers is provided by the simple expendient of 'peek' and 'poke' mechanisms supported by low level 'bit-twiddling' operations; multi-tasking relies on the use of an appropriate operating system; and error handling depends on the clever use of the ubiquitous 'goto' statement.

Although efficiency is still a consideration, it is now realised that it is much more important for a real time language to provide a high level structured approach to programming the above operations. The purpose of this chapter is to identify the language features that are necessary to be able to do this and to show how they are used.

Most of the examples given relate to the problem of programming special-purpose interupt-driven i/o devices as this characterises the special nature of real time programming and is also particularly relevant to implementers of embedded microprocessor based systems. The chapter concludes with a brief survey of the modern languages which provide some or all of the real time features identified.

7.2 ACCESSING DEVICE HARDWARE

In this section, language features for accessing device i/o registers will be examined. The basic approach here is to represent a device register by a data type and then declare a variable of that type (Young (1)). However, unlike normal program variables, a variable used to access a device register must be explicitly linked to a specific memory location or i/o port. For example, the data register of a UART located at COOBH (H denotes hexadecimal) could be accessed by declaring a variable

```
VAR uart_data:char AT OCOOBH;
```

A character can then be loaded into this data register by a conventional assignment statement eg.

```
uart_data := 'A';
```

Here the AT part in the variable declaration instructs the compiler to allocate 'uart_data' at the given memory location. If distinct i/o port addressing is used instead of memory-mapping then an additional keyword PORT can be used eg.

```
VAR uart_data:char AT PORT 2BH;
```

In this case, the PORT keyword instructs the compiler to translate subsequent assignment statements, not by normal memory transfer instructions, but by input/output instructions to the specified port.

The above language features are simple to implement yet provide a high level mechanism for accessing device registers. Not all device registers, however, are quite as simple as the above example. Control and status registers usually consist of several fields of 1 or more bits, each bit field being associated with a different function. In such cases, a RECORD data type can be used to describe the register, extended to include specific instructions on how to map the record components onto the required bit fields. As an example, the control register of an Intel 8253 timer has 8 bits whose functions are as follows:

Bit 0:	select bcd/binary	- 0 = binary
		1 = bcd
Bits 1-3:	select function	- 0 = interrupt on terminal count
		1 = programmable one-shot
		2 = rate generator
		3 = square wave generator
		4 = software triggered strobe
		5 = hardware triggered strobe
Bits 4-5:	select r/w mode	- 0 = latch counter
		1 = r/w most sig. byte

```
                              2 = r/w least sig. byte
                              3 = r/w both bytes
Bits 6-7: select timer 0, 1 or 2
```

This register can be described by the following types

```
TYPE time_func = (term_int, one_shot, rate_gen,
                  squ_wave, soft_strobe, hard_strobe);

  rwmode       = (latch, most_sig, least_sig, both);

  timer_id     = 0..2;

  timer_control  = RECORD
                     bcd:   Boolean   AT  0..0;
                     func:  time_func AT  1..3;
                     rwm:   rwmode    AT  4..5;
                     ctr:   timer_id  AT  6..7
                   END;
```

where the AT parts within the record specify which bits to use for each component. An actual variable can then be allocated to access the register as before eg.

```
VAR  tctl:timer_control AT OBOFEH;
```

Manipulation of the bit fields can now use the conventional record notation eg.

```
tctl.func   := one_shot;
```

and when all fields of a register need to be initialised then a record aggregate can be assigned directly eg

```
tctl := timer_control (true,one_shot,both,0);
```

At first sight, the above type declarations may seem very long winded and unnecessary. What after all is wrong with the following?

```
VAR tctl:integer AT OBOFEH;

tctl    := 33H;
```

The answer is a great deal. Firstly, there is no indication as to the significance of the value 33H. Subsequent maintenance of the program would therefore require ready access to the appropriate hardware reference manual. The structure of the register could, of course, be described in the program by the inclusion of a detailed comment but this would entail more effort than the proper type declarations. Secondly, the compiler is unable to check that assignments to 'tctl' are sensible. For example, a value of F3H is illegal as there is no counter number 3 but neither the compiler nor the run-time system could detect this. Finally, access to the individual bit fields requires complicated and obscure bit twiddling. In short, programs written in this way would be little better than if they had been written in assembly language.

7.3 CONCURRENT PROGRAMMING

Most real time programs of any complexity are required to handle several tasks simultaneously. With the older real time languages, this was achieved by expressing each task as a separate program. The collection of programs so-formed were then executed concurrently by using a multi-task operating system.

The main drawback of this approach is that all task communication is via calls to the operating system. These calls tend to be low level and error prone, and since the compiler is unaware of the concurrent environment, it has no opportunity to check that task communication is programmed correctly. Furthermore, the strictly sequential nature of each program means that external asynchronous events must be handled by the operating system. A direct consequence of this is that programming interrupt-driven i/o devices from within the language is very difficult. In this section, the basic features of a typical concurrent programming language will be outlined and then in the next section, it will be shown how these features provide a very natural way of programming interrupt-driven i/o devices.

The most common approach to providing concurrent programming features within a high level language is to represent each process (task) using a similar notation to that of procedures. The only difference between a process and a procedure is that when a process is called, it starts to execute in parallel with the calling program which itself continues executing immediately. Processes communicate by writing and reading from shared data areas protected by a mechanism called a monitor (Hoare(2)). The main ideas of this system are illustrated by the following example.

```
PROGRAM pipeline;

MONITOR buffer;

   CONST bufsize=64;

   VAR   buf:       ARRAY(1..bufsize)OF char;
         inx,outx:  1..bufsize;
         used:      0..bufsize;
         nonfull,nonempty: signal;

   PROCEDURE put (ch:char);
   BEGIN
      IF used=bufsize THEN wait (nonfull);
      buf(inx):= ch; used:=used+1;
      inx:=(inx MOD bufsize)+1:
      send (nonempty)
   END;
```

```
      PROCEDURE get (VAR ch:char);
      BEGIN
         IF used=0 THEN wait (nonempty)
         ch:=buf(outx); used:=used-1;
         outx:=(outx MOD bufsize)+1;
         send (nonfull)
      END;

BEGIN (initialise monitor data structures)
   inx:=1; outx:=1; used:=0
END; (buffer)

PROCESS reader;
   VAR ch:char;
BEGIN
   REPEAT
      read(ch); put (ch)
   UNTIL forever
END;

PROCESS writer;
   VAR ch:char;
BEGIN
   REPEAT
     get (ch) ; write (ch)
   UNTIL forever
END;

BEGIN (main program)
   reader;  (start reader process)
   writer;  (start writer process)
END.
```

This program simply copies an input character stream to an output character stream using two processes: 'reader' and 'writer'. These two processes execute concurrently transmitting data from one to the other via a first-in first-out buffer which smooths out any fluctations in the relative speeds of the read and write operations.

The two processes are invoked initially by being called from the main program. Once started, the 'reader' process repeatedly reads a character from the input stream and then puts it in the buffer. Similarly, the 'writer' process repeatedly gets a character from the buffer and writes it to the output stream.

The buffer itself resides within the monitor and consists of a fixed size array, a count of how many buffer slots are used and two indices to record the current input and output slots. When the program is first started, the statement body of the monitor is executed to initialise this buffer. The key feature of the monitor is that external processes are not allowed to access its data structures directly (if this were allowed, data corruption could occur when two processes attempt to write simultaneously). Instead, the only access is via the procedures within the monitor. These can always access the data safely, because the run-time system ensures that monitor procedure calls are serviced sequentially. Thus, in the example, if the 'writer' process calls 'get' at the same time as the 'reader' process calls 'put', then only one process (it does not matter which) will be allowed to proceed. The other process is made to wait until the first process has finished executing the monitor procedure (or suspends itself by issuing a 'wait for signal' request - see below). Thus, the monitor provides a safe mechanism for mutually exclusive access to shared data structures.

In the example, the buffer is normally partially full and therefore each process can get and put characters without undue delay. Special action must be taken, however, if the buffer becomes full or empty. In this case, synchronisation between the processes is needed and this is achieved through the use of signals. Each time the 'reader' process calls 'put', its last action is to send the signal 'nonempty'. If another process is waiting for this signal then that process will resume execution, otherwise sending the signal has no effect. Thus, in the example, if the 'writer' process calls 'get' and then finds that the buffer is empty, it suspends itself by waiting for the signal 'nonempty' which will be sent to it the next time that the 'reader' process calls 'put'. The case of the buffer being full is dealt with in a similar way.

Although this example is only a 'toy' program it illustrates the main features of concurrent programming using processes and monitors. The key point to stress is that the monitor encapsulates a data structure and provides the necessary procedures to access it safely. Thus, once a monitor has been properly tested, any number of processes can be introduced into a system without fear of data corruption through a fault in one of the processes. This is in contrast to earlier systems which use operating system calls (typically calls to secure and release semaphores) where every process which uses a data structure is personally responsible for accessing it properly.

7.4 HANDLING ASYNCHRONOUS EVENTS

The basic language facilities described in the previous section for representing concurrent processes provide a natural mechanism for handling external asynchrous events. All that needs to be done is to associate a signal with each event and then assign a process to monitor the event by waiting for the signal to be sent to it.

One of the most common types of external event encountered in real time systems is an interrupt from an i/o device. Interrupts can be handled using monitor-like structures in which a signal is explicitly mapped onto the appropriate interrupt vector location. As an example, the following is a simple driver for a printer on a PDP 11 computer

```
     DEVICE MONITOR printer (4);

       TYPE controlreg = RECORD
```

```
                              intenable:Boolean AT 6..6;
                              ready:Boolean AT 7..7;
                              error:Boolean AT 15..15
                            END,

      VAR int:signal AT 200C;      (C denotes octal)
          bufreg:char  AT 177516C;
          ctlreg:controlreg AT 177514C;

      PROCEDURE print (ch:char);
      BEGIN
         bufreg:=ch;
         ctlreg.intenable:=true;
         wait (int);
         ctlreg.intenable:=false
      END;

END;  (printer)
```

The printer device on a PDP11 is very simple. Characters are sent to the printer by writing them to memory location 177516C (C denotes octal). When the printer is ready to accept another character it generates an interrupt provided that this has been enabled by setting bit 6 of the control register located at 1776514C.

Given this information and ignoring errors, the operation of the 'printer' monitor is quite straightforward. Variables for accessing the devices buffer register ('bufreg') and control register ('ctlreg') are declared using the mechanisms described in section 2. In addition, a signal is declared called 'int' whose AT part specifies that it be linked to interrupt vector location 200C. Thus, when the printer generates this interrupt, the signal 'int' will be sent automatically. In order to print a character, a process calls the procedure 'print' which copies the character into 'bufreg', enables interrupts and then waits for the interrupt to occur. At this point, the calling process is suspended. When the interrupt occurs, the process is woken-up, interrupts are disabled and the process leaves the device monitor. Finally, in order to allow normal interrupt priority mechanisms to be exploited, the heading of the device monitor specifies the processor priority level (in this case 4) at which all monitor procedures must be executed.

This example shows that given the necessary language features for expressing concurrency, very few additional features are needed to be able to program interrupt-driven device handlers directly from a high level language, hence doing away with the need for assembly language device handlers and multitask operating systems altogether.

The printer driver given above is less useful than it could be since each process which uses it must wait while each character is printed. The inclusion of a first-in first-out buffer as in the 'pipeline' program of section 3 solves this problem as shown below.

```
      DEVICE MONITOR printer (4);
```

```
CONST bufsize=64;

TYPE controlreg = RECORD
                    intenable:Boolean AT 6..6;
                    ready:Boolean AT 7..7;
                    error:Boolean AT 15..15
                  END;

VAR int:signal AT 200C;    (C denotes octal)
    bufreg:char AT 177516C;
    ctlreg:controlreg AT 177514C;
    buf:          ARRAY(1..bufsize)OF char;
    inx,outx:     1..bufsize;
    used:         0..bufsize;
    nonfull,nonempty: signal;

PROCEDURE print (ch:char);
   BEGIN
     IF used=bufsize THEN wait (nonfull);
     buf(inx):=ch; used:=used+1;
     inx:= (inx MOD bufsize)+1;
     send(nonempty)
END;

PROCESS driver;
BEGIN
     ctlreg.intenable:=true;
     REPEAT
        IF used=0 THEN wait (nonempty);
        bufreg:=buf(outx); used:=used-1;
        outx:=(outx MOD bufsize)+1;
        wait (int);
        send(nonfull)
      UNTIL forever
    END;

BEGIN (initialise data structures)
   inx:=1; outx:=1; used:=0;
   driver  (start driver process)
END;  (buffer)
```

Now the monitor procedure 'print' does not attempt to output the character itself but simply puts it in the buffer. Within the monitor is a process which loops endlessly, taking characters from the buffer and writing them to the output device.

7.5 ERROR HANDLING

Traditionally, error handling has been a rather neglected topic in language design yet in the area of real time systems, good error handling facilities are crucial. There are two main requirements of an error handling mechanism.

Firstly, error handling code should not detract from the

readability of a program by distorting the normal program flow. For example, consider the following program

```
BEGIN
   inputdata(data,ok);
   IF ok THEN
   BEGIN
     computeresults(data,results,ok);
     IF ok THEN
       printresults(results)
     ELSE
        write ('Error in computation')
   END ELSE
     write ('Error in input data');

END
```

In this example, the normal error-free program flow is quite simple ie.

```
inputdata;
computeresults;
printresults;
```

but the actual program text does not reflect this linear flow since it has been grossly distorted by the error handling code. Clearly, structured control statements have little to offer when dealing with errors and, in consequence, most real time languages rely heavily on the 'goto' statement. But as is well-known, the 'goto' statement is too low level and error prone for the production of highly reliable software.

The second requirement of an error handling facility is that it should provide the same approach to handling errors detected by the underlying system as to those detected by programmer action. Examples of errors detected by the system are arithmetic overflow, array index out of bounds, etc.

Both of the above requirements are satisfied by a mechanism based on the concept of exceptions and their associated handlers. An exception denotes a particular error and when that error occurs, the exception is said to be raised. Errors detected by the implementation are predefined and are raised automatically. Errors detected by the programmer must be explicitly declared like variables and raised by a RAISE statement.

When an exception is raised, the system searches for a handler for that exception and then executes the handler in place of the interrupted sequence of statements. For example, the following is a robust integer multiplication routine

```
FUNCTION mult(x,y:integer):integer;
BEGIN
   mult  :=x*y    (arithmetic overflow can occur here)
EXCEPTION
   overflow_err:
      IF sign(x)=sign(y) THEN (exception handler)
```

```
          mult:=maxint
        ELSE
          mult:=-maxint
    END;
```

This function 'mult' has an exception handler attached to it for the predefined exception 'overflow_err'. Normally, when 'mult' is called the value of 'x*y' is computed, assigned to mult and then the function returns control to the caller. If, however, the value of 'x*y' exceeds the range of integer numbers, the underlying system automatically raises the 'overflow_err' exception. This causes control to be transferred to the exception handler which then computes the best answer it can and returns in the normal way. Note that in this case, the caller of 'mult' is never made aware that an error has occurred.

A routine does not have to have exception handlers attached to it for every possible exception that could occur during its execution. When an exception is raised for which no handler can be found, the currently active routine is terminated and control returns to the caller. The same exception is then raised again causing the system to search for a handler again. In this way, exceptions can be propagated back down a chain of procedure calls until a point is reached where the programmer considers it appropriate to handle them. As an example, the routine 'inputdata' in the earlier example could report errors detected in the input by executing the statement

```
RAISE input_fault;
```

but not contain a handler for it. The structure of the calling routine would then be

```
VAR input_fault,proc_fault:exception;

BEGIN
   inputdata(data);
   computeresults(data,results);
   printresults(results)
EXCEPTION
   input_fault:
     write('Error in input data'):
   proc_fault:
     write('Error in computation')
END
```

Now when 'inputdata' detects an error the 'input_fault' exception is raised within it but not handled locally. Hence, 'input_data' terminates immediately and control returns to the main program where the 'input_fault' exception is raised again. This time a handler can be found for it so this is executed and the program terminates. Note how the code for error handling in this second version is kept quite seperate from the normal statement flow making program operation much clearer.

The above is just a brief sketch of exception handlers and their us in error detection and recovery. A more complete discussion is given by Young (3) but it should be stressed that they are a relatively new idea and there is little in the way of real experience of their use. Nevertheless, they appear to offer a substantial improvement over existing error handling techniques.

7.6 REAL TIME LANGUAGES

The preceding sections have identified four major features which should be included in a modern real time language.

1. Facilities for mapping data types and variables onto specific memory locations and i/o ports for low level device programming.

2. Facilities for representing concurrent processes and a secure inter-process communication mechanism.

3. Facilities for associating interrupts with the process synchronisation primitives (eg. signals) to allow interrupt-driven i/o device handlers to be written.

4. Facilities for structured error detection and recovery

To conclude, some of the languages commonly used in the real time area in the UK will be briefly reviewed with respect to these features.

Coral 66 -although widely used, this is an outdated language. Basic Coral provides none of the features discussed above but a standard multi-tasking environment (MASCOT) has recently been introduced.

RTL/2 -similar to Coral but more secure. Although it has a fairly good typing system, there is no provision for representation specifications of the kind discussed here. Also like Coral, there are no in-built concurrency features but a standard multi-task operating system interface is defined. Error handling depends on 'goto' jumps but variable labels give it equivalent power to an exception handling mechanism albeit in a low level way.

PL/M -designed by Intel for programming its own microcomputers. This language is based on PL/1 but at a rather lower level. It has the basic structuring mechanisms that are now expected of a high level language and a data typing system but there is little in the way of compiler type checking. PL/M has facilities for accessing device hardware but none of the other features discussed above. It is widely used principally as a result of its high availability. The other major microprocessor manufacturers have similar languages for which the same comments apply.

Pascal -although not generally considered to be a real time language there are several Industrial Pascal systems available. Some control of data representation is provided by a 'PACKED' directive and Industrial implementations provide extensions for accessing device hardware and the interrupt system. Concurrent processes are not included in Standard Pascal but at least two implementations of Pascal provide process features as a language extension. Error handling is via 'goto' jumps but labels are fixed so it is more restrictive than RTL/2.

'C' -designed for programming the UNIX Operating System, this language is becoming popular in its own right. C is not strictly a high level language as it has many low level features. It is designed specifically to optimise the use of the PDP11 instruction set and when carefully used can compete with Assembly language on memory usage and speed. C has many features for low level programming but there is no in-built concurrency and limited error handling.

Modula -initially an experimental language but now used by several organisations for real time embedded micro systems. Modula provides all the features described here except error handling. Curiously, there is not even a 'goto' in Modula making comprehensive error handling very difficult to program.

Modula 2 -the successor to Modula. Problems with process management in Modula led to precesses being replaced by a lower level coroutine mechanism. Modula 2 is now becoming widely available and is ideal for programming embedded microprocessor systems. With the exception of error handling (which is as bad as Modula), it provides all the features described here although there are some restrictions in the mapping of data types onto device registers.

Ada -provides all the features described here without any restrictions although the process mechanism is different. Ada will doubtless come to dominate real time programming in the next few years.

REFERENCES

1 Young.S.J., 1980, 'Low Level Device Programming from a High Level Language', Proc IEE Pt E, 127. p37-64.

2 Hoare, C.A.R., 1974, 'Monitors: An Operating System Structuring Concept', Comm ACM, 17, p549-557.

3. Young,S.J., 1982. 'Real Time Languages', Ellis Horwood Ltd.

Chapter 8

MODULA-2

H.W. Thomas

8.1 INTRODUCTION

Modula-2 is a small, general purpose programming language which has been specifically designed to allow all aspects of systems programming to be written efficiently in a high-level language. It particularly aims to provide facilities for handling device programming and interrupts in a well structured manner, thereby attacking one of the last strongholds of assembly code programming, and allowing even the nucleus of a multi-tasking system to be programmed in Modula-2. The language has been developed from Pascal, from which it has inherited its rich data structures and control constructs, and Modula (1), an early attempt to define a small language suitable for multi-programming. From Modula it has taken the module concept which is so important in the development of large programs, and which has provided the base on which the "software modules" and "packages" of Ada have been built. Modula-2 is the result of over seven years experience with both Pascal and Modula, and, in the words of its designer, Professor Niklaus Wirth, "Modula-2 emerged from careful design deliberations as a language that includes all aspects of Pascal and extends them with the important module concept and those of multiprogramming".

For a language to be effective in the areas which Modula-2 has set out to serve, it must be efficient, and so, like Pascal, Modula-2's facilities are capable of efficient compilation and execution, and, unlike some high-level languages, does not provide constructs which, whilst being attractive to the programmer, carry an unacceptable overhead in their implementation. This has produced a "small" language: it can be learnt quickly by anyone familiar with Pascal, and its definition document (2) is only 30 pages long. This is in contrast to Ada, whose tome-like manuals and all embracing generality are already striking fear into the hearts of many experienced programmers. Despite this compactness, Modula-2 is surprisingly flexible, and, indeed, it conforms to most of the U.S. D.o.D. "Steelman" requirements for future high-level and real-time languages.

Consequently, Modula-2 is particularly appropriate for microprocessor based systems, where a compact, well-structured and efficient alternative to assembly-code programming is required.

The following sections will illustrate the main features of Modula-2 (hereafter abbreviated to Modula), first describing how Modula systematically solves the problems of Pascal, then expanding on the new concepts that it introduces.

8.2 A SOLUTION TO PASCAL'S PROBLEMS

Although Pascal has been enthusiastically adopted by a large section of the programming community, it has several serious restrictions, and a number of annoying limitations, generally resulting from attempts to use Pascal in tasks beyond its intended scope. The limitations have been pointed out by a number of authors, and it is interesting to take one of these papers, by Kernighan (4), and to see how Modula surmounts each difficulty.

8.2.1 Array Limitations

In Pascal, arrays are fixed in size. This makes string handling difficult, and general purpose mathematical routines (for example, the scalar product of two vectors) cannot be written for variable length arrays.

This restriction is very severe, and greater flexibility is provided in Modula by allowing a formal array parameter of a procedure to be an "open" array. In this case, whilst the types of the elements of the formal and the actual arrays must be the same, the formal array may be declared without a size as "ARRAY OF <base type>". Thus, a procedure declared as

```
PROCEDURE WriteString (S: ARRAY OF CHAR)
```

will allow calls with an arbitrary length of character string 'S'. The lower bound of the formal array is always taken to be 0, while the upper bound is obtained by calling the standard function HIGH(S), which returns the number of elements minus 1. String constants may be assigned to character arrays of larger dimension, in which case the string is terminated by a null (0) character. The body of the above procedure would then be as follows.

```
PROCEDURE WriteString (S: ARRAY OF CHAR);
VAR i: CARDINAL;
CONST null=0c;
BEGIN
  i: = 0;
  WHILE (i<= HIGH(S)) & (S[i]<> null) DO
    Write (S[i]); INC(i);
  END; (*while*)
END WriteString;
```

This example illustrates a number of additional minor improvements to Pascal. The type CARDINAL, for unsigned integer operations, allows the use of positive integers of twice the size of the type INTEGER. Octal, hexadecimal and character constants (denoted by, for example 177560b, OFFE4H, 61c respectively - the last being expressed in octal form) are introduced, and the syntax is improved by the use of keywords to begin multiple statements, and END to terminate them. This avoids the clumsy BEGIN...END of Pascal.

In addition the restrictive declaration order of Pascal (constants, types, variables, procedures) is relaxed, and any of these declarations may occur anywhere within a block. Consequently declarations may be grouped together in the most appropriate way for program readability, and the FORWARD reference is eliminated entirely.

8.2.2 Boolean Expressions

The evaluation of Boolean expressions is specifically defined as left to right, and prevents the illegal references which are possible in Pascal, where the order of evaluation is not specified.

Thus, p OR q means "IF p then TRUE otherwise q"
p AND q means "IF p then q otherwise FALSE"

This allows the above example

```
(i<= HIGH(S)) & (S[i]<> 0c)
```

to guarantee that S[i] will not be illegally referenced if i is greater than HIGH(S). Similarly, linked lists may be searched by

```
WHILE (p<> NIL) & (p↑.component <> i) DO
  p: = p↑. next
END;
```

8.2.3 CASE Statements

A particular failing of Pascal is the omission of an "otherwise" clause in the CASE statement. This is remedied in Modula, which also employs a special symbol ('|') to terminate each statement or multiple statement clause. Thus, for example:-

```
CASE ch  OF
  '0..9': number ; getnextchar
| 'A..Z': letter;  getnextchar
| '*','/',
  '+','-': operator
ELSE invalidcharacter
END; (*case*)
```

If the ELSE clause is omitted, the CASE statement does not continue, (as some Pascal extensions do) but raises a CASE error if out of range.

8.2.4 GO TO Statement

Much to the horror of many programmers, there is no 'GO TO' statement in Modula! This is a deliberate omission, made to explore the feasibility of programming without it, and to encourage (or even force!) a more structured approach. As a concession, the LOOP....EXIT....END; construction has been added, allowing exit from any point within an endless loop to the statement following it. Similarly, RETURN allows the premature exist of any procedure from any point (or points) and together, these allow all possibilities to be covered. Admittedly, even after two years of programming experience in Modula, occasions do arise where it would be useful to have a 'GO TO', and where the alternative LOOP....EXIT arrangement seems unnecessarily clumsy, but these cases are few and far between, and the change in mental approach that it forces is adequate compensation.

8.2.5 Static (or "own") Variables

Unlike Fortran, for example, Pascal procedures cannot have their own static variables which can exist from one procedure call to the next, and indeed, the problems caused by Algol's "own" type should be sufficient to amply confirm Pascal's lack of an "own" type. However, this forces the programmer to use Global variables, which are consequently much more visible than they need necessarily be. Pascal main programs are often cluttered with the initialisation of these static variables, whose function is quite specific to certain procedures, and program readability suffers. Modula's answer to this problem, and to the problem of separate compilation of program segments, is the module concept, described below.

8.3 THE MODULE CONCEPT

A module essentially constitutes a "fence" which restricts the visibility of its locally declared variables and procedures, without requiring that such variables exist only during the execution of a module. To breach this "fence" in an orderly manner, each module may have an import list, specifying which externally declared identifiers it wishes to reference, and an export list, specifying which internally declared variables or procedures it wishes to make available to the outside world.

Each module has a body, whose statements are executed when the procedure in which the module is declared is called. If several modules are declared, then their bodies are executed in order, and serve to initialise local variables. More commonly, modules are declared at the main program level, rather than inside a procedure, and so the execution of the module bodies can be considered to be an initialisation phase which precedes execution of the main program. This global existence, but restricted visibility, provides the ability to set up a program's environment whilst retaining the security of each local module. For further security, the static variables could be accessed only by procedures exported from the module, creating true "read-only" access to critical values. The following example shows a simple, dynamic storage allocation scheme which also allows read-only access to the first free storage location.

```
MODULE Storage;
  FROM SYSTEM IMPORT ADDRESS; (*see section 4*)
  EXPORT Allocate, FirstFree;

  PROCEDURE Allocate (VAR a: ADDRESS; size: CARDINAL);
  BEGIN
    a:= nextfree; INC(nextfree, size);
  END Allocate;

  PROCEDURE FirstFree( ): ADDRESS;
  BEGIN
    RETURN nextfree;
  END FirstFree;

VAR nextfree: ADDRESS;
BEGIN
  nextfree: = 0 (*initialise to start of free space*)
END Storage;
```

The module concept provides the key to the separate compilation of different program segments, and to the definition of clearly defined interfaces between them, so that a library of useful routines can be maintained. If a module is to export objects to other modules which are unknown a priori, then it must consist of Definition and Implementation modules as shown below.

```
DEFINITION MODULE Storage;
FROM SYSTEM IMPORT ADDRESS;
EXPORT QUALIFIED Allocate, FirstFree;

PROCEDURE Allocate (VAR a: ADDRESS; size: CARDINAL);

PROCEDURE FirstFree( ): ADDRESS;

END Storage.

IMPLEMENTATION MODULE Storage;
(*code to implement above procedures*)
BEGIN
   .
   .
   .
END Storage.
```

The Definition module defines the interface to other program units; recompilation of a definition module implies that all importing modules must also be recompiled, since the interface may have changed.

However, the corresponding implementation module may be changed and recompiled without affecting the rest of the program, thereby allowing library maintenance, and upgrading of inefficient routines to be effected without difficulty.

Programs which import objects from separately compiled modules must use the so-called QUALIFIED IMPORT, of the forms

```
(i)       Storage.Allocate (a,n);
(ii) FROM Storage IMPORT Allocate;
```

This simple requirement deserves further comment, since it is such an enormous improvement over the similar declaration 'EXTERNAL' found in some other languages. It both informs the programmer of the source of the imported procedure, and it allows all program linking to be done automatically. Thus, all information about the program's environment is available within the program text, where it should be.

The two forms allow objects of the same name, from different modules, to be used together, e.g.,

```
Storage.Allocate  and  Extendedmemory.Allocate
```

or, if no such name conflict exists, to "unqualify" the import, as in (ii), and refer to 'Allocate' as if it had been declared within the module.

Modula conspicuously provides no language-defined features for input and output. Instead, the module concept allows the definition of libraries of standard stream and file-handling procedures which can be supplemented where necessary with implementation-specific modules for handling special input and output. Thus, at the highest level of abstraction, sequential streams of data may be provided by appropriate modules, whilst for the highest efficiency of device handling, specific low-level modules may be programmed at the expense of program portability. At an intermediate level in this hierarchy, it is common to provide the file-handling capabilities of a particular operating system, for example, RT-11 or Unix, as illustrated by the following example taken from the version of the compiler distributed for use under RT-11.

```
DEFINITION MODULE FilesSubset; (* selection of RT-11 file operations *)

EXPORT QUALIFIED
 FILE, FileName, Lookup, Create, Delete, Release, Close;

TYPE FILE = [0..15]; (* RT-11 allows channel numbers 0..15 *)
  FileName = ARRAY [0..11] OF CHAR;

PROCEDURE Lookup (f: FILE; fn: FileName; VAR reply: INTEGER);
(* Look up file f in directory,
  reply >=0 = done, file length; reply <0 = error*)

PROCEDURE Create (f: FILE; fn; FileName; VAR reply: INTEGER);
(* Create a new file f.
  reply >=0 = done, file length; reply <0 = error*)

PROCEDURE Delete (f: FILE; fn: FileName; VAR reply: INTEGER);
(*Delete file f from directory.
  reply >=0 = done, file length; reply <0 = error*)

PROCEDURE Release (f: FILE);
(*Release file f without entering in directory*)

PROCEDURE Close (f: File);
(*close file f and enter name in directory*)

END FilesSubset.
```

The module concept is probably the most important feature of Modula, since it assists the development of large programs by a number of people. However, in order to permit all aspects of systems programming to be performed in a high level language, recognition of, and the ability to handle machine-dependent aspects of a system are also vital. Many languages avoid this by including the facility for machine-code insertions, but Modula attempts to overcome the difficulties within the language itself, and certainly, for current implementations on computers with memory-mapped peripheral devices, the attempt has been very successful.

With only a few additional concepts, device drivers can be written in an elegant manner with a readability which cannot be approached using even well-commented assembly language coding.

8.4 LOW-LEVEL AND SYSTEM-DEPENDENT FACILITIES

First and foremost in so-called low-level programming is the ability to over-rule a compiler's type checking. In general, such type-checking is a very important function of any compiler, allowing many potential disastrous errors to be detected at compile-time, but occasions do arise when it is necessary to regard an object in several different ways. Modula allows type identifiers to be used as if they were functions, denoting a type transfer function. This transfer, however, involves no computation: it exists only in the knowledge of the programmer in regarding a specific bit pattern in different ways, and in allowing the compiler to regard a variable as being compatible with different types. For example, on the PDP-11 serial line interface, bits 0-7 of the data buffer contain the received character, while bits 12–15 are used to indicate errors. Modula handles the conversion of this in the following manner.

```
CONST error=15; overrun=14; framing=13; parity=12;
VAR buffer : CARDINAL;
    ch     : CHAR;
    status : BITSET;

BEGIN
  Get (buffer);(*Read data from hardware as a 16-bit word*)
  status:= BITSET(buffer);(*'convert' to set of 0..15*)
  IF (error IN status) THEN

     IF(overrun IN status) THEN WriteString ('over-run error')
     ELSIF(framing IN status) THEN WriteString ('framing error')
     ELSIF(parityerror IN status) THEN WriteString ('parity error')
     ELSE(*unknown error-ignore*)
     END;(*if*)
  ELSE
     ch:= CHAR (buffer) (*get low byte*)
  END;
```

In order to make specific hardware locations available to a program, Modula also allows the programmer to over-ride the compiler's storage allocation scheme by adding an absolute address after a variable's declaration.

```
VAR serialstatus [177560b]: BITSET;
    serialbuffer [177562b]: CHAR;
```

Although this is designed primarily for memory-mapped peripherals, it would be straightforward matter for a compiler to issue appropriate i/o instructions for processors which have a separate i/o space.

Moving to a slightly higher level, it is still necessary in some circumstances to provide types which are machine dependent, and these are available from the predefined module SYSTEM. Thus, the type WORD is compatible with all types occupying one storage location, while the type ADDRESS is defined as POINTER TO WORD, and is compatible with all pointer types as well as the type CARDINAL, thus allowing address computations. The type transfer function can then convert a general ADDRESS into a specific pointer type, in order to reference particular components of a record.

```
TYPE ioblock  =  RECORD
       access  : Resource;
       status: SET OF iostate;
       value   : REAL;
       area  : ADDRESS; (*points to device-specific area*)
     END; (* io.block*)

VAR io: ioblock; p: deviceblockptr;

BEGIN
    p:= deviceblockptr (io.area); (*make pointer specific*)
    WITH p↑ DO...
```

For computers which have different data and address lengths (e.g., Motorola 68000) the type ADDRESS is no longer compatible with CARDINAL, but address computations are still possible using the standard generic procedures INC(x,n) and DEC(x,n), which set x to (x + n) and (x - n) respectively. The procedures ADR, SIZE, and TSIZE are provided by SYSTEM to return the address of a particular variable, the size (in bytes) of a variable, and the size of a data type respectively. In addition, SYSTEM may also provide the ability to make direct calls to the operating system facilities, giving Modula programs access to file-handling primitives, etc..

The module SYSTEM thus provides a convenient concept for gathering together all those data types and facilities which are specific to a particular computer or implementation; it is the provision of SYSTEM in each implementation that gives Modula the ability to program all aspects of the computer operating system, rather than defining an interface below which the programmer may not descend. The consequence of importing objects from SYSTEM is obviously to render a module non-portable, so that as a rule such low-level programming should be kept to a minimum, and in most installations, these low-level routines will be used to build the libraries which the majority of programmers will use.

8.5 CONCURRENCY

One of the major objectives of Modula-1 was to explore the requirements of multiprogramming, and to provide appropriate abstractions for the definition and interaction of process (or tasks) which are executed concurrently. To this end it defined a SIGNAL and a PROCESS type, together with a number of operations which allowed process communication, as shown below.

```
DEFINITION MODULE Processes;

EXPORT QUALIFIED SIGNAL, STARTPROCESS, SEND, WAIT,
                         INITSIGNAL;

TYPE SIGNAL; (*details are hidden*)

PROCEDURE STARTPROCESS (P:PROC; n:CARDINAL);
(*Allocates a workspace of size n, and starts a parameterless
  procedure P as a concurrent process which is then anonymous*)

PROCEDURE WAIT (VAR s: SIGNAL);
(*Suspend process until 's' is sent*)

PROCEDURE SEND (VAR s: SIGNAL);
(*Resumes first process (if any) waiting for 's'*)

PROCEDURE INITSIGNAL (VAR s: SIGNAL);
(*All signals must be initialised before use*)

END Processes.
```

These primitives allowed concurrent tasks, written in the form of parameterless procedures, to be started and executed in genuine or pseudo-concurrency (depending on the implementation of the Processes module). Communication between tasks could be via common, global variables, or via the SIGNAL mechanism shown. Each task, once started, was anonymous in that no other task could interfere with it, and this in turn meant that each task executed until it suspended itself by waiting for a signal from another task. Thus, in Modula-1, the process-scheduling was a fixed feature of the language, and could not be modified; allocation of the processor, in the (most usual) case of a single processor serving several processes, was defined only in that a fair share of the processor time could be expected.

In many situations this restriction was too severe, and did not allow the Modula programmer the ability to write different process schedulers implementing alternative allocation strategies (for example, giving each process a priority, or guaranteeing a given time-slice). Thus, in Modula-2, the lower-level concept of co-routines has been introduced, which then allows the process scheduler itself to be written in Modula, removing this as a language feature, and instead making it part of the implementation. This is regarded as a low-level feature, and consequently the module SYSTEM exports the type PROCESS (denoting a co-routine) and the procedures NEWPROCESS and TRANSFER.

The declaration of a new, concurrent task is then made by calling

```
NEWPROCESS (P: PROC; AREA: ADDRESS; SIZE: CARDINAL;
     VAR new: PROCESS)
```

where P is a parameterless procedure whose body constitutes the task code; AREA is the address, and SIZE the size of a workspace for the task to use, and 'new' is the process name by which the task will be referenced.

Each concurrent task which is declared requires a minimum workspace of about 100 bytes, used for its own stack and for saving its registers when a transfer is made to another task. Calling NEWPROCESS only initialises the task but does not start it; this is done explicitly by calling

```
TRANSFER (VAR from, to: PROCESS)
```

which causes the current process (saved as'from') to be suspended, and the new task ('to') to be resumed. Initially, the point at which the task is resumed will be the first statement of the procedure P declared to be the code of process 'new', but will later be the continuation of any point where the process is suspended.

With these facilities it is now possible to write an implementation for the module Processes given above for any desired strategy of processor time-sharing. This module will then 'hide' the low-level process facilities from the user, and take care of the 'housekeeping' aspects of finding the next process to run, and making the transfer to this new process.

The following module gives a flavour of the mechanism of process switching in Modula, and how higher-level facilities can be built up using these primitives. It is interesting to measure the speed of process switching in Modula, because the efficiency of this operation is critical in a multi-tasking system. Although this is highly dependent on machine architecture, (being fastest for memory-based workspace processors such as the Texas 9900 series), the time for a TRANSFER on a more typical machine such as a PDP11/34 is of the order of 50μS. The additional 'housekeeping' required by SEND and WAIT, in a simple scheme as shown will typically add an additional 50-100μS, depending on the number of processes in the run queue, so that the efficiency of a process scheduler written in Modula compares remarkably well with that achieved by assembly coding.

```
IMPLEMENTATION MODULE Processes;
(*Processor allocation is by 'round-robin'.  Processes are linked
  together to form a 'run-queue' which is searched to find a ready
  process*)

FROM SYSTEM IMPORT ADDRESS, PROCESS, NEWPROCESS,
     TRANSFER;
FROM Storage IMPORT ALLOCATE;
TYPE SIGNAL = POINTER TO ProcessDescriptor;

     ProcessorDescriptor = RECORD
        next : SIGNAL; (*link for run queue*)
        chain: SIGNAL; (*link for processes waiting for signals*)
        context: PROCESS; (*current state of process*)
        ready: BOOLEAN; (*TRUE when task can run*)
     END; (*ProcessDescriptor*).

VAR     cp: SIGNAL; (*current process-used by scheduler*)
        queue: SIGNAL; (*run queue*)

PROCEDURE STARTPROCESS (P: PROC; n: CARDINAL);
VAR this: PROCESS; workspace: ADDRESS;
BEGIN this:=cp; (*note current process*)
     ALLOCATE (workspace, n);
     ALLOCATE (cp, TSIZE (ProcessDescriptor));(*Allocate new
        process descriptor*)
     WITH cp↑ DO
        next:= this↑.next; this↑.next:=cp; (*insert into run queue*)
        chain:= NIL; ready:= TRUE;
        NEWPROCESS    (P, workspace, n, context); (*declare new
          process*)
     END; (*with cp↑ *)
     TRANSFER (this↑.context, cp↑.context);(*transfer to it*)
END STARTPROCESS;

PROCEDURE WAIT (VAR s: SIGNAL);
(*suspend cp and put into queue for 's'*).
VAR this: SIGNAL;
BEGIN
     IF s = NIL THEN s: = cp
     ELSE (*find end of queue for s*)
        this: = s;
        WHILE this↑.chain <>NIL DO this:= this↑.chain END;
        this↑.chain:=cp;
     END;
     this:=cp; (*note current process, ready for transfer*)
     this↑.chain:= NIL; (*mark end of chain for 's'*)
     this↑.ready:= FALSE; (*mark cp as 'not ready'*)
     cp:= queue; (*now search run queue for a 'ready process*)
     WHILE NOT cp↑.ready DO cp:=cp↑.next END;
     TRANSFER (this↑.context, cp↑.context);(*transfer to 'ready'
       task*)
END WAIT;

END Processes.
```

However, as can be seen, writing the process scheduler in a high-level language improves the readability and maintainability considerably, and allows the correct interface for concurrent processes to be written clearly and concisely. Since different applications often require quite different approaches to task scheduling, this is an important point which in many systems dictates the complete operating system which must be used.

This far, only the case of a single processor serving several processes has been considered, and the more difficult problems of processor interaction and mutual exclusion have been ignored. True concurrency raises these problems, and arises when input/output devices are used which signal the end of their particular process by causing an interrupt. Since this is an extremely common situation, which has caused some of the greatest difficulties in high-level languages, the approach taken in Modula is now considered in some detail.

8.6 DEVICE HANDLING AND INTERRUPTS

The most common feature of interrupt-driven devices is typified by the serial line device (e.g., a UART) where the output character may be transferred to the device as a parallel word, with hardware implementing the serialisation and transmission of this word in parallel with the further operation of the main processor. When the transmission is complete, the serial line device signifies its readiness to accept another character by causing an interrupt. Whereas a TRANSFER may be used to transfer back to the main task, (from the process depositing successive characters in the serial line buffer), such an explicit transfer cannot be used for the interrupt, since the point in the main process at which the interrupt will occur is not known. Modula extends the TRANSFER statement to handle this situation by means of the IOTRANSFER call, which incorporates an additional parameter, the so-called interrupt vector, which links the interrupt to an effective, asynchronous insertion of a TRANSFER call at the current point of execution. The transmission of a single character may then be handled in the following manner.

<u>Producer task</u>

```
Produce(ch);
.
TRANSFER(main,handler)
.
.
.
.
.
interrupt occurs
.
.
.
.
.
```

```
MODULE DeviceHandler [4];

PROCEDURE Printer; (*process 'printer'*)
VAR;
  status [177564b]: BITSET;
  data [177566b]: CHAR;
BEGIN
  LOOP (*endless*)
    status:= {6}; (*enable interrupts*)
    IOTRANSFER (printer, main, 64b);
    status:= {}; (*disable interrupts*)
    data:= ch; (*print character*)
    TRANSFER (printer, main);
  END; (*loop*)
END Printer;

END DeviceHandler
```

It is important when dealing with interrupts to prevent unscheduled transfers in critical locations. Thus, interrupts must be prohibited between enabling the interrupt bit and IOTRANSFER, whose call sets up the interrupt vector to the correct return address. This exclusion is achieved by specifying, for the processor, a hardware priority in the module heading; devices are assigned a fixed hardware interrupt level (the printer is 4 on the PDP-11) and are able to interrupt the processor only when its priority is less than this level. Consequently, interrupts can only occur when the device handler has executed its IOTRANSFER to the lower priority main process.

As in the case of the Processor module, these low-level operations are generally removed from general use and 'hidden' behind an interface in which the 'housekeeping' tasks of process management are handled. As a final example, the following procedure allows a device handler, started as a concurrent process, to suspend itself until resumed by an interrupt.

```
PROCEDURE WaitIO (vector: CARDINAL);
(*suspends current process until interrupt occurs*)
VAR this: SIGNAL; p: PROCESS;
BEGIN this:= cp; (*note current process*)
      this↑.ready:= FALSE; (*mark self as not ready*)
      cp:= queue; (*search run queue for 'ready' process*)

      WHILE NOT cp↑.ready DO cp:= cp↑.next END;

      p:=cp↑.context; (*use p for process context-cp may change*)
      IOTRANSFER (this↑.context, p, vector);
      cp↑.context:=p; (*resume here on interrupt-save context*)
      cp:= this; (*we become current process again*)
END WaitIO;
```

Once again, efficiency is important, and IOTRANSFER on a PDP-11/34 takes typically 120μS, with a further 60-100μS for 'housekeeping' in WaitIO. Many commercial operating systems take longer than this for an interrupt to be properly acknowledged, so that Modula once again provides a fast mechanism for areas of system programming which until now have been considered the preserve of assembly language.

In a practical, multiprogramming nucleus, additional features such as device timeout and message passing mechanisms might be provided. The detail of such facilities is beyond the scope of this discussion, but may be found in references 5 and 6, both of which give additional references for this type of system programming.

8.7 CONCLUSIONS

Modula has evolved from a number of years experience of the use of Pascal, and has systemmatically attacked all the major weaknesses which limit Pascal's use as a practical, professional programming language. To solve these problems it has defined a small number of elegant additional concepts which contrast with the plethora of extensions that almost every different Pascal implementation has tried to provide.

It allows for all aspects of systems programming to be carried out in a well-structured high level language, and its low-level facilities are defined in such a way that machine and data-dependent modules are clearly specified and isolated from higher levels of program.

Modula compilers are small and efficient, and eminently suitable for use on microprocessors. In achieving this efficiency through careful language design, Wirth (3) acknowledges the Modula implementation team "who not only have turned Modula into an effective, reliable tool, but have often wisely consulted against the inclusion of further fancy facilities".

When one considers the great complexity of Ada, and notes that, of the "Steelman" requirements, Modula conspicuously omits exceptions, generics, and overloading, another comment of Wirth's is significant: "An extended opportunity to use the sophisticated MESA system (7) has taught me how to tackle problems on many occasions, and on a few that it is wiser to avoid them altogether".

Although the U.S. D.o.D. investment in Ada will ensure that, as has been said, Ada is "doomed to succeed", for many aplications Modula deserves serious consideration as a language that can provide much of Ada's functionality in a simple and concise form.

REFERENCES

1. Wirth, N., 1977, 'Modula: a language for Modula Multiprogramming. Software-Practice and Experience, 7, 3-35.

2. Wirth, N., 1980, 'Modula-2' Report No. 36, Institut fur Informatik. ETH Zurich.

3. Wirth, N., 1982, Programming in Modula-2. Springer-Verlag.

4. Kernighan, B., 1981, 'Why Pascal is not my Favourite Programming Language', Computing Science Technical Report No. 100. Bell Laboratories, July 18.

5. Hoppe, J., 1980, 'A simple nucleus written in Modula-2' Report No. 35, ETH Zurich.

6. Thomas, H. W., 1982, 'Design and performance of a simple nucleus for real-time control applications', Software and Microsystems, 1, No. 6.

7. Mitchell, J. G., Maybury, W., and Sweet, R., 1978, MESA language manual. Xerox PARC, CSL-78-1.

Chapter 9

ADA

R.H. Pierce

9.1 INTRODUCTION

Ada is a programming language designed for, and promulgated by, the US Department of Defence (ALsys(1)). The language which is now called Ada was the result of a competitive design exercise, funded by DoD, to meet their requirements for a standard language for real-time, embedded computer systems. Ada is intended to replace all the present diversity of languages used in the USA for this work, and is likely to become widely adopted both in the USA and Europe. Fortunately, it is a good language despite some minor flaws, and all serious software engineers should be aware of its capabilities. In this paper we consider its aims, give a very brief introduction to its facilities, and consider its suitability for microprocessor applications.

9.2 DESIGN AIMS OF THE ADA LANGUAGE

The Ada language was designed to meet the requirements of the US Government for a language which would embody the best principles of software engineering as currently understood, and which would be helpful at all stages in the life cycle of a piece of software. It is recognised that, in professional software engineering circles at least, a program is read far more often that it is written, and read by many people other than the original author. Thus the construction of the language is intended to make Ada programs easy to read, but not necessarily easy to write. It is also designed to encourage the re-use of software components so that investment in one project can form the basis of cost reductions in other projects - something which can be difficult to achieve with current languages and methods. The language is intended to promote software reliability by a combination of program structuring methods, extensive compile-time checks, and run-time checks to catch faults which have not been prevented by the compile-time checks. Many features of programming languages which are "nice" for the user (such as free pointers or reference variables) have been eliminated from the language on the grounds that they tend to encourage unobvious programming and lead to errors - another example of easy reading and understanding being preferred to ease of writing.

Finally, machine independence and portability of Ada programs are stressed, but machine dependencies can be introduced in a controlled way, since it is recognised that in practical software engineering this may be necessary.

9.3 THE MAIN FEATURES OF ADA

This section attempts to illustrate the main features of the Ada language and to show how they can be used to promote reliable software design and implementation. In a short paper such as this it is possible to do no more than summarise the language (the reference manual runs to some 300 pages) and the reader should refer to a textbook for further details. The most authoritative and readable is Barnes (1983).

9.3.1 Program Structuring Features.

Ada has three main language constructs for expressing the structure of a piece of software - subprograms, packages and tasks.

9.3.1.1 Subprograms. Subprograms consist of procedures (which do not return results) and functions (which do). Subprograms are the most conventional of the structuring features, and are declared in a similar manner to Pascal.

```
procedure EXAMPLE (X : IN INTEGER;
                   Y : OUT INTEGER)
is
    A : INTEGER ;   -- local variable
    B : FLOAT ;     -- declarations
begin
    executable statements
end EXAMPLE;
```

X and Y are the formal parameters of the procedure. X is declared to be of <u>mode</u> "in", which indicates that its value behaves as a constant during the execution of the procedure (it cannot be written to). Y by contrast can only be used to transmit values back to the caller of EXAMPLE, in other words it can only be assigned to. To complete the scheme, a parameter may be given the mode "in out" in which case its value can be read and it can be assigned to. For scalar parameters, a copy is made of the value of the actual parameter on the call, and for an "in out" parameter the value of the formal is copied back to the actual upon return. However, for non-scalar parameters, an implementation is allowed to pass all parameters by reference to avoid the overheads of copying.

Subprogram calls are a little unconventional in that parameters can be given in either positional or named notation, e.g

```
     EXAMPLE (M,R);   -- positional
or
     EXAMPLE (X => M, Y =>R); -- named
or even
     EXAMPLE (M,Y => R);   -- mixed
```

If a parameter is given a default value on the subprogram declaration, the actual parameter can be omitted.

One of the most important features of Ada is that subprograms may be overloaded, i.e. the same name may be used for many procedures and functions, provided that they can be distinguished by the number, names and types of their parameters, and by the presence or absence of result specifications. This is useful for allowing the same name to stand for the same concept applied to various types, e.g. READ for integers and floating-point numbers (other languages use a special fudge for I/O routines). It also allows designers of different software components (especially packages, see below) to use appropriate names without fear of clashes.

Finally, Ada allows a subprogram to be specified before its full declaration appears:

```
     procedure EXAMPLE (X: INTEGER; Y: FLOAT);
or
     function SQRT (ARG: LONG_FLOAT) return LONG_FLOAT;
```

are subprogram specifications. They are vital for use with packages.

Subprograms can be marked as INLINE to tell the compiler to expand them directly at the point of call if possible.

9.3.1.2 Packages. The package is the central feature of Ada and the construct which make the language so valuable for design as well as programming. A package gathers together a collection of related types, data objects and subprograms which operate on them (they do not have to be related but logically they should be so). Packages are always defined in two parts : the specification and the body. In the specification are collected all the items which form the external interface of the package. These are the only things in the package which are externally visible. The specification part can only contain subprogram specifications. The body of the package, which provides the implementation of the external interface, contains the bodies of the subprograms defined in the specification part, and also any other local declarations and subprograms for use within the package body. The package in Ada thus embodies the concepts of encapsulation, information hiding and separation of interface from implementation, which are recognised as a vital part of software engineering practice.

The following example illustrates these points and introduces some others.

```
package SIMPLE_DB is
    type KEY is private;

    function INSERT (VALUE : in ITEM)
             return KEY;

    function RETRIEVE (KEY_VAL: in KEY)
             return ITEM;
private
    type key is
       record
          CYL_ADDR : INTEGER;
          TRACK_ADDR : INTEGER;
       end record;

end    SIMPLE_DB;

package body SIMPLE_DB is
    function INSERT (VALUE : in ITEM)
       return KEY is
    begin
    -- code of INSERT
    end INSERT;

--  likewise body of RETRIEVE

end SIMPLE_DB;
```

The body of the package need not follow the specification directly and may even be separately compiled.

This package has two functions which insert and retrieve items. The type KEY is declared as a private type; this means that no assumptions can be made about its properties outside the package. In order that the compiler can compile code which uses this package before its body has been encountered, the details of all private types must be given in the private part of the specification; nothing declared here is externally visible.

To use the items in the package specification, a selected name is quoted:

```
MY_KEY : SIMPLE_DB.KEY;
begin
    MY_KEY:=SIMPLE_DB.INSERT(MY_VALUE);
```

However, if using the package name is thought to be tedious, all the items in the visible part of a package can be made directly visible by means of a use clause (subject to some restrictions which need not be discussed here):

```
use SIMPLE_DB;
MY_KEY : KEY; --name KEY now visible.
```

The scope of the package is that of the declarative part in which it is declared. Packages may be nested as required.

9.3.1.3 Tasks. Ada is intended of real-time use, and it has an extensive tasking system built in. Tasks, like packages, have a specification part and a body part, but in the case of a task many simultaneous threads of control can be executing the body simultaneously. It is possible to declare a single task, which then executes in parallel with the program or task which declared it. More powerfully, a task type can be declared and many instances of the task type can be created. More details of the tasking system are given in section 4.

9.3.2 Separate Compilation.

Ada allows a program to be composed of a number of compilation units, which may be separately submitted to the compiler then linked to form a program. Compilation units may be library units (which are top-level program components) or subunits (which are components of other units). Library units are used for independent or "bottom up" development, while subunits are useful for "top down" design and development. Library units are also particularly useful since they are the components which form reusable software components. Subprograms, package specifications and package bodies may be library units, while subprogram, package and task bodies may be subunits.

Compilation in Ada is separate but not independent. If packages SIMPLE_DB and TEXT_IO have already been compiled into the program library, and another compilation unit wishes to use them, it must name them in a context specification thus:

```
with TEXT_IO, SIMPLE_DB;
package USER is
    .....
end USER;
```

USER can then be compiled, and the names of items in TEXT_IO and SIMPLE_DB are available by selection, or by means of a use clause. Other library units may exist in the library, but only those named in a with-clause are accessible. Note that the bodies of SIMPLE_DB, TEXT_IO need not yet have been compiled - only their specifications are needed to compile USER.

Subunits are defined as follows. Suppose the function INSERT was becoming too large, and it was decided to make it a subunit. Its specification remains the same, but in the body of SIMPLE_DB it is replaced by a body stub:

```
function INSERT (VALUE: in ITEM) return KEY is
separate;
```

The body of INSERT is then submitted as a subunit.

```
separate (SIMPLE_DB)
function INSERT (VALUE: in ITEM) return KEY is

--
end INSERT;
```

Finally, a body compilation unit can be edited and recompiled without having to recompile anything (except possibly its subunits), but if a specification is recompiled all other units which name it in their with-clauses have to be recompiled.

9.3.3 Types and Subtypes.

Ada, like Pascal, is a strongly-typed language. That is, any data object is regarded as belonging to a particular class of values, and a value of one type cannot be assigned to an object of another type (unless an explicit conversion is applied in some cases). The language supports enumeration types, numeric types (integer, floating-point and fixed-point), array types, with record types and access types (references with restrictions). Tasks are also types. Private types (used in conjunction with packages) have already been introduced.

Each type declaration introduces a new type, even if it looks the same as a previous one. Thus if

```
type A1 is array (1..100) of INTEGER;
type A2 is array (1..100) of INTEGER;
```

A1 and A2 are different and variables of type A1 and A2 cannot be assigned to each other.

In addition, Ada provides subtype declarations. A subtype is not a new type, but allows a type to be renamed and possibly additional constraints to be applied to its values. Thus if

```
subtype SHORT is INTEGER range 128..256;
```

then a value of type SHORT is regarded as an integer, but is constrained to be in the given range. A constraint check is applied if a value is assigned to a variable of type SHORT (see section 5.3.5).

The following subsections describe Ada types in more detail.

9.3.3.1 Enumeration types. Enumeration types (as in Pascal) provide a set of explicitly named values.

```
type TRAFFIC_LIGHT is (RED,AMBER,GREEN);
type COLOUR is (RED,ORANGE,YELLOW,GREEN,BLUE,VIOLET);
```

The enumeration literals (which can include character values, e.g. 'A','+','C') can be overloaded - a property which they shared with subprograms but no other sorts of declaration. BOOLEAN is a enumeration type (TRUE,FALSE) with built-in operations.

9.3.3.2 Numeric types. Ada allows three kinds of numeric types - integer, floating point and fixed-point. Implementations will always have predefined integer and floating-point types such as INTEGER, LONG_INTEGER, FLOAT, SHORT_FLOAT. However, numeric type declarations can be written as follows

```
type MY_INTEGER is range 0..40000;

type MY_FLOAT is digits 9;

type MY_FIXED is digits 6 delta 0.01;
```

The user chooses the range (and precision for a fixed-point type) and the compiler selects the appropriate representation for the type.

The normal operators are available on numeric types - +,-,*,/,**,mod and rem.

9.3.3.3. Array types. Ada allows single and multi-dimensional arrays. An unconstrained array type is declared as follows

```
type AR is array (INTEGER range <>) of
                  COLOUR;
```

An index constraint must be given when an object of this type is declared:

```
COLOURS : AR (1..100);
```

or it can be used in a subtype declaration:

```
subtype COLOUR_SET is AR (1..20);
```

9.3.3.4 Record types. An example of a record type has already been given in section 9.3.1.2. Records may have alternative sets of fields specified by variant parts as shown in this example.

```
type REC (VAR: COLOUR) is
    record
       FIELD1,FIELD2: INTEGER;
       case VAR is
       when RED=>
          A : INTEGER;
       when BLUE =>
          B : FLOAT;
       when others =>
          null
       end case;
    end record;
```

This shows a record with a common part and three variants, one of which has no data. VAR is the discriminant of the record and is part of the record data. Any attempt to access a field of a variant part (A or R in this example) causes a discriminant check, i.e. that the correct discriminant is present in the record. The discriminant field(s) - there may be more than one - can only be changed by an assignment of a complete value to the record, direct assignment to VAR is illegal. Discriminant constraints may be given in subtype or object declarations and the discriminants of such a record cannot then be changed. The bounds of an array in the record can be controlled by a discriminant.

9.3.3.5 Access types. Access types are analogous to reference or pointer types in other languages. For example,

```
type RECORD_POINTER is access REC;
```

declares that RECORD_POINTER values are references to the given record type. However, the only way to create an access value is by means of an allocator, which creates the object accessed and returns a pointer to it.

```
MY_PTR : RECORD_POINTER := new REC;
```

Values created by allocators have the lifetime of the corresponding access type. It is impossible to make MY_PTR refer to an object not created by an allocator. This scheme prevents "free" references to random data objects and is designed to improve program reliability.

9.3.3.6 Derived types. Derived types create new types which have the same properties as existing types but which have distinct names.

For example, with

```
type MASS is new FLOAT;

type LENGTH is new FLOAT;
```

MASS and LENGTH are both derived from FLOAT and have the same properties, but cannot be assigned one to another without an explicit conversion via FLOAT.

```
MASS_VAR:=MASS(FLOAT(LENGTH_VAR));
```

9.3.4 Statements.

Ada has few surprises in the way of executable statement - conditional, case, loop, procedure call, assignment, return (from subprogram) and exit (from loop) are all provided. Block statements appear as illustrated in the next section. Case statements use the syntax illustrated here, together with loop and conditional forms.

```
case EXPR is
when VALUE_1 =>
    X:= Y;
    P:= F(G);
when VALUE_2 =>
    if FLAG = V1 then
       M:= N-1;
    elseif FLAG = V2 then
       M:= N+1;
    else
       M:= N-1;
    endif;
when   VALUE_3|VALUE_4=>
    for I in 1..N loop
        S:=S+A(I);
        exit when A(I)=0;
    end loop;
end case; --NB all values of EXPR must be
          --covered by values in case arms
```

9.3.5 Exception Handling And Constraint Checking.

Ada has many run-time checks built in - some have been mentioned above, such as constraint checks on assignment, array bound checks, or discriminant checks on record field accesses. All these checks raise the predefined exception CONSTRAINT_ERROR. There are other predefined exceptions such as NUMERIC_ERROR (raised on arithmetic operation overflow or underflow), and the user may define his own exceptions as follows:

```
KEY_ERROR,            ACCESS_ERROR:            exception
```

Exceptions may be raised explicitly, e.g.

```
raise KEY_ERROR;
```

If exceptions are foreseen, subprograms and blocks may have exception handlers to deal with them

```
declare

--  local declarations

begin

--  code of block

exception
    when KEY_ERROR|ACCESS_ERROR=>........;--deal with
    when NUMERIC_ERROR=>........;--exceptions
end;
```

Whenever an exception is raised, the dynamic sequence of currently executing blocks and subprograms is unwound until a handler for the exception is reached (or the top-level program or task is encountered).

9.3.6 Generics.

Ada has a powerful generic feature, whereby packages and subprograms can be declared as generic, having generic formal parameters which may be types, subprograms or data objects. The generic operations supplied by such items can be made to apply to a specific case by means of actual parameters for the generic ones. For example, a generic stack package can be written:

```
generic
    type T is private;
package STACK is
    procedure PUSH (ITEM : T);
    function POP return T;
end STACK;
```

A specific instance can be obtained by instantiation:

```
INT_STACK is new STACK (MY_REC);
```

and INT_STACK.PUSH and INT_STACK.POP called, taking and delivering the given record.

9.4 THE ADA TASKING MODEL

As described in section 9.3.1, Ada allows one to declare task types and have many tasks operating simultaneously. Tasks communicate and synchronise with one another by means of the rendezvous mechanism, which will be described below. A task type is declared as follows.

```
task type BUFFER is
    entry SEND (INPUT : in INTEGER);
    entry RECEIVE (OUTPUT : out INTEGER);
end;
```

The entry declarations represent ports via which each task of this type communicates. It is possible to declare instances of the BUFFER task in the usual way

```
CHANNEL_1, CHANNEL_2 : BUFFER;
```

CHANNEL_1 and CHANNEL_2 are now two executing tasks. The declarative region (subprogram or block) which declares tasks like this will wait for them all to terminate before control leaves it. Allocators can also be used to create tasks in which case the task has the lifetime of the access type referring to the task.

9.4.1 The Rendezvous Mechanism.

Assume that the CHANNEL_1 task has the job of buffing values from a number of tasks and emitting them to another task. The writers call the entry SEND:

```
CHANNEL_1.SEND(X);
```

and the reader calls

```
CHANNEL_1.RECEIVE(Y);
```

Within the body of the task BUFFER, an accept statement must be executed for one of the entries in order to establish a rendezvous. If BUFFER is ready to receive an input value, it uses

```
accept SEND (INPUT : in INTEGER) do
--  place INPUT value in data
--  buffer and update buffer pointer
end;
```

If another task calls an entry for which no accept statement has been reached, it is queued until the accept is reached; similarly if an accept statement is reached and no task has called the corresponding entry, the task waits for an entry call. When both calling and called tasks are ready, the rendezvous is established and data may be exchanged. At the end of the rendezvous, both tasks proceed again. Conditional and timed entry calls allow the caller to do something else if the called entry is not ready for a rendezvous either at once or within a given time interval.

A given task may be prepared to accept a number of entry calls, e.g. for both SEND and RECEIVE, if the buffer is neither full nor empty. This is done by means of a conditional wait or select statement as shown in the example of BUFFER's body below.

```
task body BUFFER is
    BUFFER_SPACE : array (1..32) of INTEGER;
    INPUT_PTR, OUTPUT_PTR : INTEGER
                            range Ø..32;
    NO_IN_BUFFER : INTEGER range 1..32;
begin
--      initialise pointers if necessary
    loop   -- loop for ever waiting for calls
       select
          when NO_IN_BUFFER <32=>
             accept RECEIVE (INPUT : in INTEGER);
                BUFFER_SPACE (INPUT_PTR):= INPUT;
             end;  -- end rendezvous
             INPUT_PTR:= INPUT_PTR mod 32+1;
                        NO_IN_BUFFER:=  NO_IN_BUFFER+1;
       or when NO_IN_BUFFER > 0 =>
             accept SEND (OUTPUT : out INTEGER) do
                OUTPUT:=BUFFER_SPACE(OUTPUT_PTR);
             end;
             OUTPUT_PTR:=OUTPUT_PTR mod 31+1
             NO_IN_BUFFER:=NO_IN_BUFFER-1;
       end select;
    end loop;
end BUFFER;
```

This task will run for ever unless it is aborted by another task (by means of an abort statement). To overcome this problem, we can add a third alternative to the select statement consisting of the word terminate. This allows the task to terminate provided that no entry calls are outstanding and the task on which it depends (the one declaring CHANNEL_1, say) is also ready to terminate.

In addition to the above facilities, tasks can delay themselves or particular select cases can force a delay if no entry call is outstanding. Finally, there is a priority mechanism and a means of finding out whether a particular task is callable or how many tasks are waiting on a given entry call.

9.5 SUITABILITY OF ADA FOR MICROPROCESSOR SOFTWARE

9.5.1 Efficiency Considerations.

Software written in Ada will be used for applications in defence and communications which have very stringent performance criteria to meet, in terms of both of speed of execution and storage size. Despite the fact that Ada is a large and powerful language there are few features which are expensive to implement (this is because much of the language complexity is concerned with compile-time checking, not with run-time actions). The two exceptions to this rule are constraint checking and tasking, where a certain run-time overhead may be caused. In the case of constraint checking, an optimising compiler can often remove constraint checks because it can show that they will never arise, and it is also possible to suppress constraint checks (by means of a pragma SUPPRESS) if the user has sufficient confidence in the correctness of the program.

The Ada tasking model is certainly powerful, and without care on the part of the implementor and the user could lead to inefficiency. However, the facilities of the Ada tasking system have all been introduced to cater for problems of task synchronisation and communication which are common to all real-time systems, and which must be solved. There is no reason to fear that the Ada solution is particularly inefficient. The user can assist by only creating tasks where the application needs them, and the compiler can help by applying various optimisations. For example, where a task is created for the sole purpose of acting as a buffer for data between other groups of tasks, it is often possible to treat the buffer task as a passive data area with no separately schedulable existence.

The final point on efficiency is that, since the language will be used by many large projects, it will be worthwhile designing compilers with extensive optimising features, since the investment needed will be justified. This is certainly the view taken by several major implementations, among them the US Air Force and US Army compilers, and the UK Ministry of Defence/British Telecom developments.

9.5.2 Host-Target Working.

Ada is a language intended primarily for embedded computer systems. It was always envisaged that the majority of Ada programs would be developed on a host computer linked directly or indirectly to a target computer whose architecture is possibly different from that of the host. The target will often be a microprocessor or network of microprocessors. Therefore, no weight was put on the ease of compiling Ada on a small machine, and indeed no convincing evidence has yet been shown that Ada can be implemented efficiently on a machine with a 16-bit address range. The concept of host-target working is common in microprocessor work, but for Ada the host is likely to be a fairly capable machine with a 32-bit address space. However, with the advent of machines like the VAX series, Motorola 68000 and NS 16000, with their 32-bit addressing capabilities, the necessary power is becoming available even for low cost development systems.

9.5.3 Machine Dependent Ada Features.

Although it is desirable to use only high level features in any kind of software, Ada recognises that in some circumstances it is necessary to take account of hardware characteristics. For example, a peripheral driver may have a control area which contains a number of fields of particular sizes, as required by the hardware being driven. In Ada, the control area can be defined as a record in the usual way, and then its precise layout specified by means of a "representation clause".

Other kinds of representation clauses allow the user to specify the actual values to be used for enumeration literals, to state the number of bits to be used for a given numeric type, and to connect interrupts to particular task entries. There is also a machine code insertion facility, and a "unsafe conversion" mechanism to allow the normal rules on type checking to be circumvented. The use of all these machine dependent facilities should be isolated by means of packages so that they can be readily changed if needed. A good compiler should also report on any such unsafe features used in a program so that their use cannot pass unnoticed.

9.5.4 Complexity And Training.

Ada has received some criticism on the grounds that it is too complex and that the complexity will lead to unreliable programs since programmers will not understand the implications of what they have written. In the opinion of most people who have used Ada, these criticisms are ill-founded. In the first place, many of the facilities of Ada are self-contained and may be ignored by users who have no need for them. Secondly, the program structuring features of Ada encourage a clear design model, and this improves reliability rather than reduces it. Thirdly, the extensive compile-time and run-time checks built into the language should help to reveal misunderstanding on the part of the user. It is languages such as BCPL or Coral 66 (or, of course, assembler) which allow the programmer to do almost anything which lead to obscure and unreliable software. Experience shows that very high level languages such as Ada and Algol 68 do indeed improve software reliability.

Ada is also reasonably easy to learn, especially if the programmer has prior experience of Pascal, on which Ada was based. Training of staff in Ada is not thought to present any real difficulty.

9.5.5. Portability And Compiler Validation.

Ada is intended to allow ready re-use of software. A crucial aspect of this is that any implementation of Ada for any machine must have exactly the same effect for a given program (with the exception, of course, of explicitly machine-dependent features). A major problem with other so-called "standard" languages is that implementors are liable to provide only a subset of the language, or implement the same language features in different ways. Coral 66 and Pascal have both suffered from this problem. What is worse, they often introduce extra facilities which are attractive and which are almost bound to be used. The DoD was determined to stamp out this kind of abuse, and to do this they have registered the name "Ada" as a trademark. No organisation will be allowed to call their compiler an Ada compiler unless it has been validated by a registered Ada Compiler Validation Service, and this will involve successfully compiling and executing a validation suite which will eventually contain nearly 2000 tests. Validation certificates must be renewed annually. Anyone using a validated Ada compiler will thus be reasonably confident that they will be able to switch to different target hardware with ease. Perhaps more importantly, projects using more than one type of processor will be able to share common software components.

9.6 PRACTICAL EXPERIENCE OF ADA

As part of a larger project to construct a complete Ada programming support environment, the author and his team have recently completed an Ada syntax analyser program. This is a complex piece of software consisting of 19 Ada packages and some 16,000 lines of code. When the program was first built, it worked at the second attempt, and subsequent systematic testing revealed only a few additional coding errors. This remarkably short testing phase can be attributed to three aspects of the Ada language.

(i) The package structure of Ada allows confidence to be built up in the correctness of the design prior to coding, by allowing designers to separate the desired external effect of a component from its implementation, and allowing both to be monitored more easily.

(ii) Coding reviews or "structured walkthroughs" have proved to be easy and effective in Ada.

(iii) The extensive compile time checking built into Ada allowed the compiler to detect many errors which in many other languages would have persisted and become execution errors.

REFERENCES

1. ALsys, 1983, 'Reference manual for the Ada programming language', ANSI/MIL-STD 1815A, Alsys, La Celle-Saint-Cloud, France.

2. Barnes, J.G.P., 1983. 'Programming in Ada', Addison-Wesley, London.

Chapter 10

UNIX

J. Shemeld

10.1 WHAT IS UNIX?

UNIX is essentially a trademark covering a series of operating systems developed at the Bell Telephone Laboratories division of the giant American Telephone and Telegraph Company. Until recently, this regulated telephone monopoly was unable to sell software. Software was released and licensed under the following conditions:

as is,
no maintenance,
no warranties,
no patent indemnification,
no trial period,
AND, payment in advance.

Clearly, UNIX has become widely used on merit. The secret of its success lies in its origins. It did not start life as a "Project", rather its authors - Ken Thompson and Dennis Ritchie of Bell's Computing Science Research Center - wanted a "pleasant environment in which to write and use programs" and were not impressed with what was currently available (Ritchie and Thompson (1)). It was extensively tested and modified by its authors who intended it for their own use.

10.2 CHARACTERISTICS OF A UNIX SYSTEM

Today it is claimed that UNIX has been implemented on computer systems based on cpu's ranging from the Zilog Z80 to the Amdahl 470 (plug compatible with an IBM 370). What do these systems have in common? On logging in, the user expects to find an operating system with a number of characteristic features and incorporating a particular philosophy of software design.

The characteristic features concern the file system, the treatment of I/O devices, and the command line interpreter. They combine together to provide an elegant, powerful and flexible environment for program development.

UNIX is a registered trademark of Bell Telephone Laboratories

10.3 THE FILE SYSTEM

A "file" on UNIX is a generalisation of the usual data file or ASCII text file stored on disc, and covers just about anything that can be written to and/or read from and/or executed! This includes source files, object files, command scripts, the terminal, a tape drive and other devices; a directory of files is itself a file.

Three types of file may be distinguished: ordinary (disc) files, directories, and special (device) files. The inclusion of what seem at first sight to be quite disparate entities under the heading of "file" means that UNIX can avoid a great deal of unnecessary complication. From the point of view of an executing program, there need be no difference between a device, such as a paper tape reader, which cannot physically be written to, a directory on which administrative decision forbids writing, and another user's disc file that he has protected from overwriting; the program simply needs to know that writing is forbidden on that "file". Similarly, to do its job, it need not know from which of the three types of file its input comes. We will see that this generalisation and simplification is characteristic of UNIX.

10.3.1 Ordinary Files.

UNIX has a particularly simple view of disc files. An ordinary (disc) file is merely an unstructured stream of bytes. The concept of a "record" (let alone a "card") is absent from the file system. Text files are strings of characters including from time to time the new-line character and binary (object) files are streams of bytes to be placed in core memory when the program is executed. Disc files may be accessed sequentially or randomly.

All concern with sectors, tracks or cylinders is shouldered by the system. The user does not have to and is, in fact, unable to pre-allocate disc space for a file. Here UNIX is optimised for user-convenience rather than system efficiency and, for a number of specialised applications in which real time response becomes of paramount importance, attempts have been made to add provision for contiguous disc files to UNIX.

The lack of internal structure in files promotes the flexibility of the system. As is argued below, one of the most powerful features of UNIX is the way simple programs and utilities can cooperate to do a complex job. This easy cooperation would be impaired by any attempt from the system to impose structure on files.

This lack of structure is not mandatory. The system refrains from imposing structure, but it is open to a user to design a set of cooperating programs that read and write files of arbitrary structure. There are examples in the system where such strucure is natural. The connect-time accounting file is written to and read by programs which expect a particular format. Lack of system-imposed structure helps rather than hinders the creation of user-defined structure.

The UNIX authors point out (1) that this simple way of looking at files was suggested by the MULTICS system. Other features have their origins in other time sharing systems. It is generally true that the success of UNIX is not due to the large number of original ideas incorporated in it but in the clever selection and combination of already existing ideas.

10.3.2 Directories.

A directory links the name of a file with the file itself. A non-directory file may be linked to more than one directory, all the links having equal status. This means that a file can be known by more than one name and it is only deleted when the last link to it is removed. Theoretically, because a directory is a file, cross links could be created between directories resulting in a file system with the structure of an arbitrary directed graph. Directories, however, differ from ordinary files in that they can be written only by privileged system programs (they are read as ordinary files) which constrain the file system to be a conventional rooted tree.

In each directory, two special entries ("." and "..") link back to the current directory itself and up to the parent directory respectively. A file may be accessed by a path name which names the links separated by the character "/". In the limit, the character "/" on its own represents the root of the file system. Each user has his own directory in which he may create an arbitrary number of subdirectories nested to an arbitrary depth.

Using path names, the user can access files in remote parts of the file system from his home directory or he may decide to move into the remote directory and access the files directly.

In a multiple disc system, the boundaries between the discs are almost completely hidden from the user - the ONLY exception is that two users must be on the same disc if they want to link to the same file.

The file system structure was designed to make it easy for users to traverse the system reading files, and to share files. Files and directories can be sufficiently protected from access for most purposes.

10.3.3 Special Files.

Special files are interfaces to physical devices designed to hide, as far as is possible, the idiosyncrasies of their actual mechanism. Each physical device has at least one entry in the file system heirarchy. It usually resides in the directory "/dev" but that is only an administrative convenience. Requests to read or write to the device file result in the calling of the appropriate routines in the device driver.

The main advantage in blurring the differences between files and devices to the point of invisibility, is that file and device I/O become interchangeable. The redirection of output from the terminal to a disc file or to another terminal or to a lineprinter is easy and natural in UNIX. Device names and disc file names have exactly the same syntax. This redirection requires the cooperation of the command interpreter; examples will be given when the "shell" is discussed.

Besides the devices mentioned, there are also special files to correspond to physical memory and to the disc units themselves. Such files can be invaluable to the system administrator (for example to check directly the consistency of the disc file system or to copy one disc to another) but must obviously be protected from inadvertent access. The access protection mechanism is exactly the same as for a disc file.

An important side effect of the "special file" concept is that the implementation of inter-user communication is trivial - writing to the appropriate file causes output to appear on another terminal. Protection of your terminal special file will allow you to work in peace.

The protection system has a "set user identification" mechanism which can allow any user access to a protected file ONLY via a specially written program. Ordinary users are not normally allowed to put files directly into the area reserved for the lineprinter spooler, but, by using the lineprinter spooling program (which is "setuid"), they may. The spooler program, of course, makes sure that the necessary control information accompanies the file.

10.4 ASYNCHRONOUS PROCESSES

The system uses routines known as "fork" and "exec" to create separate processes to deal with each terminal and to fulfil various other tasks. Each command run by the user becomes a separate process so that each user may run as many commands simultaneously as system resources or administrative decision will allow.

The fork mechanism is also directly available to users. Having created the processes, inter process communication is rudimentary but possible. This is an area where, for some applications, UNIX is again deficient and a number of attempts have been made to provide synchronisation mechanisms.

10.5 THE SHELL

The shell is the command line interpreter. It is not an integral part of the system at all, but is just another program. It can be rewritten, extended, adapted for inexperienced or specialised users (or even replaced by a game!) on a per-user basis - all without repercussions on the rest of the system and without taking up valuable system space.

The shell can be told in which directories it is to look for the files containing utility program objects (usually they are in /bin) and in what order. User written commands are positively encouraged.

The shell automatically opens three files, the standard input, the standard output, and the standard error output. Normally these three files are associated with the user's terminal but redirection can take the input from any other file or device and send the output to yet another file or device. The program concerned remains oblivious of the change. The shell even provides a mechanism (known as a "pipe") to connect the standard output of one program to the standard input of another.

10.5.1 Redirection of Output.

If the file "hello" contains the object of the first example program in the book "The "C" Programming Language" (Kernighan and Ritchie (2)) then the command

```
hello
```

will cause "hello world" to appear on the user's own terminal. The command

```
hello > file.1
```

will cause the same output to be redirected into a file called "file.1".

```
hello > /dev/tty05
```

again causes the output to be redirected, but this time "hello world" will appear on terminal number 5.

10.5.2 Redirection of Input.

The redirection of input can be illustrated using the command

```
write jds
```

This command will warn user "jds", if he is logged in, to expect a message and will send whatever is typed in on the terminal to jds's terminal. The sequence

```
write jds < file.1
```

redirects the input to the write command so that it comes from the file "file.1" created above. Finally, the command

```
hello ¦ write jds
```

will join the output of "hello" to the input of "write jds" with a "pipe". The result is that a message consisting of the words "hello world" is sent to jds's terminal.

The addition of an ampersand at the end of any one of these command lines will mean that the command runs "in the background" i.e the prompt reappears before the command has finished executing, allowing another command to be started.

10.5.3 Argument Expansion.

A rather simple but surprisingly useful aspect of the shell is its ability to expand arguments to commands into an argument list. If you wanted to send all the files in a particular directory to the lineprinter, typing

```
lpr *
```

while in the directory in question, will do the job. The character "*" is understood by the shell to match any string. There are a number of other characters besides "*" recognised by the shell as leading to argument expansion.

10.5.4 Utilities as Tools.

We now see emerging the basis for the "toolmaking" philosophy of software design that has grown up with UNIX. If it is easy to join the standard output of one program to the standard input of another, then the most useful programs will be those that "filter" a stream of data taken from the standard input and send it to the standard output. Such programs can be combined with others in a "pipeline".

Examples of tools are:

```
diff file.1 file.2
```

which sends to the standard output the lines that differ between the files file.1 and file.2.

```
wc
```

- word count, which writes on the standard output the number of lines, words or characters received at the standard input.

grep pattern

- meaning get regular expression, which scans the standard input for the pattern specified and sends lines containing it to the standard output.

An example of a useful pipeline might be

```
diff file.1 file.2 ¦ grep pattern ¦ wc -l
```

which will write to the terminal the number of lines containing the pattern of characters that appear in only one of the two files.

It is interesting to note that the tool "diff" has an option which will cause it to produce its output in the form of an editor script that can be used to edit file.1 to produce file.2. The editor (with prompts turned off) can run the script automatically.

Many UNIX beginners are mystified by some seemingly useless 'utilities' such as "echo" which takes a string argument and merely repeats it on the standard output - by default, on the terminal! If you want a string to appear on the screen why not just type it in? Echo is designed to be used as the head of a pipeline, issuing a command string to a (normally interactive) progam.

A similar situation arises with error messages. As a rule, experienced users do not want the screen to be covered in explanatory error messages every time they make a typing mistake and UNIX diagnostics are notoriously terse - often just "?" appears on the screen when you have done something wrong. This is not wholly a matter of taste. The usefulness of a program in a pipeline is seriously impaired if it insists on producing prompts and diagnostics besides its useful output. Beginners, however, require a little more help than "?". The problem has been solved by including verbosity as an option on programs often used by beginners (for example the editor) or by writing menu-driven shells for a particular application.

10.5.5 Programming with the Shell.

Combined with the previously mentioned ability of the shell to run more than one command at once, these capabilities already offer a powerful facility to the user, but the real power of the shell stems from the fact that it is just another program. The shell can call itself recursively (or call another version of the shell) and the new incarnation can have its standard input connected to a disc file rather than the terminal special file. The shell can thus be made to execute a prepared list of commands. From here it was only a short step to require the shell to take parameters, conditionally branch and repeatedly execute sets of prepared commands. Two main versions of the shell with these capabilities exist. One has evolved at Bell and mimics the syntax of Algol68; one at the University of California, Berkeley which has a syntax similar to the UNIX system language "C". These are in one sense very high level programming languages which manipulate programs and files.

10.6 THE ENVIRONMENT AND THE PHILOSOPHY

Ritchie and Thompson (1) summarise the facilities so far described as follows:

1. A heirarchical file system incorporating demountable volumes.
2. Compatible file, device, and inter-process I/O.
3. The ability to initiate asynchronous processes.
4. System command language selectable on a per-user basis.

It is the combination of these facilities which provides the programming environment which is the UNIX system. It is worth looking at the design philosophy that evolved with the environment and which it promotes and encourages.

The point of departure from traditional thinking was succinctly put by Kernighan and Mashey (3):

"Too much design without any experience may well lead to a first class solution of the wrong problem."

In contrast, the UNIX approach is:

"to design and build software, even operating systems to be tried early, ideally within weeks. Don't hesitate to throw away clumsy parts and rebuild them."

Such an approach is not possible unless the software is highly modular with simple interfaces. They also advocate-

"Make each program do one thing well. To do a new job, build afresh rather than complicate old programs by adding new "features".

and

"Expect the output of every program to become the input to another, as yet unknown, program."

In other words, write software tools - small, elegant programs that concentrate on a single function and therefore are easy to build, understand, describe and maintain. UNIX is its own advertisement in this respect. The tools that come with the system were often invented to help with its development and were continually tried, discussed, thrown away and redesigned.

This is encouraged by the environment. Programming in the shell can provide a quick, easy route to a first experimental version; programs designed to interact with files may be tried out on the terminal; the file system encourages sharing and discussion; the flexibility of the shell facilitates redesign. It is likely (but not guaranteed!) that software produced on UNIX will be flexible and modular with clean, simple interfaces.

10.7 THE PROGRAMMING LANGUAGE "C"

The decision, early in its development, to recode UNIX in the high level language "C" (2) (designed for the purpose) contributed substantially to its success. Since then, many compilers have been written to provide such languages as Fortran, Pascal, Lisp, APL, Modula2 and Ada under UNIX, but not all of these are available on all versions of UNIX. "C" is the only language common to all UNIX systems and is the one that interfaces most naturally with the system.

What sort of language is it and what facilities does it offer?

"C" is a small, versatile language which confines itself to dealing with operations that are easily mapped to machine instructions - it is not very high level. The more complex functions (including I/O) are covered by library routines. It has a rich set of operators, including bit manipulation.

It was designed by expert programmers who new what they wanted the machine to do, so that they could write programs with the minimum number of key strokes and the minimum of restrictions from the language. They wrote clear code without being forced to by the syntax and did not require extensive compile time checks. "C" cannot be described as encouraging good programming habits in the same way as UNIX encourages good software design. The emphasis is on what can be done rather than on attempting to set programming standards. It is possible, in "C" to write programs that are indecipherable, compile without error, give ludicrous results at run time, and are impossible to debug. On the other hand it is possible to write UNIX in "C". With Pascal, for example, you do not get as much rope.

10.8 A BRIEF UNIX HISTORY AND GUIDE

The first version of UNIX was not written in "C" but in assembler and ran on DEC PDP-7 and -9 computers in 1969-70. PDP-11 UNIX dates from 1971 and the first version written in "C" dates from 1973. This was also the first to incorporate multiprogramming. The first ports to machines other than DEC PDP-11's were done in 1977.

The versions of UNIX licensed by AT&T's subdivision - Western Electric - are snapshots of systems that were in use in the Bell organisation.

The main systems on offer at present are listed below. The numbering conventions may make some sense to Western Electric - they certainly seem almost random to an outsider.

Mini UNIX:	Version for small DEC machines.
UNIX Version 6:	First widely available version on PDP-11's. (It was in fact the THIRD version of UNIX produced, but the manual that went with it was the "Sixth Edition".)
PWB/UNIX:	The Programmer's Workbench - designed for large software development projects and used in the Business Information Systems Programs (BISP) area of Bell Laboratories. PWB/UNIX is specifically discussed later.
UNIX Version 7:	An enhanced V6 that runs on the PDP-11/70.
UNIX 32V:	Bell's version for the DEC VAX series.
UNIX SYSTEM III:	The latest version to be released. It incorporates features from UNIX 32V and PWB/UNIX.

The first release that AT&T will sell and support following their recent settlement with the US Department of Justice seems to be fairly similar to System III but is to be called System V!

10.8.1 The Programmer's Workbench.

The Programmer's Workbench UNIX system is particularly relevant to the present discussion. It was developed specifically for software development. The target systems, however, were generally machines of the size of the IBM System/370. Among the requirements identified by the developers of PWB/UNIX (Dolotta et al (4)) were:

1. A good interactive computing service.

2. A file structure designed for convenient interactive use.

3. Good, uniform tools for the manipulation of documents, source programs and text.

4. A command language simple enough for everyone to use, but one that offers enough programming capability to help automate the tasks of project development.

5. Adaptibility to frequent and unpredictable changes in target environment.

The UNIX system as developed in the Computing Science Research Center was identified as fulfilling many of these requirements without modification. New facilities added included most significantly the Source Code Control System described later. Other new facilities, such as Remote Job Entry and the simulation of "cluster controllers" were specific to the very large target machines.

The original system was also modified to increase reliability. The Research system typically ran well within the limits of the machine, whereas in the production environment the system ran much closer to the limit of resources such as disc space, process table size etc. The modifications made have become standard on most UNIX systems.

The more sophisticated aspects of the shell evolved out of the apparent need for groups cooperating on a project to write their own commands and share them - "to customize their work environment". This "need" has probably more to do with social psychology than with the objectively perceived requirements for software development, but it has apparently been observed to make a significant contribution to productivity!

10.8.2 Berkeley UNIX.

UNIX 32V and System III are swapping systems and do not make use of the paging facility available on the DEC VAX series of machines. The United States Advanced Research Projects Agency (ARPA) - an offshoot of the Department of Defense - funded a project at the University of California, Berkeley to produce a paging system. The resulting system also incorporates a number of other enhancements and there have been two releases:

Berkeley Software Distribution 4.0
BSD 4.1

System III represented an effort by Bell Labs to unify in one product the best features from the various development strands within the organisation, but the Berkeley versions represent a totally separate development path.

It must be said that the Berkeley software has not been subjected to as much discussion and redesign as the original Bell system. Liberated from the restrictions of the PDP-11 address space, some of the utilities have grown to an enormous size and sprouted numerous "features". Similarly, it is difficult to see what some of the improvements are improving. Berkeley UNIX was a "project".

The economic situation being what it is, however, not many organisations can prevent excessive swapping exclusively by buying more memory or more machines - which is the Bell solution. A paging system is therefore a requirement.

Many of the extra facilities provided by Berkeley UNIX are excellent. Their Pascal system is very good - especially for tutorial purposes. Facilities provided by the Berkeley shell include the ability to suspend a program running in the foreground and restart it in the background and a "history" mechanism. The history mechanism allows previous commands to be recalled, modified and rerun. Bell Laboratories run Berkeley UNIX on many of their VAX machines and some "Berkeley features" have been incorporated into System V. The next release of Berkeley UNIX (BSD 4.2) is due in the Autumn of 1983 and promises network facilities and a much faster file system.

10.9 TOOLS FOR SOFTWARE DEVELOPMENT

Unix is an environment for software development but there are also some tools specifically designed to do software development jobs.

10.9.1 Partial Recompilation.

"Make" is a utility to recompile only those parts of a large system that have been modified since the last recompilation. "Make" must be supplied with a file specifying dependencies between source modules - those conventionally connected with the "C" language it already knows about. The success of this utility in saving time and trouble when only a small section of a large system has been modified depends on the modularity of the system. For example, in the operating system itself, one file contains all system parameters. Almost all the programs in the system depend on this file. If it is modified, make will recompile all the source modules even if only one parameter has been adjusted and is referred to in only one of them.

10.9.2 Control of System Modifications.

The Source Code Control System is a small set of commands that records changes made to files of source code (or other text). It is able to deal with branching development paths - when two programmers start work on the same original source file - and is able to recreate the file as it existed at any point in time.

SCCS files consist of six parts:

1. A checksum of all the characters in the other five sections of the file.

2. A table specifying the changes ("deltas") to the file - lines inserted, deleted or unchanged, date and time of the change, the name of the user concerned, the serial number of the change.

3. A list of users who may change the file.

4. A list of flags to the SCCS system, specifying such things as whether branches in the development are to be allowed.

5. A comment section typically containing a description of the file's purpose.

6. The body of the file, consisting of text lines and control lines specifying insertion and deletion of passages of text for various version numbers.

The tools include programs to create and administer SCCS files, make a change to an SCCS file and to recreate a certain version of an SCCS file.

10.9.3 Sdb: A Symbolic Debugger.

Sdb is designed to work in conjunction with the "C" compiler which produces sufficient information to allow sdb to interact with a running program at the "C" language level. Facilities for placing breakpoints and single stepping through the program examining variables by name in their correct format are provided. The core image of an aborted program may be examined in a similar way.

10.9.4 Language Development Tools.

Two of the provided tools are "C" program generators. They are known as "yacc" - standing for "yet another compiler compiler" and "lex" a generator of regular expression recognisers. Lex may be used to generate lexical analysers, while yacc generates LALR(1) parsers. They have been used together to produce a portable "C" compiler and the macro preprocessor for "C".

10.10 CONCLUSION

Recently UNIX has become fashionable. It is mentioned almost every week in a headline somewhere in the computing press and also features prominently on the vacancies pages. In the amateur magazines, alongside the articles entitled "Pascal versus Basic" (in which BASIC comes out on top) are appearing "UNIX versus CP/M" articles (in which CP/M wins every time!). Even the technology page of the Financial Times has recently seen fit to make its readership aware of UNIX.

With this popularity have come claims from manufacturers that they have now incorporated "the main features of UNIX" in their own operating systems. On closer inspection, this often means they have a "C" compiler, or something similar to the Source Code Control System, or even a command interpreter that does a minimal amount of argument expansion. Conversely, UNIX is sometimes criticised for its lack of applications programs. With the wide recognition of the underlying merits of the system, this situation is being rapidly remedied. Those now committed to reselling and supporting UNIX include Perkin Elmer, Hewlett Packard, Intel, Motorola, National Semiconductor and DEC.

The identification of UNIX with the particular utilities available on it is to miss the essence of the system. UNIX is essentially a way of thinking about operating systems and software design. The UNIX approach is as applicable to the new workstations (Perq, Appollo, Sun...) with high resolution bit-mapped graphics and local area networks, as it was to the teletypes on which it was originally developed.

REFERENCES

1. Ritchie, D.M., and Thompson, K., 1978, Bell System Tech. J., 57, 6, 1905-1929.

2. Kernighan, B.W., and Ritchie, D.M., 1978, "The C Programming Language", Prentice-Hall.

3. Kernighan, B.W., and Mashey, J.R., 1979, Software-Practice and Experience, 9, 1-15.

4. Dolotta, T.A., Haight, R.C., and Mashey, J.R., 1978, Bell System Tech. J., 57, 6, 2177-2200.

Chapter 11

Development environments and run-time support in ADA

P. van der Linden and R. Spencer

1. ABSTRACT

The Ada programming language is a modern development in the software world. It incorporates many new ideas, while building on a foundation of established technology. Ada was originally designed for programming very large dedicated real-time military systems, but it appears likely that it will be widely used outside this domain. The language is therefore of interest and relevance to systems engineers working in all areas of applied computer technology. This paper outlines some of the unique features of an Ada development environment, and then describes the demands which are made on a run-time support system for the language.

2. INTRODUCTION

Ada is practically unique amongst programming languages in that it was the subject of a lengthy and detailed design process, before any implementations were attempted. Thus the designers of Ada were able to devise and refine ideas, to present an integrated whole, without considering "downwards compatibility" with existing installations. This is a marked contrast with say, FORTRAN, where the millstone of obsolete technology is worn around the neck of every new standard for the language.

Designing a new language ab initio has permitted a radical break with established software development practices. In a conventional system, the term "development environment" refers to the surroundings and means by which software is produced: the host computer, a compiler, an editor and so on. In an Ada installation, the term has a much less nebulous meaning. Every installation where Ada programs are developed is supposed to implement an Ada Programming Support Environment or "APSE".

3. DEVELOPMENT ENVIRONMENTS

The Ada Programming Support Environment is a practical result of recent research into programming languages. An APSE is a software system which is designed to produce software systems. It attempts to use the computer to speed up the process of software development.

A programming development environment is comprised of many software tools and a central database. The software tools will consist of existing programs such as compilers, pretty-printers, and linkers, along with other less familiar processors such as dynamic trace analysers, network interfaces, and structure editors. The information in the database will concern the software under development. Typically it will cater for multiple target computer profiles, system maintenance history and version control, documentation and project management information.

Some of these features are present in existing programming development environments, such as the InterLISP system. The APSE goes beyond these however, and attempts to present a comprehensive coherent and consistent model. It is no coincidence that all the existing APSE prototypes borrow heavily from the Unix system in their architecture. Other items which the APSE may eventually incorporate include a programmer training facility, and program verification aids.

The APSE approach is useful for other programming languages too, but specific parts of the Ada design have an impact. Ada programs are comprised of a set of compilation units, which contain packages. Each package has a specification and a body; the specification part contains declarations of all procedures, variables and types that are available for use by programs in other packages. The package body contains the actual executable program and declarations of any data that must be protected from outside interference. The major advantages of this approach are that:

- The software system can be modularised with the assurance that only certain well-specified cross-module interactions can take place.

- If a package specification is compiled separately from its body, then subsequent changes to the implementation described in the body will not affect any users of this package. This "fire-wall" is of great benefit in program maintenance, allowing changes in implementation to be made with a minimal input on the total software system.

- Tasks. The language provides full support for parallel processing including relative priorities, synchronisation, and interprocess communication. The run-time system must provide the appropriate scheduling and dispatching mechanisms. A multi-processing system is required, but this may by implemented on either single processor or multiple-processor hardware. Ada tasks have quite complex semantics. The run time system must support the creation, and termination of tasks as well as inter-task communication (via the rendezvous mechanism). For example, if a group of tasks are declared inside a procedure, then that procedure will not return until all the child tasks have terminated.

- File handling. There is a rich set of file-handling primitives, including support for sequential and direct I/O. A comprehensive text I/O package is also provided.

- Date-time concept. Ada requires a target system to maintain a real-time clock, which includes calendar dates. Obviously this requirement falls on the run-time system, though it may be implemented in terms of the underlying machine model of time.

- Interrupt processing. User interrupt-handling is quite feasible in Ada, and may be selected (by the compiler-writer) for implementing certain exception conditions. The run-time system must be aware of this and manage the appropriate context saving and switching.

Any Ada development environment must support this approach. For example, the development system for the Intel iAPX432 microprocessor:

- allows separate compilation of package specifications and bodies

- type-checks all references between packages

- ensures that if a package specification is changed, that all dependent packages (i.e. those that reference the specification) are recompiled

- allows the modified package(s) to be linked to the existing object code where the updated package(s) will replace the old version(s).

In addition the Intel 432 Ada development system supports debugging of Ada programs at the source code level.

The package construct opens up the possibility of using software modules in a similar manner to the way integrated circuits are used in hardware design. One of the great benefits of integrated circuits is that details of the implementation of each type of circuit is not available to the user. He designs his system based on his understanding of the operation of each type of integrated circuit from the published specifications. In the same way, it is anticipated that a library of standard packages will be built up for use in the construction of complex systems.

Since program development environments are a relatively new idea, the design and implementation of APSEs has lagged behind that of Ada Compilers. At the time of writing (June 1983) the first Ada compiler has been officially validated, but no APSEs are yet fully operational. The ROLM Corporation has an advanced prototype, whilst products from other vendors are in varying stages of development. The United States Department of Defense, which is the prime mover in the Ada effort, views the development environment as the key aspect of the language. It proposes to apportion its (considerable) funding in the ratio 20%-80% between compilers and environments, with the environments getting the lion's share.

4. RUN-TIME SUPPORT

Ada is a large and sophisticated programming language, and contains features which make considerable demands on a run-time support system. Among these features are the following:

Memory allocation. Most variables in an Ada program will be simply declared either in a package or in a procedure. Package level variables will be static and thus require no memory management. In common with many other languages Ada procedure-level variables need to be created (allocated) when the procedure is called and destroyed (deallocated) when the procedure returns. The run time support required here will vary depending on the architecture of the underlying machine. Some sophisticated computers (e.g. the iAPX432) allocate memory for procedure-level variables as part of the procedure call instruction. Ada also allows the creation of variables that have no name, but are referenced via access variables (variables which store the address of another variable). These variables have a lifetime that is not tied to the procedure in which they are declared. Each variable must be destroyed when there are no access variables referencing it. The run time system detects this condition and deallocates the memory used. This reclamation of unused memory, ready for reallocation is termed "garbage collection".

Clearly the naive single-user control programs found on modern commercial microcomputers are inadequate for the job. Nonetheless, Ada code may be executable on even these processors by rewriting the monitor. The run-time support is considerable compared with other languages (e.g. FORTRAN) but it does not necessarily incur an undue overhead. For example, the process management routines for the York University Ada compiler require about 4K bytes of storage.

A further important consideration concerns software portability. In the past, run-time support has usually been regarded as an operating system function. Tasking, for instance, is implemented in C, Modula, and PL/I through system calls. By moving this functionality into the programming language software portability is ensured.

In general, an Ada system will be developed on a host computer, for execution on a target computer. Where the host and target systems are identical, one may regard these run-time requirements as a further responsibility of the Ada programming support environment.

5. CONCLUSION

This paper reviews two of the more important aspects of the programming language Ada. In both cases the language represents an improvement over existing technology. In both cases the benefits of these improvements are purchased by placing more of the burden on the computer system rather than the programmer. As programming continues to evolve into the central systems discipline, we expect this trend to be increasingly emphasised. Therefore Ada constitutes an important introduction into the software systems of the future.

In exploiting these aspects of Ada and its support environment, programmers will find themselves using design approaches that may be unfamiliar to them. It has been the experience of those using Ada that these new approaches and the support provided by the language do give an appreciable increase in software productivity and reliability.

Some Ada compiler implementations

Organisation	Host System	Target	Availability
New York University USA	VAX, IBM 370	same	full Ada validated March 83
Rolm Corporation	MV-range	same	full Ada validated June 83
Western Digital	WD 1600	same	full Ada validated Sept 83
Intel Corporation	VAX	iAPX432	comprehensive subset now validation planned end 84
York University England	VAX/UNIX	same	subset available now
Intermetrics	IBM 370 PDP-10	same	subset available now
Yokosuka Laboratory NTT, Japan	DIPS	same	subset available now
Softech	VAX/VMS	same	subset available now
Telesoft	VAX, IBM 370, 68000, 8086	same	subset available now
Verdix Corporation	VAX	same	subset available now
DEC	VAX/VMS	same	no date known
Honeywell	Multics	L6,DPS-6	subset available now
Univac	1100 range	same	subset available now
Amdahl	470 range	same	subset available now
Carnegie-Mellon University	VAX, Perq	same	subset available now
University of Karlsruhe	Siemens 7760	same & 68000	subset available now

Note : There are literally dozens more Ada implementations under way in both Europe and the USA. This list is subject to rapid development, and gives details of :

(i) hardware manufacturers who have made public announcements of Ada compiler plans,

and

(ii) those organisations which are in an advanced stage of Ada compiler development.

Some Ada Programming Support Environment implementations :

Organisation	Tool Title	Host System	Availability
Softech	Ada Language System	VAX/VMS	Beta version now
Intermetrics	Ada Integrated Environment	IBM 370 Perkin Elmer 8/32	under development
University of California, Irvine	Arcturus	VAX/Unix	Beta version now
TRW	Prototype Advanced APSE	VAX/Unix	under development
ROLM Corporation	Ada Development Environment	MV-range	first field release available now
Olivetti	not known	Olivetti 6000	under development
Ada Group Ltd. (a consortium of SPL, Systems Designers Ltd. Software Sciences & ICL)	MCHAPSE (Minimal Chill-Ada PSE)	ICL 2900	under development

Note : There are other APSE implementations currently under development or being planned in both Europe and the USA. This list gives details of some manufacturers, and other furthest advanced in their projects.

It is probably true to say that Ada can today be successfully and beneficially substituted for other programming languages (without an APSE) on most projects, even small scale ones. Indeed, a small pilot-project forms a useful way for an organisation to evaluate and acquire this new software technology. To support very large scale projects however an APSE would be desirable.

Chapter 12

Specifications, testing and the contribution of quality systems

N.C. Sedgwick

12.1 SUMMARY

The concept of the system development life cycle is introduced as a model of the work to be done on a development project. The output of the system development life cycle is a working item that can be manufactured or replicated. This item is defined in terms of its static sub-items and sub-sub-items in a strictly heirarchical fashion. There are five stages of work to be done on each item: specification, design, implementation, internal tests and external tests. For each stage of work, for each item-type, standards and procedures will be defined for methodology, documentation and validation. Standards are also required for configuration management and change control.

A distinction is made between "Client Requirement" and "Acceptance Testing" and specification and testing of the top level item. Separate documents should be produced to allow for differences in emphasis, detail and presentation between client and contractor documentation. The use of national, international or industry standards is recommended.

Quality assurance systems are introduced and justified on the grounds of efficiency and confidence for both the client and the contractor. The features of quality assurance systems and the contents of quality assurance plans for development projects are summarised.

Finally some of the more awkward features of software engineering for microprocessors are discussed and the importance of quality assurance in identifying these problems in advance is stressed.

12.2 SYSTEM DEVELOPMENT LIFE CYCLE

In order to consider the contribution of quality assurance we must have a model of the software development process. The model presented here is not the only correct model but it is self consistent and has been used successfully in developments in my own company. The model is also applicable, in general terms, to hardware developments, software developments and to mixed hardware and software developments.

The model says that a development goes through five distinct stages, each of which has a well defined interface with the other stages. The names and definitions of these stages are given below. The flow of work from stage to stage is shown in Figure 12.1.

12.2.1 Specification

This is a description, of what the item to be developed will do. It describes the item in terms of its inputs, outputs and the transformation between them (processing). The specification must concentrate on what the item is to do; not how which is design, nor why which is rationale. All statements in the specification should be of a provable nature. Quantitative statements are preferable to qualitative statements. Vague aims should be avoided at all costs. Statements concerning flexibility, contingency for increased workload and the ability to enhance or upgrade the item should also be given in similar provable and definite terms. The specification should also give constraints on the design and implementation; for example the target hardware and programming language to be used.

12.2.2 Design

The design document describes how the item meets its specification. It is a description of the insides of the item in terms of its sub-items and the interactions between them. The design must be complete; it must describe how all statements in the specification are met. It must be unambiguous; interpretation of the number of sub-items and their interconnections should not be left to the reader. It must be possible to validate that the design meets the statements on performance given in the specification.

12.2.3 Implementation

Implementation consists of making the sub-items specified in the design and connecting them together (which is sometimes called integration). Making, in this sense, means building a prototype rather than manufacturing or replicating copies of an already proven prototype. Making (in the case of software engineering) means writing computer programs or subroutines or (as will be expanded on later) going through the system development life cycle for all sub-items.

12.2.4 Internal Testing

Testing is proving that the item meets its specification. This is usually done by selecting suitable inputs to the item, calculating by some independent means the way in which the item should operate with those inputs and then confirming that it does operate in the expected way. The internal test plan will specify the inputs and expected operation of the item.

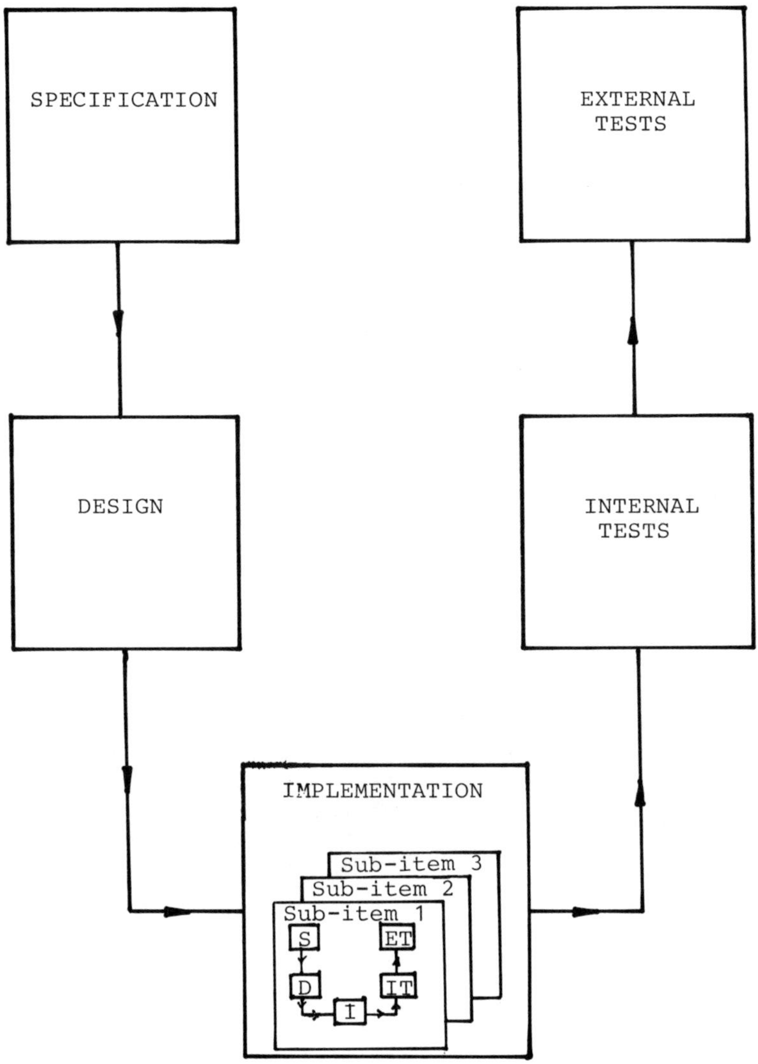

Fig 12.1 U-curve for system development life cycle.

Internal tests are those that are specified with knowledge of the specification and, particularly, with knowledge of the design. Inputs may be injected into some sub-item and operation may be observed by looking at the output of some sub-item. In the case of software development this is best summarised by saying that debug statements, traces and memory dumps are allowed.

12.2.5 External Testing

The purpose of external testing is the same as that of internal testing; namely to prove that the item meets its specification. The external test plan will also specify the inputs and the expected operation of the item.

External tests differ from internal tests in that they are produced only with knowledge of the specification; knowledge of the design is excluded. As a result of this: inputs may only be injected into the item and not into any sub-item; operation of the item may only be observed by monitoring the outputs of the item and not those of any sub-item. In software terms this means debug statements, traces and memory dumps are not allowed.

12.2.6 Heirarchical Decomposition

It is reasonable to suppose that the work done on a small development project will require a similar approach to that taken on a similar part of a larger development project. The similarity of approach would cover the five stages of the system development life cycle, the project planning and costing and project control. To deal with this in a consistent way we extend our model of the system development life cycle to say that the five stages apply to each sub-item of the item to be developed. This is further extended to <u>sub-sub-items</u> and so on.

All items, sub-items and sub-sub-items that are conceptually similar and require similar work to specify, design, implement and test we refer to as an <u>item-type</u>. The identification of the item-types and the techniques or standards to be applied to each one are of major importance in quality assurance.

Figure 12.2 shows the hierarchy of items and sub-items to four levels for a software development in which MASCOT(1) terminology has been used. This example is discussed in more detail in the next sub-section. However it is worth saying here that the strictly heirarchical and rigorous approach to the system development life cycle given so far can lead to duplication of effort in two main areas. The first is that the specification of a sub-item may replicate part of the design of its parent item. The second is that the external tests of a sub-item may largely overlap with the internal tests of its parent item. The solution to this is to agree, for each item-type, where the single copy of the documentation is to be kept: in the documentation of the item, the sub-items that constitute it, or split between the two in an agreed way.

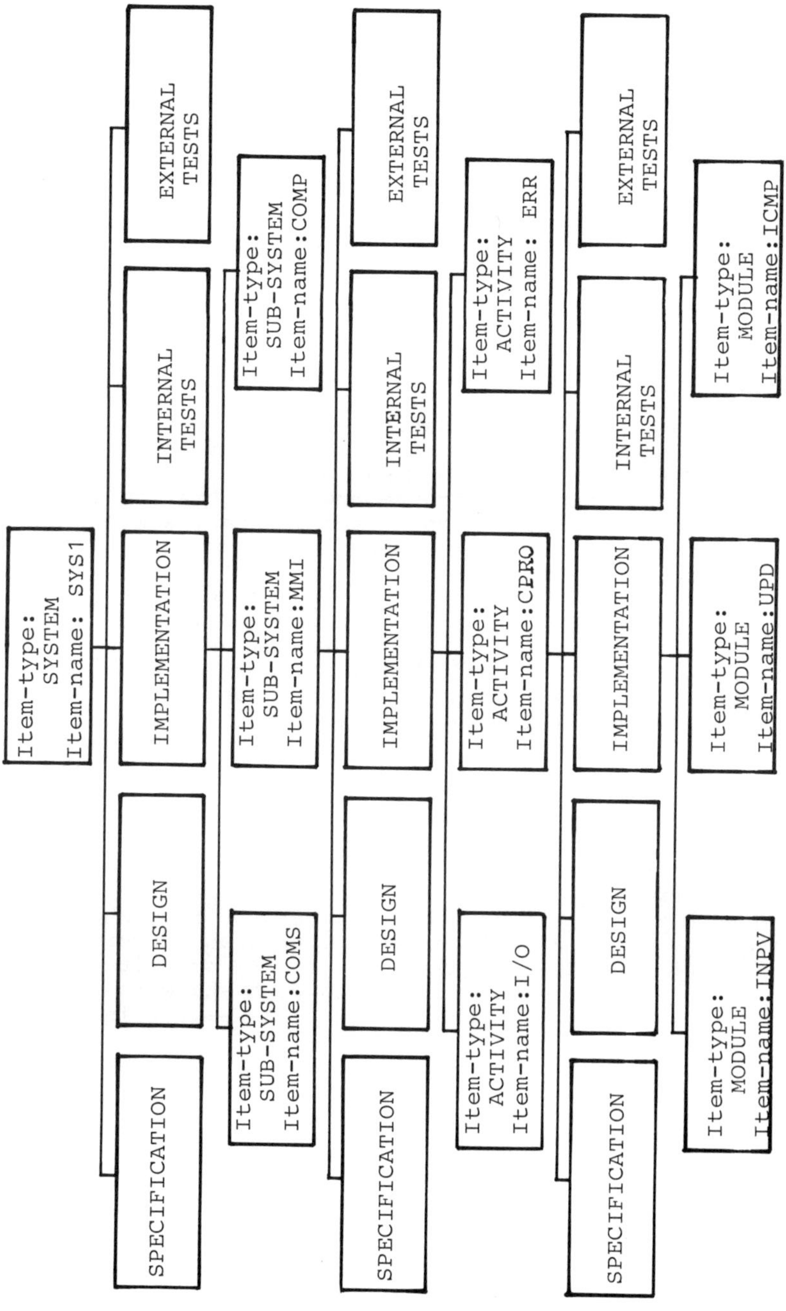

Fig 12.2 Example heirarchy of items and sub-items using MASCOT terminology.

12.2.7 Methodology, Documentation and Validation

From the quality assurance viewpoint, it is highly desirable to identify (for each of the five stages of work for each item-type) a methodology of working, a documentation standard, and validation procedures to ensure that the work has been carried out correctly. Example methodologies, documentation standards and validation procedures for the software development summarised in Figure 12.2 are given in Table 12.1.

12.2.8 Configuration Management and Change Control

Configuration management is the method of labelling items and of specifying the sub-items that go together to make each item (the configuration).

Change control is the method of changing the configuration such that new items or sub-items are created and inter-relationships are changed. Change control procedures should ensure that the new configuration is known, an audit trail of changes can be traced back and finally that all components of the new configuration are self consistent. This final point should cover all documentation and all items and sub-items.

Configuration management and change control has always been a strong discipline in hardware and there is a lot that software engineers can learn from hardware engineers in this area. In general terms the approach is the same; a tree diagram shows the relationship between items and sub-items. In electronic hardware this may identify boards, sub-assemblies, assemblies and major assemblies. In software the equivalents may be source code modules, object code modules, loadable programs, suites of programs etc. In each case items should be labelled with:

- item name
- variant identification
- version, issue or revision number
- serial number

The term variant is used here to mean an item whose specification in functional terms (rather than performance terms) is identical to other variants of the same item. Examples in software terms are modules with and without run-time error checks or with different trade-offs in memory and execution requirements.

Serial numbers are only of concern for manufacture and replication and normally refer to delivery media. For software these are generally magnetic media devices (discs or tapes) but for microprocessor developments they will frequently include read only memories (ROMs).

The number of items that exist as part of a software development usually exceeds those of a hardware development of similar cost by one or two orders of magnitude. The importance of configuration management is therefore greater but so is the cost and this frequently discourages correct use. For software developments of any size, configuration management is essential for maintenance purposes.

TABLE 12.1 Example Standards

Item-type	Stage	Sub-Stage	Example Approach
System	Specification	Methodology	De Marco (2) Structured Analysis
		Documentation	De Marco New Physical System Diagram and Data Dictionary
		Validation	Technical review by peer group.
Subsystem	Design	Methodology	Consideration of a number of alternative designs and selection of the best by subjective and objective scoring against flexibility, elegance, efficiency, cost of implementation etc.
		Documentation	MASCOT (1) ACP Diagram
		Validation	Technical review by peer group.
Module	Implementation	Methodology	Line by line manual translation from Program Design Language to CORAL-66.
		Documentation	Heavily commented source code listing to an agreed layout standard.
		Validation	Code review by immediate supervisor on a sample basis. Validation that all source code meets the BSI language standard (3) and only contains valid code constructs (of nested sequence, selection and iteration) using an automatic code analyser.
Activity	Internal Tests	Methodology	Confirmation that all statements have been executed at least once without failure. Input test data is chosen using knowledge of the design to exercise all paths. The execution path trace option of the particular compiler is used to log all statement numbers as they are executed. A post processor lists the number of executions of each statement and checks for any zero executions.

Table 12.1 (continued)

Item-type	Stage	Sub-Stage	Example Approach
Activity	Internal Tests	Documentation	Test plan to an agreed standard identifying all input test data and paths executed for each test. Test run log and listings of post processor analysis.
		Validation	Approval of test plan by immediate supervisor and random sampling of 5% of test cases to ensure actual path execution (recorded by the trace log) matches that given in the test plan.
System	External Tests	Methodology	Confirmation that testing the system satisfies each statement (of a functional rather than performance related nature) in the specification of SYS1 using an individual set of test inputs for each statement.
		Documentation	Test plan to an agreed standard identifying all input test data, cross references to the statements in the specification and expected output from each test. Test run log and manual log of observed outputs.
		Validation	Approval of test plan by a technical review team consisting of peer group, client representative and quality assurance representative. Attendance at tests and certification of results by quality assurance representative.

12.3 SPECIFICATION AND TESTING OF THE TOP LEVEL ITEM

So far I have been careful in the use of terminology and have gone to some trouble to define meanings. I have avoided the use of "functional specification", "system design", "integration tests", "system tests", and "acceptance tests". I have only used the terms "system", "sub-system" and "activity" in the MASCOT sense and I have not defined "module" even though I have used it.

This care is purposeful. The justification is that these terms are not defined, they are in widespread use, and everyone thinks they mean something different. The introduction of a consistent set of terminology within your own company or working environment is highly beneficial as if you don't know what each other are talking about how can you expect anyone else to do so. If your terminology follows a national or international standard such as BS3527(4) then you will be able to communicate more effectively with people from similarly enlightened companies.

12.3.1 Contractor/Client Relationships

All developments have clients and contractors. There may be a legally binding contract between companies or a more informal relationship between parts of the same company. Clients reasonably expect to approve, or even write, the specification and external tests for the top level item that constitutes the deliverable of the development. Unfortunately, despite the wide availability of suitable national and international standards, clients and contractors rarely use the same terminology and documentation standards. There are three general approaches to solving this communication gap:

i) The client accepts the contractor's terminology and documentation standards.

ii) The contractor accepts the client's terminology and documentation standards.

iii) The contractor uses his own terminology and format for all of his work and translates only the necessary documents into the client's terminology and format.

The significance of this problem of contractor/client communications is frequently under-rated. The third approach usually requires that the specification and external test documentation of the top level item be translated into new documents and a conformity matrix be produced as a separate document. It is important to recognise that translation produces new documents and they need different titles. I use the titles "Client Requirements" and "Acceptance Test Plan" for the translations of "Specification for Top Level Item" and "External Tests for Top Level Item".

The emphasis that the client and the contractor place on different parts of the work are different. The contractor will be concerned with higher level aspects of the work. This may even extend to missing out a lot of information that should appear in the "Client Requirements" and "Acceptance Test Plan" if they were strict translations of the contractor's internal documents. Alternatively this text may be relegated to appendices. The client is also likely to be much more concerned about the documentation than methodology and validation.

The client's interests in the lower level and more detailed aspects of the development work are usually limited to feeling confident that the delivered goods will work and be maintainable. The modern trend is for the contractor to inspire this confidence in the client by operating a formal quality assurance system.

12.3.2 Contents of the Client Requirements Document

The contents should be the same as for specifications in general (as given in sub-section 12.2.1) applied to the top level item. In summary these are:

i) A functional description of the item in terms of inputs, outputs and processing.

ii) Performance requirements in terms of, for example, inputs per hour. This should also cover degraded operation in the event of partial failure of equipment.

iii) Constraints on the design and implementation in terms of target hardware and programming languages etc.

iv) Contingency in terms of, for example, spare processing capacity and spare memory.

v) Flexibility. This means taking into account likely additional functions when designing the items and any associated increases in performance to be satisfied out of contingency or by upgrading the hardware and software.

12.3.3 The Break between Hardware and Software

The nature of microprocessor systems is such that they are used in embedded real-time applications. In these cases the client requirement is usually for an equipment embodying hardware and software. The split of the workload in the equipment between hardware and software is a design decision and the client views this as a detail below his level of interest.

In these cases the development life cycle model described in section 12.2 can be extended to higher levels to include hardware aspects. This would typically be done by introducing item-types for hardware items such as each processor, each intelligent interface board and possibly any conditioning of analogue and digital signals. This approach has been used successfully in my company for a turnkey computer system based on a conventional mini- computer and an array processor for a real-time signal processing application.

12.3.4 Testing against the Client Requirements

Acceptance testing should follow the same general methods as those given in sub-sections 12.2.4 and 12.2.5. Namely each statement in the "Client Requirements" should be proved. If the feature is not required it should not be stated as required. If it is required then its existence in the finished item should be checked. Statements about constraints and flexibility can generally only be checked by manual inspection. Functional, performance and contingency statements are usually checked by objective tests on the item or sub-items.

Functional requirements are normally checked using external tests only. There are no differences to checking these things on microprocessors, minicomputers or mainframes. Test inputs are selected to prove compliance with each statement of a functional nature in the "Client Requirements".

Performance is much more difficult to check and internal tests are usually necessary. This raises problems as the measurement can affect the performance. This is discussed further in section 12.5.

Contingency requirements can usually be checked by, for example, manually examining linkage-editor maps for memory utilisation and having a null activity (in the MASCOT sense) that measures free CPU time. However there are problems with equipments that use dynamic memory allocation and whose execution load is highly data dependent. Once again the measurement itself may affect the performance.

12.3.5 Test Selection, Planning and Monitoring

To some people testing is boring. It is not like debugging; the thrill of the chase is missing. It requires the approach of the auditor with its attendant mundane clerical aspects. To some people testing is fascinating. It is a battle of wits against the designer and coder. It requires the investigative approach where there may not even be a crime. Test staff can also be thought of as needing destructive rather than creative instincts. Many companies use different staff for testing (especially on large projects) and these staff may be attached to the quality assurance, rather than the project, side of the company. This approach recognises the different staff requirements and ensures independence and separate and adequate costing. However it can be expensive and is not applicable to small developments.

What is true is that testing is essential, test selection is an activity needing intelligent and skilled staff and that conducting tests, correcting deficiencies and re-testing is a significant part of any development. It requires careful planning and monitoring if it is not to get out of hand or be skimped.

12.4 QUALITY ASSURANCE ASPECTS

As has been mentioned, quality assurance is a method of inspiring confidence in the client that the contractor knows what he is about.

The second aspect of quality assurance is efficiency. The client obtains his confidence in the contractor without watching his every move. He delegates the responsibility of monitoring the contractor's quality to the contractor himself. He requires the contractor to introduce a quality assurance system that is independent of the contractors development and manufacturing operations. The client is willing to pay higher prices for this service as it is more cost efficient than monitoring individual contracts in detail himself.

The third aspect of quality assurance is that it increases the contractor's own confidence and efficiency. Confidence increases because responsibility for quality is delegated within the company in an independent manner. Efficiency is increased because of the introduction of standard working practices and procedures. This reduces training costs and means that the wheel is not re-invented throughout the company again and again.

Quality assurance systems are now widespread in all areas of development and manufacturing. This is largely due to pressure from large organisations such as government, nationalised industries and large companies who demand confidence in their contractors in an efficient way. The Ministry of Defence has been a leader in this area in electronics and computing in the United Kingdom through the introduction of the quality assurance system requirements in DEFSTAN 05-21(5) and DEFSTAN 05-24(6). More recently the British Standards Institute has introduced similar requirements in BS5750 but these have not yet been extended to cover computing and software aspects in an adequate manner.

12.4.1 Definition of Terms

Quality assurance is the method of building quality into a development. It requires knowing what is to be done and how it is to be done before doing it. Every worker is his own quality assessor and every supervisor is the quality assessor of his staff.

Quality control is the measuring and checking of quality in a manufacturing environment, providing an audit trail so that the cause of quality deficiencies can be diagnosed, and providing a procedure for corrective action to restore quality to the required level.

Inspection is the method of checking on both quality assurance and quality control procedures independently from the development or manufacturing parts of a company.

12.4.2 Quality Assurance Systems

The requirements for a contractor's quality assurance system are well defined in DEFSTAN 05-21 and BS5750. The MoD expands on the requirements for software development in QTM16(8) but this is soon to be replaced by DEFSTAN 05-22/Part B.

The requirements can be summarised as follows:

i) The quality assurance system shall be managed independently of the development and production departments and shall report directly to senior management. Its operation shall be defined in a quality assurance manual.

ii) Clients shall have the right to assess the contractor's quality assurance system (Contractor Assessment).

iii) The contractor shall have standards for procedures and deliverable items covering management, methodologies, documentation, verification, manufacturing, replication, etc.

iv) The contractor shall have an internal procedure for reviewing his own quality assurance system and quality assurance manual.

v) For each development project, there should be a quality assurance plan that describes the standards and procedures to be used in conducting the work on that project.

vi) The contractor shall have internal inspection procedures for development and manufacturing that are independent of those departments.

vii) The contractor shall have procedures for monitoring the quality of delivered products, diagnosing the cause of any drop of quality and taking corrective action on all affected delivered products.

viii) There shall be a formal procedure for isolating and handling non-conforming materials (e.g. faulty or substandard components) and obtaining concessions to use such materials in certain circumstances.

ix) The contractor shall have formal procedures for assessing his sub-contractors and suppliers.

x) The contractor shall have formal procedures for configuration management that provide an audit trail.

12.4.3 The Quality Assurance Plan

The quality assurance plan for a development project has two main uses:

i) It describes the standards and procedures to be used on

the project. It is not practical to enforce a single standard or procedure across the whole of the contractor's company in a development environment; this is especially true of software which is a rapidly developing engineering discipline. It is therefore essential to have a reference document that informs all project staff what standards and procedures to work to.

ii) Its production, at the beginning of the project, forces the project team to think through all aspects of the project in advance and in some detail. They therefore have a better understanding of the work before starting it.

The quality assurance plan is therefore written by the project team for the project team.

The content of the quality assurance plan will vary from company to company according to the number of compulsory procedures and standards and from project to project according to the type of project. The standard set of chapter headings for project quality assurance plans in my company is as follows:

1) Objectives. This lists the deliverables, the contractual conditions including cost, timescale and QA requirements. It also briefly describes the work to be done and the reason for doing it.

2) Client-contractor liaison. This names the people, job titles and responsibilities for all significant points of contact. It also defines the reporting procedures.

3) The contractor-project team relationship. This describes how the project team will obtain the internal facilities and resources it needs to undertake the work. It also describes the internal reporting procedures.

4) The project team structure. This describes the responsibilities and relationships within the project team. It also defines the reporting procedures within the team.

5) Work definition. This describes how pieces of work are allocated to individuals and the method of confirming that the work is complete.

6) Records. This describes the project filing system for correspondence, work plans, project control, technical reports and working papers and the organisation of computer files etc.

7) Acceptance of bought-in goods. This describes (for each significant item purchased by the project) how it will be tested prior to formal acceptance and use by the project.

8) Working practices. This chapter gives the breakdown of the project work into item-types and identifies the standards for methodology, documentation and verification for each item type. (See Table 12.1).

9) Acceptance testing. This gives the agreed acceptance tests that the client accepts as an adequate demonstration of completion of the project. This chapter is often issued as a separate document part way through the project.

10) Technical reviews. This is a list of the types of technical reviews (including design reviews, walkthroughs etc.) that will be conducted on a formal basis throughout the project. It gives the stages of the project at which they will be conducted, the items to be reviewed and who will do the reviews (identifying in particular the need for technical staff independent of the project).

11) Configuration management. The details of configuration management of all deliverables must be specified in detail. This is usually done by reference to standards.

12) Identification of re-usable material. This chapter identifies those items that the contractor could use elsewhere in his business and how they will be generalised (if necessary), documented and made available throughout the contractors company.

13) Standards. This is a summary of all standards referenced throughout the quality assurance plan. It is structured as a quick reference index.

12.5 SPECIAL FEATURES OF SOFTWARE ENGINEERING FOR MICROPROCESSORS

Nearly everything I have covered so far has been applicable to software engineering in general. There are however some special features of developing software for microprocessors that make life more difficult; I am not aware of any that make it easier.

1) Firmware. The program images are often stored in read only memory (ROM) rather than loaded from some magnetic storage media. This means that either a development version of the target hardware has to be used with the ability to download the program images or that the debugging cycle is considerably lengthened to include re-programming of EPROMs. Configuration management is also complicated by the need to deal with ROMs, several of which may be needed to contain one program image.

2) Host/target development. To overcome the problems with ROMs and other problems, software development is often done on a host computer. This is no real problem as far as cross compilers etc. are concerned but if some testing is to be done on the host and the host architecture differs from that of the target then new stages of testing are introduced to confirm correct operation.

3) Confidence in the target hardware. Often the software and hardware are developed in parallel and the integration

of the two introduces problems in identifying the causes of errors. Timescales must therefore allow for this.

4) Use of bare machines. One can usually rely on the operating system of a mainframe or minicomputer to provide basic run-time support facilities as well as program development facilities. On a bare machine these must be provided from scratch. Unfortunately these facilities include peripheral handling and real-time aspects that are the most difficult to test.

5) Testing. Testing is typically done using test harnesses and injecting test data. In microprocessor systems, especially embedded ones, there may not be sufficient memory to include test harnesses and input data and there may not be adequate peripherals to output the test results. These problems become worse as testing is done at higher and higher levels and also as performance aspects are considered.

6) Real time aspects and special peripherals. Microprocessors are often used in real-time situations involving interfaces to peripherals with critical access times.

7) The client often requires a black box and specifies acceptance tests for hardware and software working together.

All of these features mean that software engineering for microprocessors needs staff with skills in both software and electronics. Companies with historical biases to either of these disciplines can find problems with their first moves into microprocessor developments because of a lack of understanding of the other side. Fortunately these problems are becoming less frequent and this is at least partially due to the wider introduction of quality assurance in the software environment.

REFERENCES

1. MASCOT Supplies Association, 1980, 'The Official Handbook of MASCOT', Royal Signals and Radar Establishment, Malvern, U.K.

2. De Marco, T, 1978, 'Structured Analysis and System Specification', Yourdon Inc., New York, USA, ISBN: 0-917072-07-3.

3. British Standards Institute, 1980, 'Specification for Computer Programming Language CORAL 66', British Standards Institute, BS5905.

4. British Standards Institute, 1976 to 1980, 'Glossary of Terms used in Data Processing', British Standards Institute, BS3527 (Parts 1, 2, 3, 4, 5, 6, 7, 10, 11, 12, 14, 16, 19).

5. Director of Standardisation, 1973, 'Quality Control System Requirements for Industry', UK Ministry of Defence, DEFSTAN 05-21/1.

6. Director of Standardisation, 1976, 'Inspection System Requirements for Industry', UK Ministry of Defence, DEFSTAN 05-24/2.

7. British Standards Institute, 1979 to 1981, 'Quality Systems', British Standards Institute, BS5750 (Parts 1, 2, 3, 4, 5, 6).

8. Defence Quality Assurance Board, 1976, 'Quality Assurance in the Programming and Use of Computers', UK Ministry of Defence, QTM16.

Chapter 13

Principles of real-time operating systems

D. Jenkins, M.K. Crowe

13.1 INTRODUCTION

In this chapter we discuss some of the considerations which should be kept in mind when the design of algorithms for Real Time work is underway. The tools which must be to hand are discussed.

13.2 CONCURRENT SEQUENTIAL PROCESSES

Separation of concerns is one of the major strategies in reducing the complexity of algorithms and hence increasing their reliability. We achieve separation of concerns in real time by using the concept of cooperating concurrent sequential processes. This concept allows us to look at small sets of interactions with the real world and design separate computing processes to deal with each set as a different design task. Complex sequences can be divided into sub-sequences and so on.

13.2.1 Processes

It is very easy to use the term "process" in a general and intuitive sense: it is quite proper to talk of a process transforming inputs into outputs at the general systems level (e.g. the economy), or at the business level. We can use the term "process control" without explanation in the context of chemical processes. However the term has a specific sense in computing science in relation to operating systems and real time computing. We define:

A process is a sequence of operations carried out one at a time.

We assume that an operation, once started, concludes within a finite time and that its output is a time-dependent function of its input. We also state that the variables operated on by a process are private to it. Common variables accessible to more than one process are considered to be a message passing mechanism and to be "system interfaces" (see below).

13.2.2 Concurrent Processes

Processes whose executions overlap in time are concurrent: that is, their effects appear together. In a multiprocessor computer the concurrency may be actual, that is, separate processes are executed by separate processors. In a multiprogrammed timeslicing computer system the individual operations from the concurrent processes are interleaved by the computer system. There are two ways of viewing the sharing of central processor time. In the interrupt view, a process in the background is stopped and the central processor is used to execute some interrupt response code. In the process view, processes are given the central processor until they stop, or wait, or are forceably suspended. The waiting state is entered voluntarily by the process which is suspended, that is, has no time allocated to it, until the event awaited occurs. The state of the process (see below) is regarded as maintained in the private data of the process, being changed through a history of values by the bursts of activity attained by the process when a processor is made available to it. If the bursts are fine enough the activity appears continuous.

13.3 SYSTEMS AND INTERFACES

Any two systems can be said to communicate through an interface:

```
                ----------------------
               :          :           :
               :          :           :
               :          -           :  ----SYSTEM
               :         :*:          :
SYSTEM-------  :         :*:  --------------INTERFACE
               :         :*:          :
               :          -           :
               :          :           :
               :          :           :
                ----------------------
```

A real time system must communicate over interfaces to the system to which it is dedicated. At the lowest level, any interface can be modelled at some point by one or more binary devices which can take up a series of values of 0 or 1. What each of these values represent is a property of the system to which the computer system is connected. In process control the stream of bits presented say 11 at a time represent a measurement, perhaps, of flow through a valve into a reactor: in missile control they might represent a bearing: in communications an encoded symbol in an alphabet, and so on. In practice the interface is likely to be a semiactive system. e.g. an analog to digital convertor which takes a message meaning "find the value of input 07" and returns messages meaning "51%". The situation which looks like this:

```
       -------------   -------------
      :             : :             :
      :             :*:  COMPUTER   :
      :    PLANT    :*:  CONTROL    :
      :             :*:  SYSTEM     :
      :             : :             :
       -------------   -------------
```

is really like this:

```
   ------------- -------------   -------------
  :             :             : :             :
  :             :             :*:  COMPUTER   :
  :    PLANT    :     A/D     :*:  CONTROL    :
  :             :             :*:  SYSTEM     :
  :             :             : :             :
   ------------- -------------   -------------
```

The interface system itself has two (passive) interfaces e.g.

```
             -         -----
   convert = : :       : : : :    = address
             -         -----
    STROBE   0..1      0..7    ADDRESS
```

and

```
             -         -------------------
            : :       : : : : : : : : : : :
             -         -------------------
  FINISHED  0..1          0..17777(base 8)   VALUE
```

These diagrams show the static detail of the two interfaces. Associated with them is dynamic information about the order and effect of the events ocurring in each interface, the protocol of its use. The protocol for this interface is:

> To obtain a value of a process variable, place its address in register ADDRESS. After 1 microsecond, send "1" to STROBE. Wait for FINISHED to go to "1", read the value (0 - 99.98%) from VALUE.

English statements like this are unsatisfactory for formal definition of protocols. There are complementary ways of discussing and defining protocols for communication across an interface. An abstract process, state transition diagram and message exchange sequence chart are three of them. We shall consider state transition diagrams and abstract processes briefly.

13.4 STATE TRANSITION DIAGRAMS

Any system can be described by writing down values of its attributes (a state vector) but in many cases an exhaustive list would be too long. The art of systems analysis is to reduce the list to the minimum needed to solve a problem. All cars possess colour, weight, registration number, registered keeper, tyre pressures, velocity, acceleration, position .... and so on. An accident investigation is likely to use position, velocity and acceleration to attach blame to one party or another but to use other attributes to draw up the charge. The state in the first case is (position, velocity, acceleration) and something else in the second! The system formed by a computer obeying a program posseses state vectors. The values are digital rather than analogue but the idea is the same. In the case of a car, we can divide the system's history into a series of different states. Usually we partition the history into fairly large periods of time by using ranges of values of a variable to describe one state - e.g. at rest, travelling slowly, exceeding the speed limit. The categories we choose depend on the problem. We select values of declared variables to represent states of interest to us. Suppose we are modelling the state of a car in a computer program. We use a variable "state" to model the computer process. We have used a Pascal user defined type,

state = (stopped, slowly, excessive)

The state transition diagram for this is:

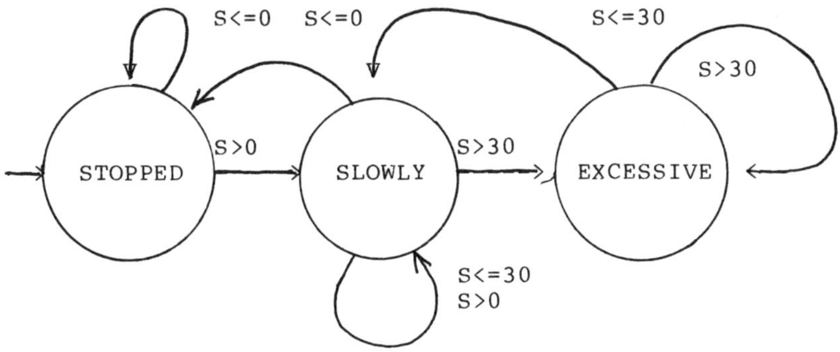

State transition diagrams have three elements

1. States, represented by named circles
2. Transitions from one state to another, represented by arrowed lines
3. The value(s) of the state vector elements causing the transition.

In this model of a car we are not using any velocity or acceleration information explicitly but the transitions missing from the state diagram represent physically impossible changes of speed. We cannot go from stopped to excessive and from excessive to stopped by any transaction possible in physical reality. Data purporting to represent this must be in error and we can add error states to the diagram to report their occurrance. Implicit in this discussion has been the assumption that engineering systems can be modelled as finite state automata.

13.5 PROCESS STATES AND PROCESS CODE

Suppose we wish to report the state of the car only when a transition has occurred. We derive our code from the state transition diagrams, noting that the transitions form one state to another must generate a message.

```
process 1;
begin
  state:=stopped; send(state);
  forever do
  begin
    case state of
     stopped:   begin
                  repeat get speed until speed>0;
                  state:=slowly
                end;
     slowly:    begin
                  repeat get speed
                  until speed<=0 or speed>30;
                  if speed>30 then state:=excessive
                  else state:=stopped
                end;
     excessive: begin
                  repeat get speed until speed<=30;
                  state:=slowly
                end
    end;   (* of case *)
    send(state,(* to *) process 2)
  end;  (* of forever loop *)
end;  (* of process 1 *)
```

We write a repeat loop for each state which consumes all values of speed which will not cause a transition out of the state. We also modify the code to deal with errors:

```
process 1;
begin
  state:=stopped;  send(state); sound:=true;
  while sound do
    case state of
     stopped:   begin
                  repeat get speed until speed>0;
                  if speed>30 then state:=error
                  else state:=slowly;
                  send(state)
                end;    (* of stopped *)
     slowly:    begin
                  repeat get speed
                  until speed<=0 or speed>30;
                  if speed>30 then state:=excessive
                  else state:=stopped;
                  send(state)
                end;   (* of slowly *)
     excessive: begin
                  repeat get speed until speed<=30;
                  if speed<=0 then state:=error
                  else state:=slowly;
                  send(state)
                end;   (* of excessive *)
```

```
        error:     begin
                     sound:=false;
                     sendmessage('Suspect speed measurement',
                   (* to *) boss)
                   end
       end;    (* of case and of while loop *)
   end;  (* of process 1 *)
```

where "boss" supervises the system in some way and we have added "error" to be the state vector. Process 1 now sends messages both to Process 2 and to Boss. The error sequence is reported on to both.

13.6 TIME CRITICALITY

The requirement in Real Time computing that the results be available on a timescale dictated by the application introduces the concept of time criticality. Informally, we can say that an event in the system requires a response from the Real Time system within a critical time. A faster response may produce a better performance overall or may not. A slower response produces no performance (total failure).

13.6.1 Response To One Event Using One Process

The simplest algorithm for a computing process to provide a response to one external event is

```
   initialise process;
   forever do:
     wait for event;
     compute response;
     respond.
```

13.6.2 Multiple Events And One Process

If we consider multiple events and use one "process" (one processor) the algorithm becomes:

```
   initialise process;
   forever do:
     wait for any event;
     identify event case
     select case of:
       event 1: compute response 1; respond.
       event 2: compute response 2; respond.
     otherwise: error response.
```

13.6.3 Inter-Dependence Between Events

At first sight this looks entirely satisfactory but a moment or two of reflection shows that there could be problems. Suppose event 2 has a long computation time and a long critical time and event 1 is much shorter, with little or no computation and a short critical time. The ability to respond to event 1 depends whether event 2 has just occurred or not. Depending on the interface between system and process, response 1 is either delayed beyond the critical time by the computation of response 2 or is never recognised and responded to at all. In either case the overall system will fail.

13.6.4 Single Processor Solution

We can propose and use a solution involving a single "process" using this algorithm below:

```
initialise process;
forever do:
  wait for event 1 or event 2
  identify event case
  if event 2 then
     do part of computation 2
     if event 1 has now occurred then do
        computation 1, respond.
     do more of computation 2
     if event 1 has now occurred then do
        computation 1, respnd.
     do rest of computation 2;
  else do computation 1, respond.
```

We can tidy the code by having a subroutine "respond to 1":

```
initialise process;
forever do:
  wait for event 1 or event 2
  if event 1 then
     do part of computation 2
     if event 1 ... then do respond to 1.
     do more ....
     if event 1 ... then do respond to 1.
     do rest ...
     respond
  else do respond to 1.
respond to 1:
computation 1; respond.
```

13.6.5 Reliability Implications

Perfectly reasonable applications have been programmed in this way but for more than two or three events the coding becomes very complex, without any consideration of the actual detail of the application. Notice too how the detail of one element, response to event 1, affects the code written to implement a second element, response to event 2. The size of the "part", "more" and "rest" bits of the event 2-response 2 computation are derived from considering the critical time requirements of event 1-response 1. Thus a relationship has been introduced between the detail of one concern and the detail of a second. This is hostile to the attainment of reliability! We can improve on this via two strategies, interrupt driven coding and multiple processors. The first dates from the early days of computing; the second is now feasible because microprocessors are cheap. There is (as we mentioned) also a third strategy, multiprogramming but this is actually number two implemented using strategy one, that is we use interrupts to give the effect of having a multiprocessor by employing a real time operating system

(RTOS) to give us the ability to design as if we did possess more than one processor.

13.7 CONCURRENT PROCESSES AND INTERRUPTS

13.7.1 The Origins Of Concurrency

The first computers were expensive and few in number. They also used a pair of slow input and output devices: a paper tape reader and punch typically. The "wait for event" statement in an algorithm is implemented by testing a bit in a register in the interface hardware between computer and system. In this case, the event waited upon was reading of the next character. If the bit is reset (0) then the event has not occurred since the last test was made. If the bit is set (1) then the event has occurred; the register may be designed so that testing the bit resets it to zero, otherwise we include a "clear bit" statement in the subroutine associated with the event (e.g. "respond 1"). The elaboration of "wait for" is:

```
wait for event = repeat
                     test bit "1"
                 until bit "1" is set;
```

This technique is known as "looping on status bit". Since input/output steps were 1000x slower even then than computational steps, the time wasted in looping waiting for the next character to be available in the input register (or for the last output character to be punched) represented a very significant (up to 90) percentage of the time used, even in tasks dominated by the computation to be carried out. Expensive, scarce resources could not be wasted in this way. Observing that the tasks had the structure "input-computation-output", which we will represent as:

```
<-I-><-C-><-O->
```

they batched tasks together

```
<-I-><-C-><-O-><-I-><-C-><-O-><-I-><-C-><-O->
```

and added features to the hardware interface to allow a single step in the input of output subtasks to interrupt the progress of the main computational task. This allowed the overlap of input and output with the computation.

```
<-I-><-C-><-O->
     <-I-><-C-><-O->
          <-I-><-C-><-O->
```

Now almost no time at all is unused for computation! These additional features added to the hardware are called the interrupt mechanism or interrupt hardware. The event in the (external) system which cause this interruption is the "interrupt event". The minimum necessary interrupt mechanism is one that will allow an interrupt handling routine to be obeyed without disturbing the effect of the computational task. This is obviously essential since in the "batch" the order of jobs is random and the jobs are totally independent.

13.7.2 The Interrupt Mechanism As A Forced Subroutine Jump

If we inspect the last version of the two-event problem, we see that a subroutine "respond 1" is called at various points in computation 2. Obviously "respond 1" has no effect on computation 2 whenever it is called otherwise computation 2 would be unreliable. So the interrupt mechanism must be such as to allow a subroutine such as "respond 1" to be executed once the interrupt event has occurred. In my code for computation 2 I have selected points at which the computation may be suspended by the recent occurrance of event 1 and resumed after the computatio of response 1 by the inclusion of conditional calls of "respond 1". Using the interrupt mechanism, I do not have to select these points. The mechanism will cause the "interrupt handling subroutine" or "interrupt handler" to be obeyed and returned from without affecting the computation which has been interrupted. Thus, given that event 1 will cause an interrupt, I can write an algorithm for the two-event problem:

```
   initialise process;
   forever do
      wait for event 2;
      compute reponse 2;
      respond.
   on interrupt do
      compute response 1; respond.
```

The code for each event is independent of the other and separation of concerns is achieved. We can now see that the effect of the interrupt mechanism is "a forced subroutine jump". Usually we find that much of the detail of the interrupt mechanism in a computer is decided by the detail of the subroutine handling mechanism.

13.8 THE REAL TIME OPERATING SYSTEM (RTOS)

13.8.1 The Basic Task Of The RTOS

We started earlier that the alternative to interrupts was the use of multiple processors. Here we assume we have an infinite number of processors (or more than we will ever need). Each sequence of events derived from one element of the external system is handled by one processor, or, rather, one process. This minimises the complexity of the software since the effect of other sequences of events can be ignored (if not part of the application). That is, we can simplify the state transition diagram, and the resulting code, by partitioning the set of states into subsets with few transitions between the subsets as compared to those within them. The processors may or may not share memory. Intercommunication between processors may be via memory or special I/O channels. In practice, multiprocessors of this type are still few in number. Is there another solution? The answer is yes; we can run more than one computing process (or computation) on one processor if we can organise the sharing of the central processor resource between processes using a RTOS.

13.8.2 Use Of Interrupts To Allow Processor Management

Consider the handling of interrupts and the situation in which the process for event 2 was interrupted by event 1. The computation for event 1 uses the cpu and that for event 2 is successfully interrupted and returned to using the save/restore sequence. The quiescent state in this case is process 2 waiting on the status bit for event 2, i.e. executing "test, branch" repeatedly, and with interrupts enabled so that event 1 can interrupt this loop. Suppose we modify this so that process 2 is suspended on the first status test and not given any cpu time until immediately after the status is set. All the cpu cycles saved can be allocated to a another process. This process (process 1) now uses the same solution, being suspended on the first status test and waiting until just after event 1 has occurred.

13.8.2.1 The save-restore area. In the quiescent state both process 1 and process 2 will be suspended and the cpu will be carrying out a background "do nothing" process. The state of each process is saved in a set of locations associated with each process in which the values of the processor registers, etc. at the time of suspension are stored. This is a voluntary version of what happened at an interrupt and the identical mechanism can be used. So in the quiescent state we have:

```
                process 1        process 2        process 3
                                                 (do nothing)
               ------------     ------------     ------------
   save      : last PC1     : : lact PC2     : : last PC3     :
   and       : last SP1     : : last SP2     : : last SP3     :
   restore   : register     : : register     : : register     :
   area      : values       : : values       : : values       :
             :              : :              : :              :
             :------------: :------------:    ------------
             :              : :              :
             : process      : : process      :
             :              : :              :
             : data         : : data         :
             :              : :              :
               ------------     ------------

               ------------     ------------     ------------
             : process      : : process      : : process      :
             :              : :              : : code         :
             : code         : : code         :   ------------
               ------------     ------------
```

PC1 and PC2 will point to the instruction immediately after the "wait for" instruction in the respective code areas. The interrupt code is now simplified to carry out the mapping between the interrupt and the process waiting for it. An interrupt will suspend the "do nothing" process and the process required to service the interrupt has its state restored into the cpu registers before the execution of the "return from interrupt" command is obeyed.

13.8.2.2 Required modification to interrupt coding.
Comparision of the task of the original interrupt mechanism and that of the new one will help here:

```
   original:
      a. preserve values of the volatile registers of
         the processor,
      b. determine cause of interrupt,
      c. execute code to service interrupt,
      d. reload values of volatile registers.
   new:
      a. preserve values of the volatile registers of
         the processor in the save and restore area of
         the interrupted, current process,
      b. determine cause of interrupt,
      c. select process waiting for this cause,
      d. add this process to list of processes able to run,
      e. reload values of volatile registers from the save
         and restore area of the highest priority process
         able to run, thus causing resumption of
         its execution.
```

13.8.2.3 Resulting simplification of the algorithm. We can now represent our algorithm as:

```
   process 1: initialise;
              forever do
                 waitfor (event 1);
                 respond 1.
   process 2: initialise;
              forever do
                 waitfor (event 2);
                 respond 2.
```

13.8.3 The Basic RTOS Kernel Coding

The basic RTOS kernel is as follows:

```
   wait:   suspend the calling process, associating
           it with the indicated event;
           run the most suitable program which is
           not waiting.
   on interrupt do:
           suspend the interrupted process, add to
           the list of processes which are not waiting;
           find the process associated with this event;
           add it to the list of programs which are
           not waiting;
           run the most suitable process from those
           which are not waiting (i.e. runnable).
```

Generally, in Real Time work we consider that the most suitable process will be the one of the highest priority. We can achieve this by modifying "add process to the list of processes which are not waiting" by appending the qualifier "according to its relative priority". This relatively minor change allows this approach to deal with the priority and arbitration issues raised above.

The "wait for" and "on interrupt do" coding is application independent. We can supply them as part of the toolkit availabe to the Real Time programmer: as a result, such a programmer has more to work with than the actual hardware of the machine. A "virtual" machine consisting of "actual hardware capabilities" PLUS "Real Time operating system kernel primitives" MINUS "instructions withdrawn to protect the kernel" has been created. An "infinite" number of processes can be written for this machine using the additonal command "waitfor".

13.8.4 Hardware Events And Software Events

So far we have considered the events to be occurrances in the external system. For example, suppose we are detecting changes in the state of a telephone line, an event being the crossing of a boundary voltage. We could have a programmable device to detect the crossing of a boundary set by an output command to the device. This could be complex, might be costly and can only detect one event. If the voltage were digitised at sufficiently small intervals of time, we could track the voltage fast enough to detect these events, and more flexibly. A high priority process could do this while a low priority one would analyse the course of events and take the required action. But to do this we need to be able to signal the occurrance of an event from one process to another. We augment our "virtual" machine by the "signal (event)" command. This requires but little extension to the kernel code: it becomes:

```
   wait:  suspend calling process;
          associate this event with it;
          run first process on runnable list.
   signal:   suspend calling process;
             add to list of processes which
             are now waiting;
             add process associated with event to list
             of runnable processes according to priority;
             run first process on runnable list.
   interrupt: suspend interrupted process;
              add to list of processes which are runnable
              according to priority;
              add process associated with this (hardware)
              event to runnable list according to priority;
              run first process on runnable list.
```

As we might expect, "signal" and "interrupt" have very similar coding. If "signal" were implemented by a "software interrupt" mechanism, then nearly all the code would be common: the event number would be supplied by the hardware (e.g. the device) in a hardware interrupt or by the (self) interrupting process in a software interrupt.

13.8.5 Dijkstra's Semaphore

The software mechanism used to implement secure/release and signal/wait is the Dijkstra semaphore; the term come from the railway analogy. Dijkstra's semaphore is an information stucture consisting of

(1) an integer variable and
(2) a list of processes waiting on the semaphore.

For our purposes, we restrict this slightly to
(1) a non-negative integer and
(2) a list of processes waiting on the semaphore in order of priority.

13.8.6 Detail of Signal and Wait

Understanding the full detail of Signal and Wait depends on knowing the detail of the data structures managed by the kernel: here is the pseudo-code of both:

```
wait(s):
   disable interrupts;
   if s <> 0 then s:=s - 1
   else
      add processess to list in priority order;
      process.status := unrunnable;
      delete process from central processor list
   endif
   dispatch.
signal(s):
   disable interrupts;
   if list of waiting processes is empty then s:=s + 1
   else
      remove the first process from the list of
      waiting processes;
      process.status := runnable;
      add process to list of runnable processes
      according to priority;
   endif
   dispatch.
dispatch:
   move first process in list of runnable processes to
   central processor list;
   restore status of process in central processor
   list, return from interrupt, enabling interrupts.
```

13.8.7 Kernel And User State

Kernel (or Supervisor) state and User state may be contrasted. Kernel code is executed in a priviliged mode in which the whole instruction set, including operations for memory management, input, output and interrupt management, can be carried out. User (process) code is executed in non-privileged mode and these operations can only be carried out by using a supervisor call (software interrupt) to enter the kernel in privileged mode, saving the user process status meanwhile. Signal and Wait are invoked using this mechanism.

13.9 MESSAGE BASED SYSTEMS

Upto now, we have used "events" and common data structures to communicate between processes. Message-based systems behave differently. The kernel is extended to offer a message delivery service to all user processes. Direct access to a data structure, e.g. a queue, within a critical section of code by a process is replaced by a message of the form (operation,record) sent via the message system to a third process which owns the structure. Since messages are transmitted via "ports" to and from the message sub-system, this type of system is also known as a "port-driven" system.

A thoroughly implemented message-based system regards all exchanges within the system and across its interfaces as being the exchange of messages. If the message has values (nil,nil), say, it has the effect of a Signal-Wait pair. Thus a message-based system can emulate an event based one. The basic mechanisms used to implement message sub-systems are consumer-producer pairs implemented using semaphores and buffers. However, the important difference is that the data areas are protected by use of memory management from any access by user processes and the message system is inviolable. Additional hardware features can be provided to make message transfer fast, e.g. by switching a small block of memory between address spaces without physical movement.

13.9.1 A Basic Communication Mechanism

One possible basic communication mechanism is to regard a single byte in memory as the buffer used in the consumer-producer relationship. The mechanism consists of a byte of common memory, into which the producer place a byte of information and two semaphores. One indicates that a byte has been deposited, the second that a byte has been read by the consumer process. Any more complex message sub-system could be implemented using this.

13.9.2 Distribution Of This Mechanism

If these two processes (on one processor) communicated back-to-back, we could represent them thus:

```
             --------------------------------------
            :    -------------------------------    :
            :    :        ------------          :   :
            :    V        :           V         :   V
            -    -   ----------  ----------     -   -
          -: :-: :--:         :-:         :---: :-: :-
         :  -    -   ----------  ----------     -   -  :
         :                                             :
         :     ------------           -------------    :
         :    :            :         :             :   :
         :    : producer   :         : consumer    :   :
         :    :            :         :             :   :
         :     ------------           -------------    :
         :                                             :
          ---------------------------------------------
```

If we now place the two processes on seperate processors,

the diagram hardly requires amendment:

```
            -------------------------------------
           :    -----------------------------     :
           :   :        -------------        :   :
           V   :        :             V       :   :
           -   -    -------       -------     -   -
      ----: :-: :--:        :-  -:       ---: :-: :------
     :     -   -    -------   : : -------     -   -       :
     :                        : :                         :
     :   ---------------      : :   ------------------    :
     :  :               :     : :  :                  :   :
     :  :  producer     :     : :  :  consumer        :   :
     :  :               :     : :  :                  :   :
     :   ---------------      : :   ------------------    :
     :                        : :                         :
      ------------------------  --------------------------
```

This demonstrates that a message based system can be distributed over many processors provided that the appropriate ports can be connected and identified to the processes. The message exchange system built using the consumer-producer pairs can manage a process name scheme across all the processors and direct traffic appropriately. Since the consumer-producer pairs implementing a simple, one-way channel uses a register-to-register model, any pair of interface adaptors (with additional code), can be used to carry out the physical transfer, using an appropriate low-level protocol.

Chapter 14

Validation techniques

B.A. Carré

14.1 INTRODUCTION

The reliance placed on microcomputer software in many engineering systems - for instance in aircraft, nuclear power station control, and railway signalling - is such that the correct functioning of the software is of paramount importance. Considerable efforts have been made to improve software reliability, for instance by systematizing the programming task through the use of Structured Programming, by the development of languages such as Pascal and Euclid which encourage one to program "tidily", and by the development of flexible program documentation and testing aids. Nevertheless, the debugging of software remains an extremely difficult task. Program testing - which is still performed on an ad hoc basis, because it is usually impossible to construct sets of test data which will fully exercise a program - falls far short of present needs, especially in the case of real-time systems. The advent of the microcomputer has also high-lighted the enormous cost of software development: the price of each line of code in a microcomputer program is now of the same order as the cost of the chip on which it is to be run, and much of this cost can be attributed to (usually inadequate) testing.

As opposed to program testing - which involves checking the behaviour of a program with particular values of input ("test") data - program validation is the process of showing that a program has no errors, for <u>any</u> possible execution. Our purpose here is to describe the principal methods of program validation, and to indicate the nature of the software aids being developed for this purpose.

The tools for program validation fall into two categories. In the first we have a variety of purely mechanical methods of analysing the structure of a program, and checking program code for inconsistencies and bad coding practice. The most important of these are control-flow analysis, data-flow analysis, and information-flow analysis. The second category of validation methods comprises techniques for checking the behaviour of a program at a semantic level, with the ultimate aim of showing that it meets its "specification".

14.2 FLOWCHART PROGRAMS

The term "flowchart" will be used here to describe a directed graph (such as Fig.14.1) which contains the following kinds of labelled nodes and arcs:

(i) a single START node, which has no predecessors, and only one successor;

(ii) assignment nodes, each labelled with a single assignment statement of the form

<variable> := <expression>

and each having only one successor;

(iii) test nodes, each labelled with a predicate, and having two arcs (labelled true and false) incident from them;

(iv) input-output nodes, labelled with a statement of the form

read A

where A is a variable, or

write B

where B is a variable or constant, and each having one successor;

(v) one or more HALT nodes, which have no successors.

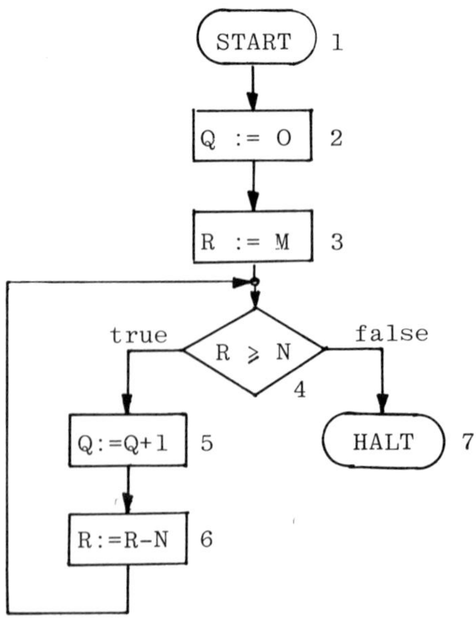

Fig.14.1 Flowchart of a program for the integer division of M by N. On termination Q is the quotient and R is the remainder.

In drawing a flowchart it is sometimes also convenient to use "junction points" to join some arcs together (see Fig.14.1); however, these are only introduced for aesthetic reasons, and we do not consider them as a special kind of node.

A flowchart program is essentially a program which can be represented by a flowchart, with each node (and the arcs incident from it) corresponding to a statement, or possibly a sequence of statements, of the program text.

Throughout our discussion it will be assumed that programs to be analysed are flowchart programs. This presupposes that if a program in a high-level language is to be analysed, its conditional and repetitive statements (such as if-then-else and while-do statements) will have been decomposed into more rudimentary assignment and test statements, which correspond to elements of a flowchart (see Fig.14.2).

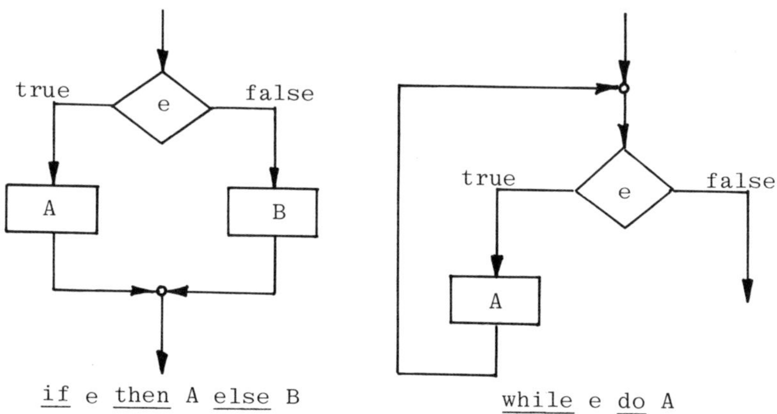

Fig.14.2 Flowchart representations of conditional and repetitive statements.

Such transformations can be achieved by a "translator" specially designed for the purpose (and indeed, this is the method used in a validation system which will be described below). Alternatively, the original program may have been transformed by the "front end" of a compiler into an intermediate form, such as quadruples (Gries (1)), from which the flow of control is easily derived; optimizing compilers usually perform control and data flow analysis on programs at this intermediate level.

The unlabelled form of a flowchart (as in Fig.14.3) is called the control flow graph of a program.

In the following sections we shall present some "flow analysis" methods which can be applied to a flowchart program, and which provide systematic tests for certain kinds of errors and anomalies. These methods use only weak

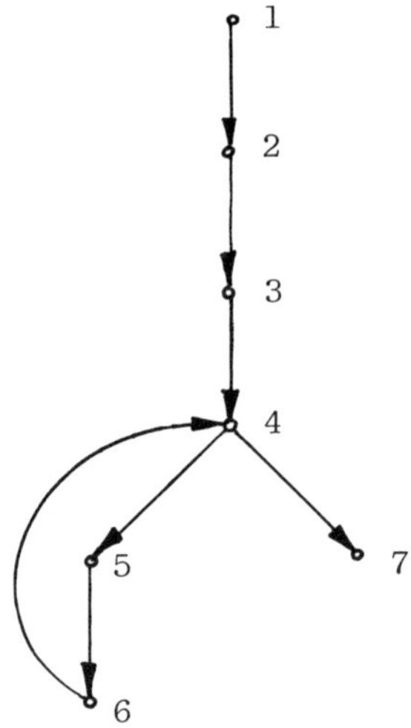

Fig.14.3 Control flow graph of the program of Fig.14.1

(essentially syntactic) information, so they cannot, by themselves, make us confident that a program will perform its intended function. However, they may uncover a large proportion of the "silly" mistakes in a program, such as misuse of labels and transposition of variable names, and they have been known to uncover errors even in programs which had run successfully for some months, and which were believed to be correct. We consider it useful to subject programs to these tests before proceeding to semantic analysis - particularly since the flow analysis tests can be entirely mechanised, and the algorithms to perform them are fast.

14.3 CONTROL FLOW ANALYSIS

To quote the authors of the programming language Euclid (Popek et al. (2)) " ... one of the main lines of current programming language development is to transfer more and more of the work of producing a correct program, and verifying that it is consistent with its specification, from the programmer and the verifier (human or mechanical) to the language and its compiler".

In using a language such as Euclid, the programmer is compelled to produce software which is "well-structured"; the flow of control in a program is obvious in the program text, and all the information relating to control structure which could be required (for instance in proving that the program meets its specification) is obtained conveniently by the syntax analyser of a compiler. Some other languages (such as Pascal and Ada) encourage good programming; but with any language which allows for instance the use of goto statements, it is possible to create "undesirable" control structures (such as multiple-entry loops) which render validation and verification particularly difficult, and even to introduce serious defects (such as "unreachable code"). And with such languages, the precise nature of the control structure is not immediately obtainable from a syntax analysis. In using machine code and primitive assembly languages, where it is particularly easy to introduce errors, the control structure may be quite lost in a mass of hieroglyphics.

For these reasons, it is often useful to check the control-structure of a program systematically, in the following ways.

14.3.1 Accessibility Tests

A program should not contain (a) jumps to non-existent labels, (b) labels to which no jumps are ever made, (c) statements which cannot be reached from the START statement, and (d) statements from which one cannot reach a HALT statement.

Methods of detecting the faults (a) and (b) are rather obvious and will not be discussed here. Faults of type (c) can easily be detected by the following "labelling algorithm" (Carré (3)), which successively marks all the nodes of a control flow graph that can be reached from its START node.

```
begin
   clear stack;
   mark START node;
   push START node into stack;
   while stack is not empty do
      begin
         n:=top node in stack;
         pop stack;
         mark all unmarked successors of n
         and push them into stack
      end
end
```

On termination, any nodes which are not marked represent unreachable code.

Faults of type (d) can be detected in a similar manner (the algorithm for this purpose is obtained from the above simply by changing "START node" to "END nodes" and "successors" to "predecessors").

14.3.2 Structural Analysis

The advantages of "structured programming" in aiding the writing, comprehension and testing of programs are well-known, and to produce very reliable software, programmers are commonly required to respect certain stylistic rules which ensure that their software will be "well-structured" in some sense.

As an example, Fig.14.4 shows the kinds of "stepwise refinement" which are permissible in the form of structured programming first advocated by Dijkstra (4). In this figure, each node containing an "E" is expansible, and can be replaced by one of the structures to the right of a ::= sign.

Readers familiar with syntactic definitions of computer languages will recognize Fig.14.4 as an informal "flowchart grammar", (in which each diagram represents a production rule), defining the class of Dijkstra-structured flowcharts.

Just as a compiler can parse a program, using the production rules of the language in which it is written, so one can perform a bottom-up parsing of a flowchart, using the production rules of a flowchart grammar (Aho and Ullman (5)). In this way it is possible to verify that prescribed structuring rules have been obeyed in writing a program, and if so, to obtain the syntactic tree relating its constituents. As well as revealing any flaws in control structure, this information is useful in applying the further analysis methods which will be described below.

Of course, the rules of structured programming given in Fig.14.4 are very restrictive, and some extensions are usually allowed. For instance, one may wish to allow the use of a <u>loop</u> construct with multiple exits, as in Euclid or Ada. (Obviously, these <u>loop</u> statements may be "simulated" in any other language, using conditional <u>goto</u> statements.) As has been pointed out by Knuth (6), the use of such a construct may lead to improvements in program clarity, and it does not necessarily make the task of proving correctness of a program any more difficult. Although the task of checking that a flowchart is "well-formed" becomes much more complicated if we admit such constructs, it remains feasible, as do our other kinds of flow analysis.

For further discussion of control-flow analysis the reader is referred to Hecht (7) and Muchnick and Jones (8).

14.4 DATA FLOW ANALYSIS

Historically, data flow analysis emerged from the need for compilers to produce efficient object code, and the techniques were mainly aimed at code optimization (Allen (9), Schaefer (10), Hecht (7)). More recently, these techniques have also been used successfully in validation systems (Fosdick and Osterweil (11), Osterweil and Fosdick (12), Osterweil (13)), for detecting certain program errors, such as references to undefined variables; they also detect data flow "anomalies", such as re-assignment of previously unused variables, which are important because they are often symptomatic of common programming errors such as mis-spellings, confusion of names, and omission of statements.

The aim of this section is to present the principles of data flow analysis, and to show the kinds of program errors it can reveal.

14.4.1 A Data Flow Problem

If the execution of a program statement can change the

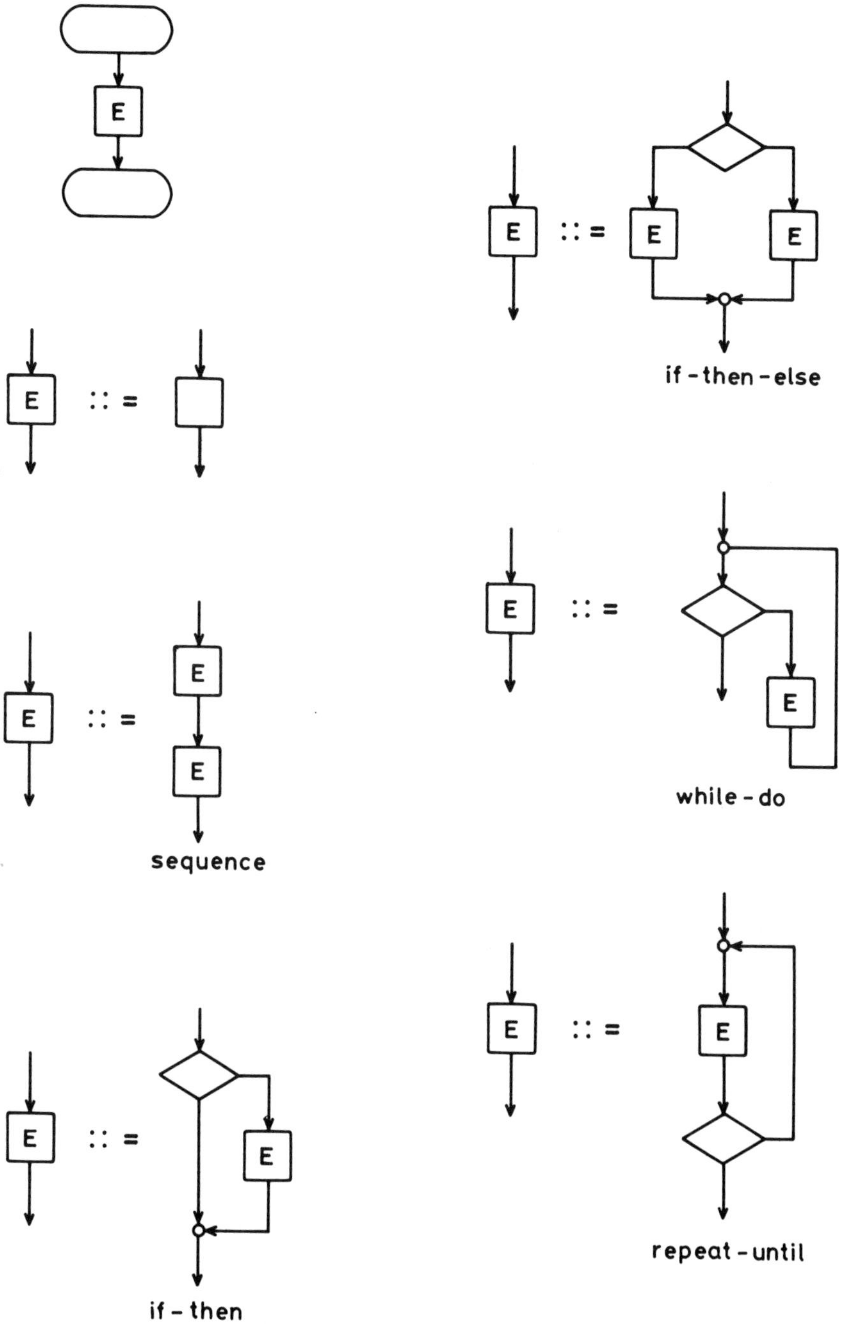

Fig.14.4 A flowchart grammar

value of some program variable v, we say that v is defined by the statement; and if the execution of a statement involves obtaining the value of a variable v from memory we say that the statement refers to v. For instance, the statement

x := y + z

defines x and refers to y and z, whereas the statement

if y > z then goto exit

only refers to y and z; the input statement

READ x

defines x and the output statement

WRITE x

refers to x. Execution of a statement can also undefine a variable; for instance, in FORTRAN, the DO index becomes undefined on normal exit from a DO-loop.

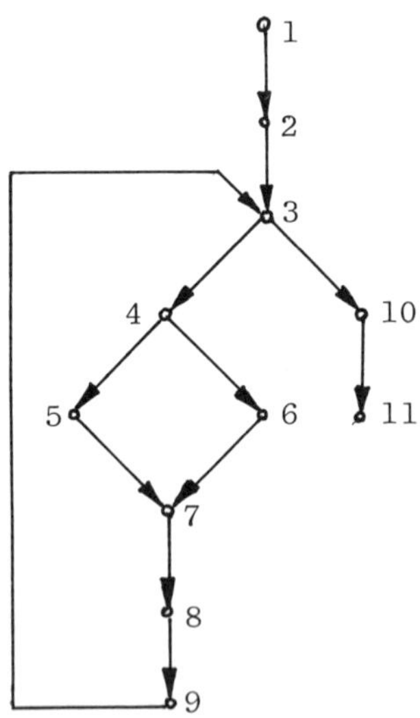

Node	Defined variables	Referenced variables
1	x, y, z	
2	x	w, x
3		x, y
4		y, z
5	y	v, y
6	z	v, z
7	v	x
8	w	y
9	z	v
10	z	z
11		z

Fig.14.5 Control flow graph with variable definitions and references.

Fig.14.5 shows the control flow graph of a small program, and indicates which variables are defined and referred to by each of its statements. (It is assumed that none of the statements undefine a variable). It will be observed that the START statement defines three variables x, y, z. This means that values are assigned to those variables outside the program; for instance, Fig.14.5 could represent a procedure or subroutine with input parameters x, y, z. In the same way, the fact that the HALT node refers to z indicates that the value of z is returned to the outside environment.

This program contains two errors:

(a) statement 2 uses a variable w which has not been previously defined, and

(b) statements 5 and 6 use a variable v which has not been defined at the first iteration around the loop.

In addition, the program contains two anomalies:

(c) the definition of z by statement 6 is never used, and

(d) the definition of w by statement 8 is never used.

Of course, a program can contain anomalies such as (c) and (d) above and yet be correct. However, such features indicate that either the program contains errors, or that its text could be made more comprehensible - which would simplify its verification and subsequent maintenance. (Removal of unnecessary statements will also usually reduce execution time, but that is not our primary concern here.)

The way in which such data flow errors and anomalies can be detected automatically is described below.

14.4.2 Reaching Definitions

Formally, a definition of a variable v is a program statement which modifies the value of v. If statement i is a definition of v, we may denote this definition by v_i. A path in a control-flow graph is definition-clear for a variable v if there is no definition of v on that path. A definition v_i is said to reach the entry (respectively:exit) of a node j if there exists a definition-clear path for v from node i to the entry (respectively:exit) of node j. Finally, a definition v_i is said to kill all other definitions of variable v which reach node i (and to preserve all definition of other variables).

We shall now establish which definitions reach each of the nodes of a program. For any node i, let us denote by s_i and t_i the sets of definitions which reach the entry and exit of i respectively; also, let p_i be the set of all definitions preserved by node i, and let c_i be the set of definitions created in node i.

Now for each node i, these sets are related by

$$t_i = (s_i \cap p_i) \cup c_i . \qquad (14.1)$$

Also, it is clear that the set of definitions which reach the top of a node i is the union of the sets of definitions which reach the exits of its predecessors: denoting the set of predecessors of node i by X_i, we can express this condition as

$$s_i = \bigcup_{j \in X_i} t_j. \tag{14.2}$$

Combining equations (14.1) and (14.2) we obtain

$$s_i = \bigcup_{j \in X_i} ((s_j \cap p_j) \cup c_j) \tag{14.3}$$

or

$$s_i = \bigcup_{j \in X_i} (s_j \cap p_j) \cup d_i, \tag{14.4}$$

where $d_i = \bigcup_{j \in X_i} c_j.$

For an n-node graph, we have a set of n simultaneous equations of this kind (for i = 1, 2, ..., n). As is shown by Hecht (7), such systems of equations may have more than one solution, but they always have a "least" solution, which gives the required reaching definitions.

This solution can be obtained by a "round-robin" iterative algorithm in which we initially set $s_i = d_i$, for i = 1, 2, ..., n, and then repeatedly solve the equations (14.4) for s_1, s_2, ..., s_n in turn, always using latest values for the terms s_j in their right-hand sides. When the s-values cease to change, we have the required solution. The algorithm is described more precisely in Fig.14.6.

```
begin
   for i := 1 step 1 until n do s_i := d_i;
   CHANGE := true;
   while CHANGE do
   begin
      CHANGE := false;
      for i := 1 step 1 until n do
      begin
         TEMP := ∪ (s_j ∩ p_j) ∪ d_i;
               jεX_i
         if TEMP ≠ s_i
         then
         begin
            CHANGE := true;
            s_i := TEMP
         end
      end
   end
end
```

Fig.14.6 Round-robin algorithm

It will be noted that each set s_i can be represented by a binary vector, with one entry for each variable definition of the program, this entry taking the value 1 if the corresponding definition belongs to s_i, and 0 otherwise. If the sets p_i and d_i are represented similarly, the set operations $\cup$ and $\cap$ in the round-robin algorithm can be replaced by the OR (bitwise sum) and AND (bitwise product) operations respectively.

To demonstrate the process, Table 14.1 gives the binary vector representation of the sets d_i, as defined in equation (4), for the program of Fig.14.5. Using these as initial approximations for the s-values, the first complete iteration of the round-robin algorithm gives the s-values shown in Table 14.2; the results of the second iteration are shown in Table 14.3. The third iteration does not change any of these values, so Table 14.3 gives all the reaching definitions, for each node of the program.

14.4.3 References to Undefined Variables

From the table of reaching definitions it may be possible to detect some references to undefined variables, as follows. For each node i, we consider in turn each variable to which statement i refers: if for any such variable v, no definition of v reaches i, then the program contains an error.

As an illustration, when we consider node 2 in our example, we find (from the list of referenced variables) that this statement refers to variable w. However, we then discover from Table 14.3 that no definition of w can reach node 2, and therefore the program must contain an error. (This is error (a) listed above.)

Unfortunately, the fact that some variable definition v_i reaches node j does not imply that v will always be defined before statement j is executed (unless statement i is always executed before statement j). For this reason, the test described above does not necessarily reveal all references to undefined variables; for instance, it fails to reveal error (b) in our program. Such errors can be detected however, by the iterative solution of another system of equations, of a form very similar to equation (14.4). (Hecht (7), Kennedy (14), Osterweil (13)).

14.4.4 Unused Definitions

It may also be possible to find some unused definitions, as follows. For each variable definition v_i, we consider in turn each node j of the programs which is reached by v_i: if none of the corresponding statements refer to variable v, then the program contains an anomaly.

For instance in our example, when we consider definition z_6, we find (from Table 14.3) that this definition reaches nodes 7, 8 and 9. However, we see from the list of referenced variables that none of the corresponding statements refer to variable z. (This is our anomaly (c).) Anomaly (d) is also discovered by this process.

Of course, it cannot be assumed that any of the paths by which definitions of a variable v reach the nodes where

TABLE 14.1

	v_7	w_8	x_1	x_2	y_1	y_5	z_1	z_6	z_9	z_{10}
2	0	0	1	0	1	0	1	0	0	0
3	0	0	0	1	0	0	0	0	1	0
4	0	0	0	0	0	0	0	0	0	0
5	0	0	0	0	0	0	0	0	0	0
6	0	0	0	0	0	0	0	0	0	0
7	0	0	0	0	0	1	0	1	0	0
8	1	0	0	0	0	0	0	0	0	0
9	0	1	0	0	0	0	0	0	0	0
10	0	0	0	0	0	0	0	0	0	0
11	0	0	0	0	0	0	0	0	0	1

TABLE 14.2

	v_7	w_8	x_1	x_2	y_1	y_5	z_1	z_6	z_9	z_{10}
2	0	0	1	0	1	0	1	0	0	0
3	0	1	0	1	1	0	1	0	1	0
4	0	1	0	1	1	0	1	0	1	0
5	0	1	0	1	1	0	1	0	1	0
6	0	1	0	1	1	0	1	0	1	0
7	0	1	0	1	1	1	1	1	1	0
8	1	1	0	1	1	1	1	1	1	0
9	1	1	0	1	1	1	1	1	1	0
10	0	1	0	1	1	0	1	0	1	0
11	0	1	0	1	1	0	0	0	0	1

TABLE 14.3

	v_7	w_8	x_1	x_2	y_1	y_5	z_1	z_6	z_9	z_{10}
2	0	0	1	0	1	0	1	0	0	0
3	1	1	0	1	1	1	1	0	1	0
4	1	1	0	1	1	1	1	0	1	0
5	1	1	0	1	1	1	1	0	1	0
6	1	1	0	1	1	1	1	0	1	0
7	1	1	0	1	1	1	1	1	1	0
8	1	1	0	1	1	1	1	1	1	0
9	1	1	0	1	1	1	1	1	1	0
10	1	1	0	1	1	1	1	0	1	0
11	1	1	0	1	1	1	0	0	0	1

v is used can actually be followed in a program execution, so the above test does not necessarily reveal all redundant definitions.

14.4.5 Extensions

Here it has only been possible to demonstrate one of the most basic methods of data flow analysis; however, a number of other more elaborate techniques have been devised. For instance, techniques of the kind described above, used in conjunction with a structural analysis of a program, give stronger tests for references to undefined variables and unused definitions; it is possible also to perform inter-procedural data flow analysis, as well as intra-procedural analysis of the kind presented here, (Flavigny (15), Hecht (7)). Error-detection systems based on these principles have been implemented, and found capable of uncovering spelling errors even in a program which had run successfully for several months, and was believed to be correct (12).

In the context of optimizing compilers, data flow analysis has been used for a number of purposes other than those we have described, one example being constant propagation: if all definitions of a variable v which reach a particular statement referring to v assign to this variable the same known constant, the reference to v can be replaced by that constant. As a trivial example, the sequence

```
a := 4
b := a + 1
    .
    .
    .
c := 3*(a + b)
```

can be replaced by

```
a := 4
b := 5
    .
    .
    .
c := 27.
```

As well as improving execution time, constant propagation sometimes improves the clarity of a program text, and validation systems can usefully signal the possibility of making such changes.

Another example is the detection of invariant definitions within a loop, i.e. definitions which do not refer to any variables whose values could be changed in executing the loop. In an optimizing compiler, the detection of an invariant definition is important because it may be possible to move this definition either forwards or backwards out of its loop, and thus reduce the number of times it will be executed. In the context of program validation, we are also interested in invariant definitions, because they suggest careless programming.

14.5 INFORMATION-FLOW ANALYSIS

Until now, information-flow analysis has been used primarily to verify that information transmission between program variables cannot violate security requirements (see for instance Denning and Denning (16) and Cohen (17)). However, it has recently been found possible to derive information-flow relations for a program, which provide a very useful tool for software development and validation.

To indicate the nature of this analysis, Fig.14.7 shows the program of Fig.14.1 in textual form, with each of its assignment and repetitive statements numbered, and for this program, Fig.14.8 gives tabulations of three relations. The

```
statement
number:        begin
   1              Q := 0;
   2              R := M;
   3              while R >= N do
                     begin
   4                    Q := Q + 1;
   5                    R := R - N
                     end
               end
```

Fig.14.7 Integer-division algorithm

first of these (Fig.14.8(a)) indicates the variables whose

	M	N
1		
2	√	
3	√	√
4	√	√
5	√	√

(a)

	Q	R
1	√	
2	√	√
3	√	√
4	√	
5	√	√

(b)

	Q	R
M	√	√
N	√	√

(c)

Fig.14.8 Relationships between input values, statements and output values for the integer-division algorithm.

input values may be used (directly or indirectly) in the execution of each statement. For instance, it is evident from the text that the input value of M is used (directly) in the execution of statement 2, and since this statement 'transmits' the value of M to R, the initial value of M is also used (indirectly) in statements 3 and 5. Furthermore, since the successive values of the expression "R >= N" in statement 3 determine the number of repetitions of statement 4, which in turn determines the values assigned to Q by this statement, the value of M is also used indirectly in statement 4.

The second relation (Fig.14.8(b)) indicates those statements whose executions may directly or indirectly affect the final values of the output variables. It will be noted that all the statements may affect the quotient Q; whereas statements 1 and 4 could be removed without affecting the value of the remainder R.

The final relation (Fig.14.8(c)) shows which input values may affect output values, directly or indirectly.

For "well-structured" programs, fast (polynomial-time) algorithms have been found to construct these relations Bergeretti and Carré (18)), and they are extremely useful in program validation. For instance, the first relation reveals all the possible references to undefined variables. The second relation is also useful in error detection; for instance, if a computed value of a variable is inadvertently over-written before it is used, this is revealed through the existence of statements which do not affect any output values. The possibility of isolating those statements whose execution can affect the value of a particular variable, at any chosen point within a text, is very useful in debugging and formal verification. The third "input-output" relation also provides a check, that each output value is derived from appropriate input values, and no others.

14.6 PROVING CORRECTNESS OF PROGRAMS

We now consider ways of proving that a program meets its "specification". Since this specification may be very complex, and is possibly provided only in informal terms, proving correctness necessarily involves a great deal of disciplined mental work on the part of the programmer; at this level, software aids can only assist him in his task by relieving him of some of the more tedious, mechanical processes involved in reasoning about a program. Here we shall simply outline a basic method of proving program correctness, and indicate the types of software aids which are becoming available to help in this work.

Usually it is most convenient to prove the correctness of a program in two separate steps. First we prove its <u>partial correctness</u> i.e. we prove that if the program terminates, its outputs bear the intended relationships to its inputs; then we prove its termination.

14.6.1 Partial Correctness

The basic method of proving the partial correctness of a program is to attach to each of a number of points in the program an <u>assertion</u>, i.e. a precise statement of what we believe to be true about the program variables at that point. For instance, an assertion attached to an "output" node of a program may state that the data output at that point bears the required relationship to the input. Then, by systematic techniques to be described below, an attempt is made to prove that the truth of the assertion at each point follows from the truth of assertions at previous points in the program.

To apply the method, we must first choose an appropriate set of points at which to "plant" assertions. These are (i) the points at which data is input, together with (ii) the points at which data is output, and (iii) a set of points called cutpoints, chosen in such a way that every program loop traverses at least one of them. For instance, for the integer-division program of Fig.14.9, the nodes α, β, and γ form an appropriate set. Readers familiar with the testing of logic circuits will see here a strategy analogous to that involved in choosing a set of test-points for monitoring a circuit's behaviour. For a program without goto's we have a natural choice of cutpoints - namely the loop entry nodes.

The next stage is to assign assertions to the chosen points. For instance, in our example of Fig.14.9 we have placed at point α an assertion about the nature of the input data. At point γ we have an assertion relating the output to the input, which is essentially a "definition" of integer division. At point β, which is a loop-head, we have an assertion which we suppose to be a loop-invariant, i.e. a statement which always holds when the program execution reaches this point - that is on first entering the loop, and

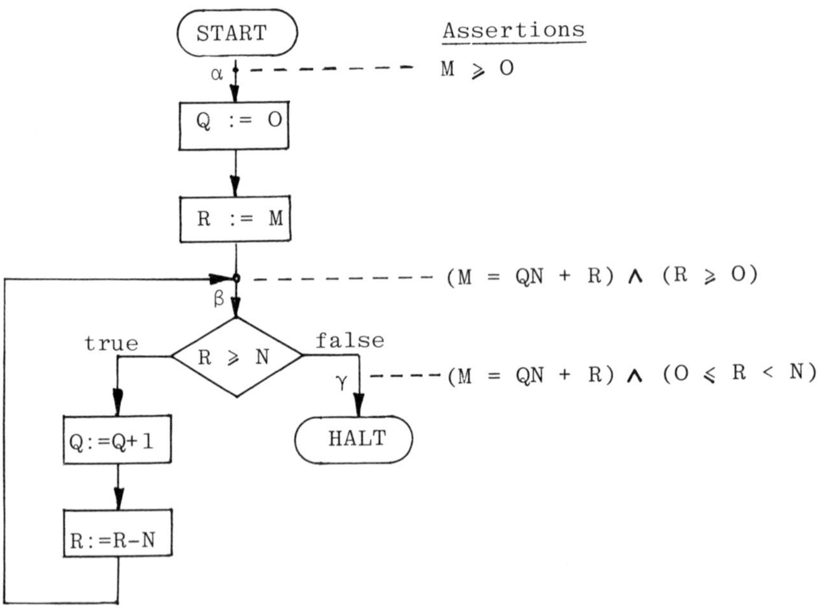

Fig.14.9 Program for integer division of M by N. On termination Q is the quotient and R the remainder

also after any finite number of iterations. The choice of appropriate loop invariants is obviously going to be a non-trivial problem, and we shall return to it; for the moment, let us simply suppose that we have somehow chosen assertions (good or otherwise).

Now it will be observed that the choice of nodes at which we plant assertions naturally decomposes a program into elementary paths. For instance, in Fig.14.9 we have three such paths:

path 1: from α to β,

path 2: from β to β, around the loop,

path 3: from β to γ.

Every execution of the program traverses first path 1, then path 2, (zero, one or more times), and finally path 3. The final stage of program verification involves taking each such path in turn, and checking the "consistency" between the assertions at its endpoints. More precisely, for each path, with initial endpoint s and terminal endpoint t say, and with assertions A_s and A_t at these points respectively, we must check that if A_s is true when the program execution reaches point s, then A_t will be true on reaching t. The simplest way of doing this is to "hoist" the assertion A_t backwards up the path, transforming it as we go, by taking into account the effects of all the assignment statements and the outcomes of all the tests which are encountered on the way to s. The result is a modified form A_t' of A_t; clearly, if the program execution traverses the path from s to t then A_t will be true at t if and only if A_t' was true at s. Hence the truth of A_s at s implies the truth of A_t at t if and only if:

$$A_s \Rightarrow A_t', \text{ or equivalently } \sim A_s \vee A_t'.$$

(The notation used here is that of the <u>predicate calculus</u> (Manna (19)). The symbolism "p $\Rightarrow$ q" means "if p is true then q is true". The symbols $\sim$, $\wedge$, and $\vee$ stand for "not", "and", and "or" respectively.) This statement is called the <u>verification condition</u> for the path from s to t.

If all the verification conditions hold, then for any program execution in which the assertions for the inputs hold, (and for which the program terminates), the assertions on the outputs will also hold.

As an illustration, for path 1 (from α to β) in Fig.14.9, we must hoist the assertion

$$(M = QN + R) \wedge (R \geqslant 0)$$

from node β to node α. When we hoist this assertion through the assignment statement "R := M" it becomes (by substitution of M for R)

$$(M = QN + M) \wedge (M \geqslant 0)$$

and then, after hoisting it through the statement "Q := 0"

we obtain

$$(M = 0Q + M) \wedge (M \geqslant 0)$$

or more simply

$$M \geqslant 0$$

which is obviously implied by the assertion originally planted at α (since these assertions are identical).

For path 2 (from β to β, around the loop), we take the assertion

$$(M = QN + R) \wedge (R \geqslant 0)$$

backwards round the loop. Hoisting it through the assignment statement "R := R - N" changes it to

$$(M = QN + R - N) \wedge (R - N \geqslant 0),$$

which can be written as

$$(M = (Q - 1)N + R) \wedge (R - N \geqslant 0),$$

and then, hoisting it through the assignment statement "Q := Q + 1" we obtain

$$(M = QN + R) \wedge (R - N \geqslant 0).$$

Then (since we follow the "true" branch of the test on $R \geqslant N$), it becomes

$$(R \geqslant N) \Rightarrow ((M = QN + R) \wedge (R - N \geqslant 0))$$

or equivalently

$$\sim (R \geqslant N) \vee ((R \geqslant N) \wedge (M = QN + R)).$$

The verification condition for path 2 is therefore

$$((M = QN + R) \wedge (R \geqslant 0)) \Rightarrow$$

$$(\sim (R \geqslant N) \vee (R \geqslant N) \wedge (M = QN + R))$$

which is easily demonstrated to be true.

In a similar way, for path 3 (from β to γ), we obtain the verification condition

$$((M = QN + R) \wedge (R \geqslant 0)) \Rightarrow$$

$$((R \geqslant N) \vee (0 \leqslant R \leqslant N) \wedge (M = QN + R))$$

whose validity is again easily demonstrated.

14.6.2 Termination

We have proved that if $M \geqslant 0$, and the program terminates, then the final values of Q and R will be the values of the quotient and remainder, as required. However, to have a complete correctness proof we must also show that the program does terminate.

It will be observed that the program does not terminate for $N = 0$, but we can easily prove termination for every input M and N such that

$$(M \geqslant 0) \wedge (N > 0).$$

Indeed, if this condition holds at α, then it can be shown by the hoisting method that the condition

$$(R \geqslant 0) \wedge (N > 0)$$

always holds at β. Since we always have $N > 0$ at β, the value of R decreases each time the program loop is traversed, by an integral amount. Since also $R \geqslant 0$ whenever we reach β, the loop cannot be traversed infinitely many times; consequently the computation must terminate.

14.6.3 The Role of Formal Verification

Much progress has been made in program verification, but there are still severe practical difficulties. Obviously, a correctness proof of the kind given above only establishes the validity of a program with respect to the assertions used to specify it. In practice it is usually very hard to specify the requirements of a program formally, and to relate specifications to implementations in a rigorous way.

Even for a simple program where we are satisfied with the precondition (i.e. the assertion stating our assumptions on the input) and the postcondition (specifying the required relationship between input and output values), the proof of correctness can still be onerous. In choosing the loop invariants, proving the verification conditions and developing the code (which should proceed hand-in-hand), it is necessary to prove a large number of theorems. In the example given above the theorem-proving seemed easy, because the proofs only involved familiar rules of integer arithmetic, but in this respect the example was not typical. Software aids have been developed for this work, ranging from automatic theorem-provers (Boyer and Moore (24)) to primitive theorem-checkers, which simply check the validity of the successive steps of a proof supplied by the user; such tools can be helpful, but automatic provers can follow many blind alleys and theorem checkers are very tedious to use.

For these reasons the rigorous proof of correctness of software will not become commonplace for some time to come. However, in some practical situations, where the importance of the software has justified the work, programs have been verified satisfactorily (Cheheyl et al (25)). And certainly, every software designer should become familiar with the principles of formal verification; at the very least this will give him a better insight into the craft of programming, and lead to some improvement in the quality of his work.

A comprehensive survey of specification and verification methods has been written by Berg et al (27).

14.7 SYMBOLIC EXECUTION

By the symbolic execution of a program we mean its execution with symbols or symbolic expressions as the input values, in place of real data objects, e.g. integers or real numbers. For given paths through the program, the values of all the variables encountered are recorded as formulae - which are kept in as simple a form as possible. (When the process is mechanised, this can often be achieved, at least partially, by using algebraic simplification routines.) By examining these formulae, one can determine to some extent whether the successive program statements will produce the intended results.

The symbolic execution of assignment statements is straight-forward. If two program variables P and Q have been assigned the symbolic values "p" and "q" say, then after symbolic execution of the statement R := P + Q, R would be assigned the symbolic expression "p + q". The subsequent execution of the statement S = 2*R - 1 would assign to S the expression "2(p + q) - 1".

When a program is executed symbolically and one reaches a test node, it is often impossible to "resolve" the test: in other words, it may be impossible to determine, from the symbolic expression representing the test predicate, whether this takes the value true or false. In this case both possible outcomes must be explored, and the execution from this point on breaks into two parallel executions. Notice that, in pursuing each of these two executions, we have some additional information on the program variables. (In one case we know that the test expression is satisfied, and in the other we know it is not.) This information may enable us to resolve some tests encountered subsequently and is conveniently recorded by associating with each step in a program execution a symbolic logical expression, called a path condition. At the beginning of the program execution the path condition is set to true; it is then built up, as execution proceeds along a particular path, by accumulating the symbolic unresolved test outcomes. (At any point in an execution, the path condition is seen to represent the condition under which that point is reached.)

The process of symbolic execution can be represented naturally by an execution tree; for instance, Fig.14.11 shows the symbolic execution tree for the program of Fig.14.10. Each tree node represents the execution of a particular program statement, and is numbered accordingly; all nodes have one successor, apart from nodes representing unresolved tests, which have two successors. Clearly, each path from the root of the tree corresponds to an execution path through the program; the labels on the arcs of the tree represent the path conditions.

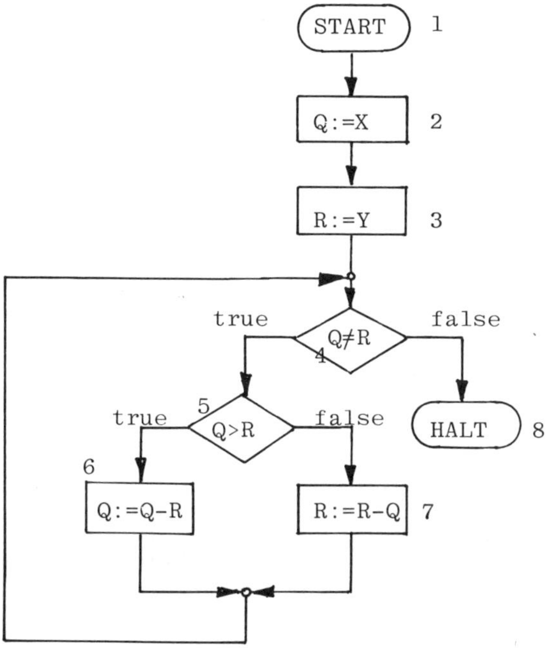

Fig.14.10 Program for calculating the greatest common divisor Q of two integers X and Y

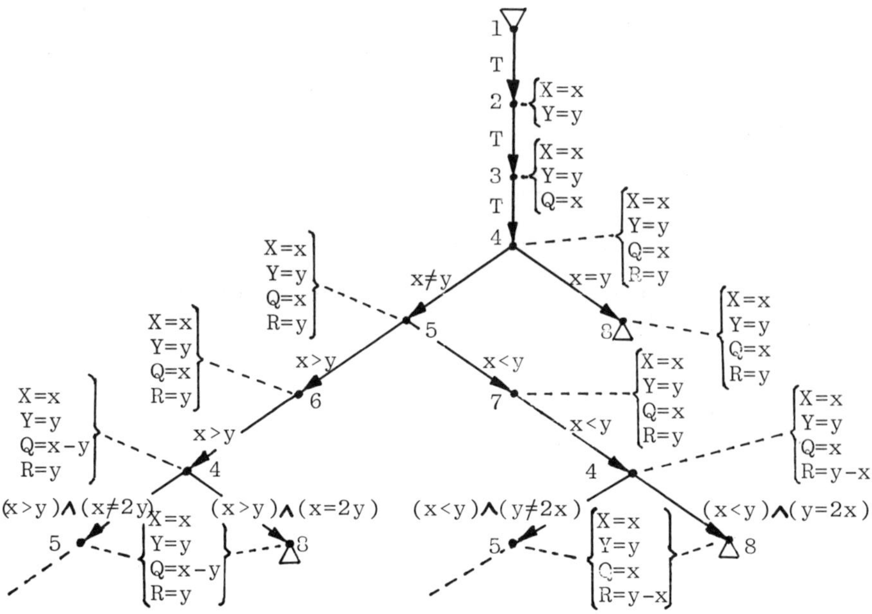

Fig.14.11 Symbolic execution tree for program of Fig.14.10

The intelligibility of such a tree will depend on the extent to which algebraic simplification can be performed in the course of its development. (In developing the tree of Fig.14.11 we have for instance simplified "$x \neq y \wedge x > y$" to "$x > y$", and "$y - x = x$" to "$y = 2x$".) However, the tree given for our very simple example does reveal an inherent difficulty in using symbolic execution, namely that as the executions proceed for a program containing numerous unresolved tests we get a "combinatorial explosion" in the number of tree branches; and of course, if a program contains a loop for which the number of iterations depends (directly or indirectly) on input values, the tree will continue to grow indefinitely.

A number of software systems have been developed for symbolic execution (Boyer, Elspas and Levitt (27), King (28), Clarke (29) and Howden (30)), and they try to solve the problem of "tree growth" in different ways. For instance, in the EFFIGY system (28) symbolic execution is pursued for all paths shorter than a specified number of statements. Alternatively, one may perform a symbolic execution along a single execution path in interactive mode, the programmer being asked which way the program should branch at each unresolved test, or one may limit the number of iterations around each loop.

The principle of symbolic execution is appealing, because of its familiarity; in fact, all programmers use it extensively though in an informal, even unconscious way, both in writing and debugging programs. The notion of a symbolic interpreter is a powerful one - especially since one can allow input values to be not only symbols but symbolic expressions (which may relate the input variables), and one can associate path conditions with input statements (to restrict the range of values of input variables). Thus a symbolic interpreter can be used either for a completely general symbolic execution, or for more restricted executions - which in the limit become ordinary test runs with particular values of the input variables. The potentiality of symbolic execution, with reference to symbolic testing, test case generation, and formal program verification is discussed in more detail by Darringer and King (31) and Clarke and Richardson (32). However, even a very versatile symbolic execution system can in general only partially solve the verification problem, because the number of executable paths through a program is usually very large.

14.8 SOFTWARE DEVELOPMENT ENVIRONMENTS

Many of the techniques outlines in this chapter have been well-known for some time: for instance data-flow analysis has been used since the early days of optimising compilers, and symbolic interpreters have existed for a decade or more. Despite this, very few software development aids are available in a form useful to program designers. To some extent this is because the tools have been produced to analyse texts in specific languages (or worse, uncommon dialects of them), and because they are not portable.

Another very important reason is that tools have been developed in a piecemeal fashion, and are mutually incompatible.

In an attempt to overcome these difficulties, serious attempts are now being made to construct "software engineering environments" in which a set of software development tools are integrated. An important example is the FORTRAN development system TOOLPACK (which is available through the Nag organisation); several other systems are described in Hunke (33).

As another example, in Southampton University work has been in progress for several years on SPADE - the Southampton Program Analysis and Development Environment. In this system, a program to be analysed is represented in a 'functional description language', FDL. Translators to FDL have been developed, from a subset of Pascal, and from a subset of M6800 assembly language. SPADE contains control-flow, data-flow and information-flow analysers, a program for computing program path functions (as required for formal verification), an algebraic simplifier and a symbolic interpreter. Most of these tools have been completed, and it is anticipated that a version of the system will be available for production work within a year.

14.9 CONCLUSIONS

The specification of a program, and the proof of its correctness, will always require a great deal of disciplined mental activity on the part of the programmer; and complete formal verification will often remain intractable, at least in the foreseeable future. The present difficulties in verification may be overcome to some extent through the development of new methods of programming (such as applicative programming), and by refinements in verification techniques and tools. However, it is important to appreciate that programming is a much more complicated activity than we generally admit, and that the difficulty which a programmer may experience with formal analysis can be largely due to his lack of comprehension of the software which he is creating. Even if a programmer will not be expected to produce complete correctness proofs, he should become familiar with validation and verification methods, to achieve a deeper understanding of his craft.

In the near future we should see many more software aids to support validation and verification, incorporated for instance in compilers or "intelligent editors" or other program development environments. They will not always enable us to obtain complete correctness proofs, but they should encourage more systematic program development, and lead to improvements in the quality of the final product.

REFERENCES

1. Gries, D., 1971, 'Compiler Construction for Digital Computers', Wiley, New York, U.S.A.

2. Popek, G.J., Horning, J.J., Lampson, B.W., Mitchell, W.G. and London, R.L., 1977, SIGPLAN notices, 12, No.3, 11-18.

3. Carré, B.A., 1979, 'Graphs and Networks', Oxford University Press.

4. Dahl, O.-J., Dijkstra, E.W., and Hoare, C.A.R., 1972, 'Structured Programming', Academic Press, New York, U.S.A.

5. Aho, A.V. and Ullman, J.D., 1973, 'The Theory of Parsing, Translation and Compiling, Volume 1: Parsing', Prentice-Hall, Englewood Cliffs, U.S.A.

6. Knuth, D.E., 1974, Computing Surveys, 6, 261-301.

7. Hecht, M.S., 1977, 'Flow Analysis of Computer Programs', North-Holland, New York, U.S.A.

8. Muchnick, S.S. and Jones, N.D., (editors), 1981, 'Program Flow Analysis', Prentice-Hall, Englewood Cliffs.

9. Allen, F.E., 1969, Annual Review of Automatic Programming, 5, 239-307.

10. Schaefer, M., 1973, 'A Mathematical Theory of Global Program Optimization', Prentice-Hall, Englewood Cliffs, U.S.A.

11. Fosdick, L.D. and Osterweil, L.J., 1976, Computing Surveys, 3, 305-330.

12. Osterweil, L.J. and Fosdick, L.D., 1976, Software - Practice and Experience, 6, 473-486.

13. Osterweil, L., 1981, 'Using Data Flow Tools in Software Engineering', in 'Program Flow Analysis', (eds. S.S. Muchnick and N.D. Jones), Prentice-Hall, Englewood Cliffs.

14. Kennedy, K., 1981, 'A Survey of Data Flow Analysis Techniques', in 'Program Flow Analysis', (eds. S.S. Muchnick and N.D. Jones), Prentice-Hall, Englewood Cliffs.

15. Flavigny, B., 1975, Rev. Française d'Automatique, Informatique et Recherche Operationelle, 9, 43-59.

16. Denning, D.E. and Denning, P.J., 1977, Commun.ACM, 20, 504-513.

17. Cohen, E., 1978, 'Information Transmission in Sequential Programs', in 'Foundations of Secure Computation', (ed. R.A. Demillo), Academic Press, New York.

18. Bergeretti, J.-F., and Carré, B.A., 1983, 'Information-Flow and Data-Flow Analysis of while-Programs', to be published.

19. Manna, Z., 1974, 'Mathematical Theory of Computation', McGraw-Hill, New York.

20. Alagic, S. and Arbib, M.A., 1978, 'The Design of Well-Structured and Correct Programs', Springer-Verlag, New York.

21. Gries, D., 1981, 'The Science of Programming', Springer-Verlag, New York.

22. Jones, C.B., 1980, 'Software Development: A Rigorous Approach', Prentice-Hall, Englewood Cliffs.

23. Polak, W., 1981, 'Compiler Specification and Verification', Springer-Verlag, New York.

24. Boyer, R.S. and Moore, J.S., 1981, 'A Verification Condition Generator for FORTRAN', in 'The Correctness Problem in Computer Science', (eds. R.S. Boyer and J.S. Moore), Academic Press, London.

25. Cheheyl, M.H., Gasser, M., Huff, G.A., and Millen, J.K., 1981, Computing Surveys, 13, 279-339.

26. Berg, H.K., Boebert, W.E., Franta, W.R. and Moher, T.G., 1982, 'Formal Methods of Program Verification and Specification', Prentice-Hall, Englewood Cliffs.

27. Boyer, R., Elspas, B. and Levitt, K.N., 1975, 'SELECT - A Formal System for Testing and Debugging Programs by Symbolic Execution', Proceedings of International Conference on Reliable Software, Los Angeles, U.S.A.

28. King, J.C., 1976, Comm. ACM, 19, 385-394.

29. Clarke, L.A., 1976, IEEE Trans. on Software Engineering, 2, 215-222.

30. Howden, W.E., 1977, IEEE Trans. on Software Engineering, 3, 266-278.

31. Darringer, J.A. and King, J.C., 1978, Computer, 11, 51-60.

32. Clarke, L.A. and Richardson, D.J., 1981, 'Symbolic Evaluation Methods for Program Analysis', in 'Program Flow Analysis', (eds. S.S. Muchnick and N.D. Jones), Prentice-Hall, Englewood Cliffs.

33. Hünke, H., (editor), 1980, 'Software Engineering Environments', North Holland, Amsterdam.

Chapter 15

Top-down versus bottom-up testing

D.A. Stuart

15.1 INTRODUCTION

This chapter begins by examining the reasons why it is necessary to test software at all, and will thus identify the proper role of the testing process during software system development. This will provide a basis for the main discussion. Testing strategies other than pure top-down and pure bottom-up testing will also be examined briefly.

15.1.1 Terminology

In the following discussion it will be necessary to use certain terms. These are: module, program, subsystem and system (Fig.15.1). These terms will be given the following meanings:-

15.1.1.1 Module. A "module" is a unit of software that performs a small task and would usually be coded as a procedure or routine.

15.1.1.2 Program. A "program" will here mean a hierarchy of modules (Fig.15.2). Reading the top-level module would give one an understanding in broad outline of the function of the complete program. Successively lower-level modules in the hierarchy solve successively smaller problems but in greater detail.

15.1.1.3 Subsystem. Particularly in large software systems, the first level of design identifies a set of system components that are often called "subsystems". These are groupings of programs and data areas that together usually achieve some identifiable large-scale function. A system may consist of several such subsystems, and subsystems may overlap (i.e. may share programs).

15.1.1.4 System. This term will be restricted to mean the software part of a computer based system, i.e. is the total set of programs together with any operating system components, such as a program scheduler.

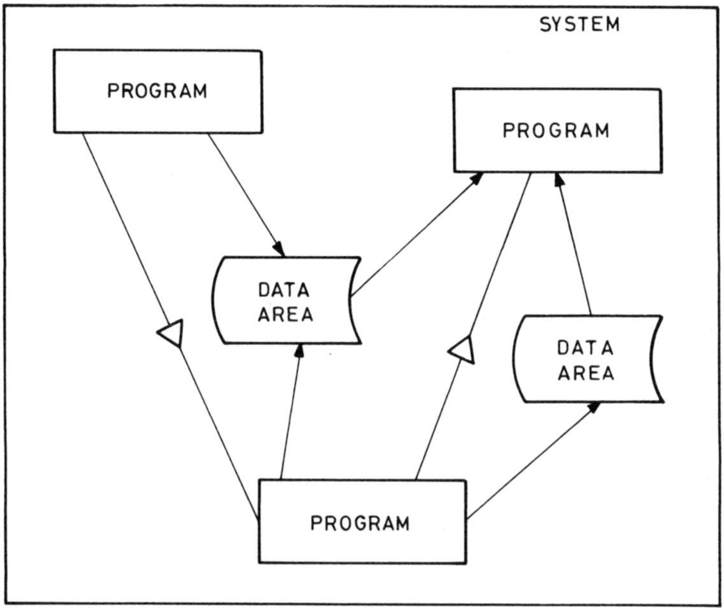

Fig.15.1 Software system components

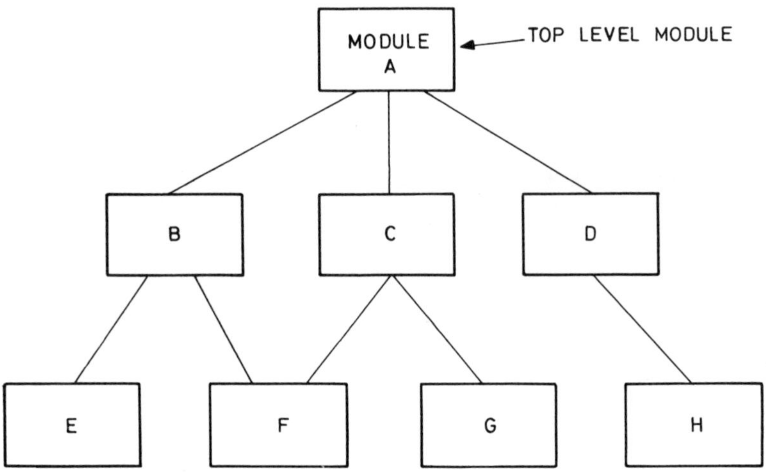

Fig.15.2 Program structure

15.2 THE RÔLE OF SOFTWARE TESTING

15.2.1 Software Development

The development of any software system takes place in a sequence similar to that shown in Fig.15.3. This sequence consists of a succession of transitions in each of which one or more specifications are translated into one or more "lower level" specifications. The actual sequence will be dependent to some extent on the nature of the system. For example, very large systems will usually require the high-level design phase to be carried out in two stages.

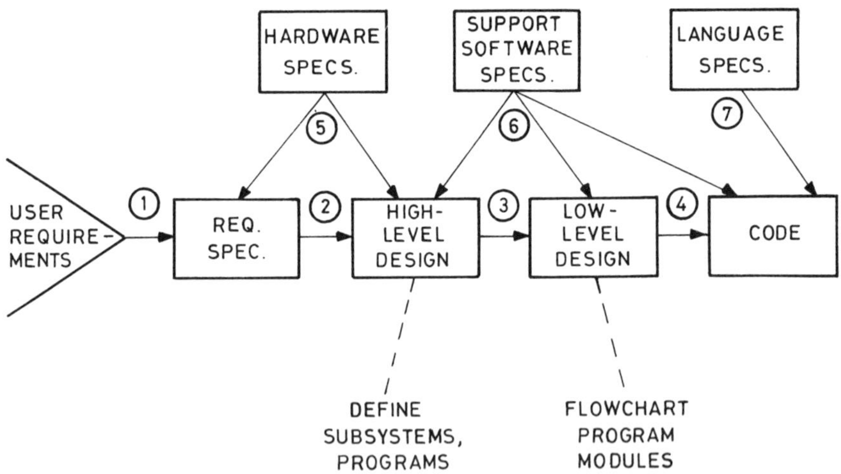

Fig.15.3 Software development sequence

In the first stage the system will be designed in terms of subsystems, and in the second the subsystems will be designed in terms of programs.

15.2.2 Error Generation

It is this process of conversion (steps 1 to 7 in Fig.15.3) that results in the generation of errors in a software system. Step 2 illustrates the risk well. The requirement specification may be complete, clear and unambiguous. The system designer may have a perfectly correct understanding of the requirement. However, should the designer himself have an indifferent ability to write clearly and unambiguously, then his output (the system design) may lend itself to more than one interpretation in the subsequent stages.

Step 7 affords a further example. The coder may have a correct understanding of the flowchart he is basing his implementation on. The danger is that he may attempt "clever" code, using rather sophisticated features of the chosen language. In this case there is a risk that the code will not achieve the intentions of the designer, even though it may successfully compile.

15.2.3 Implications of Error Generation

It should be clear that errors generated in the early stages are likely to be the most serious. Unless detected early on in the project, such errors can pose a real threat to the success of a software project in terms of costs and timescales. They can also affect morale of project team members because they will force a considerable amount of "back-tracking" over work that the team had presumed complete. The true cost of such errors can be very considerable because, being in the design from an early stage, they give rise to further errors - an error cascade can be the result.

15.2.4 Project Aims and Methods

From the above discussion it is apparent that two important aims must be recognized by all members of a software development team:-

1) minimize the incidence of errors

2) of the errors that do occur, remove as many as possible as early as possible.

Methods for achieving the first of these aims are well established: top-down design, good documentation, avoidance of obscure, language-specific code, etc.

The second aim is partly met by the use of techniques such as design reviews, formal configuration control, project audits, etc.

These methods provide justification for some degree of confidence in the software. However, provided that a definite objective is identified, testing will add considerably to confidence in the system. From the above discussion, it can be seen that this objective must be to carry out testing with the intention of discovering remaining errors in the software as early as possible. This view can be taken further. Since the transitions 1 to 4 (Fig.15.3) are the main nodes of error generation, the most productive approach is to have distinct test phases, one for each of these nodes. A test phase would focus on detecting the errors generated at its corresponding development node. Focussed testing of this kind is likely to be more effective than any random testing (by which is meant random selection of tests. Random test data, on the other hand, may well be used as the basis of a carefully planned test).

15.2.5 Test Phases

The concept of focussed testing is illustrated in Fig.15.4. It should be noted that the diagram is not intended to imply any particular sequence of testing. Indeed, as will be shown later, certain phases may sensibly be carried out in parallel.

There are several strategies for sequencing the testing. In the rest of this chapter, two of these approaches will be examined and compared in some depth. They will be discussed firstly in relation to module and program testing and then in connexion with system level testing.

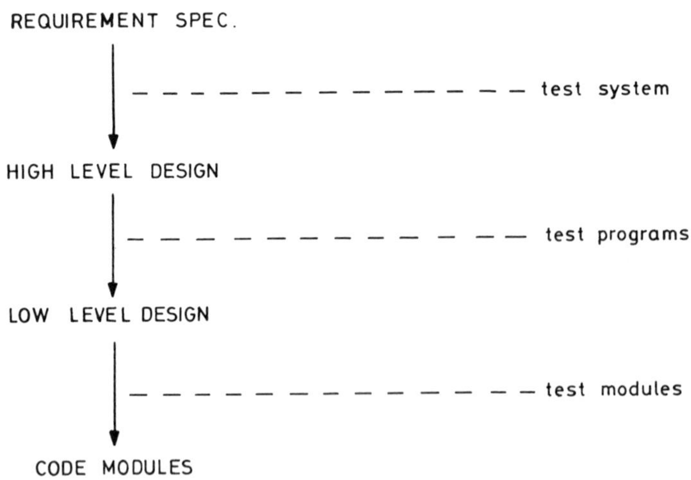

Fig.15.4 Test phases

15.3 OUTLINE OF TESTING STRATEGIES

15.3.1 Top-down Testing

For the program structure illustrated (Fig.15.2), module A is tested first. Since module A uses (calls) modules B, C and D, the interfaces A-B, A-C and A-D must be catered for when testing module A. Since B, C and D are untested at this stage, special modules called "stubs" are written to stand in for them. Their purpose is to satisfy the interface requirements, and are (it is hoped) much simpler than modules B, C and D.

When it is considered that A performs satisfactorily against its test data (i.e. it has "passed" its tests), the stubs for B, C and D are replaced by the actual modules B, C and D so that they can now be tested in conjunction with the previously tested module A. As before, stubs must be provided, this time to replace modules E, F, G and H.

Finally the actual modules E, F, G and H are tested in the presence of modules A, B, C and D. Since E, F, G and H are all at the lowest level in the case illustrated, no further stubs are needed.

15.3.2 Bottom-up Testing

In this method, no stubs are used. The first modules to be tested are those at the bottom of the program hierarchy (E, F, G and H). Each is tested in total isolation from other modules. Once these are "working", the modules in the next level up are tested, using the previously tested lower level modules. This process is continued up to the top-level module.

15.4 COMPARISON OF TEST STRATEGIES

The two strategies outlined above each have advantages and disadvantages, and it is important to know what these are, as the choice of approach will usually need to be made on a project-wide basis. This choice has a considerable influence on the way test cases are written, the amount of work involved in constructing and performing tests, and possibly also the thoroughness of test.

15.4.1 Top-down Testing

15.4.1.1 Constructing stubs. It is often assumed that stubs are always of a trivial nature, consisting perhaps of a message to indicate entry, followed by a simple return to the calling module. Unfortunately this is often not the case. For example, the calling module may require data to be returned by the stub, that data depending upon the test selected. If the data responses needed are in the nature of status indicators (e.g. VALID, INVALID, TYPE x), then the problem may not be too serious. In such a case it may be sufficient to construct one stub for each possible response, linking in the stub appropriate for a test. Of course this would mean many more stubs than contemplated in the outline description of top-down testing. The problem would not be so easily resolved if the different responses were needed at different stages in one test. One stub would then have to be constructed, capable of supplying the responses in the appropriate sequence.

Of even greater difficulty is the problem of supplying unpredictable responses. For example the function of the module that the stub replaces may be to place a value passed to it by the calling module into an ordered list, returning the position allocated to the value back to the calling module. A stub for such a module would not be much simpler than the module it replaces.

<u>15.4.1.2 Advantages of top-down testing</u>. One of the strengths of the top-down approach to testing is that not only are modules tested against their specifications, but also integration testing occurs automatically in the process. Top-down testing is also sensible where the feasibility of the design is under question, since major problems will tend to be located in the higher levels of a program, and will thus be detected early on.

<u>15.4.1.3 Disadvantages of top-down testing</u>. In addition to the problem of writing stubs, there are dangers inherent in top-down testing. One such danger is illustrated in Fig.15.5. Program design is essentially an iterative process, and this implies that the designer may need to modify the design of higher level modules when designing a lower level module. The design-test loop shown in Fig.15.5 (a) should therefore be avoided. Not only could it lead to time being wasted in testing a succession of versions of a module, but, more seriously from the point of view of product quality, it could lead to the designer distorting the structure of his program in order to avoid modifying previously tested modules.

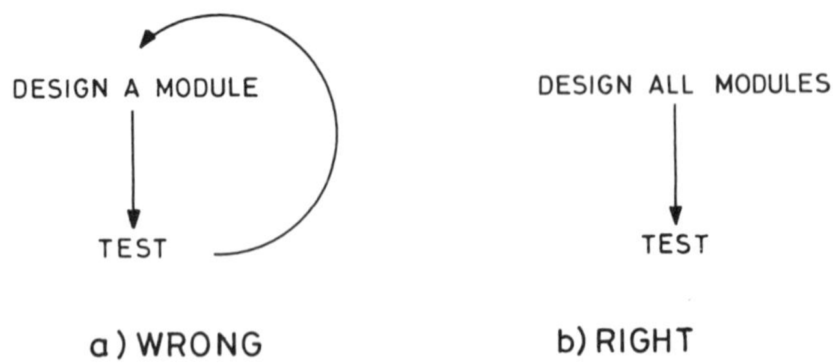

Fig.15.5 Design-Test sequence

Another disadvantage arises from the fact that high level modules act as filters of the data passed down to lower level modules. Bearing in mind that one of the desirable aims when designing software is that of design portability, this ought to be an important consideration, when using a top-down strategy. For example, it may not be possible for module E (Fig.15.2) to be fed negative values in the program under test. Although that may not be a problem for the program under test, subsequent incorporation of module E in another program in which negative values are possible could prove troublesome.

15.4.2 Bottom-up Testing

15.4.2.1 Advantages of bottom-up testing. As noted earlier, bottom-up testing does not involve the use of stubs, thus avoiding the difficulty that can be encountered in stub construction. In order to "drive" the module (i.e. supply test data, execute the module, and print out results) some sort of test harness is required. This can either be a program written for each module, providing pre-set data and a fixed sequence of module calls, or it may be a more general purpose program designed to drive any module in accordance with a set of commands. Writing a dedicated test harness or a command set is normally considerably easier than constructing an equivalent set of stubs, especially where multiple calls of the module under test or of its subordinate modules are needed.

As with top-down testing, one of the strengths of bottom-up testing is that, in addition to testing the modules themselves, the linkages between modules are also tested.

A natural consequence of the bottom-up approach is that the design of all modules of the program must be completed before testing can begin. The dangers of premature testing are thus avoided, in contrast to the situation with top-down testing.

Another advantage of bottom-up testing is that the thoroughness of test is independent of the position of the module in the program's module hierarchy, since modules higher in the hierarchy than the module under test are not present during the test, so that data filtering does not take place.

15.4.2.2 Disadvantages of bottom-up testing. The main problem with bottom-up testing is that major flaws in the design tend not to be found until late, assuming that such flaws reside in the higher levels of a program. Correction of the program's design could then mean that the previously tested modules have to undergo considerable modification, or even complete replacement.

A related limitation may be of significance when testing stand-alone programs such as editors. These programs interface directly with the operator. If such a program is tested top-down, then it may be possible to supply test data via the external input interface, thus reducing the complexity of the stubs used. The main point is however, that operational difficulties with the program will become apparent early on with top-down testing. A bottom-up strategy will prevent the discovery of such problems until the end, when the top-level module is linked in.

15.5 ALTERNATIVE STRATEGIES

Pure top-down and pure bottom-up approaches to testing are not the only strategies available. In "big bang" testing, for example, each module is tested in total isolation from the other modules. Both test harnesses and stubs are needed. Because the modules are tested in isolation, integration testing does not take place, so this must be done separately as a subsequent test stage. For this purpose the modules are linked together in one operation (hence the term "big bang"), making isolation of integration faults more difficult than with either top-down or bottom-up testing. This is unlikely to be a problem with small programs, but generally big bang testing offers few advantages in comparison with the other strategies, yet incorporates the less desirable features of each.

Other strategies are available, these being varied combinations of top-down, bottom-up and big-bang testing. All these attempt in varying degrees to overcome the difficulties discussed above. For example, replacing the big-bang integration stage of the big bang strategy with a top-down integration sequence provides a strategy that is an improvement on either of the two basic strategies used alone. The problem of test data filtering (top-down) is removed, as is the difficulty of isolating integration errors (big bang). However, integration faults are still discovered late, after the isolated testing of modules.

15.6 PROGRAM TESTING

So far the discussion has centred on the subject of module testing and module integration testing. Fig.15.3 shows that, although each module may satisfy its own specification, and although the modules may integrate (i.e. with no interface discrepancies), the program itself may not satisfy its specification because of the errors that can creep in when converting the program specification into the specifications for the program modules. The next stage for each program is, therefore, to test it against its specification. Essentially a bottom-up strategy is the result - the program's modules are tested first, followed by testing of the program as a unit.

15.7 SYSTEM INTEGRATION TESTING

15.7.1 Inadequacy of a "big bang" Approach

With small systems, consisting of only a few programs, it may be adequate to bring all the previously tested programs together in one integration operation and then apply tests to the total system. In other words, a "big bang" strategy may be followed. With larger systems this policy is likely to prove little short of disastrous in terms of product quality, schedules, and costs. There are several reasons for this:-

a) The number of programs is usually very much larger than the number of people on the project available to develop them. The complete set of programs therefore becomes available only in the late stages of the project. This leaves little time for system integration testing, which as a result is not likely to be as thorough as it should be. Should serious errors be discovered, project slippage will be inevitable.

b) As with big-bang integration of modules, isolation of errors is made unnecessarily difficult.

c) The larger the system, the greater the problem of ensuring that the conditions under which a test is run are precisely known and exactly repeatable. For example, the exact sequence in which programs are scheduled may impact on the value of a test, but may be difficult to fix.

15.7.2 A Strategy for System Integration Testing

15.7.2.1 General aims. It was stated at the beginning of this chapter that Fig.15.4 is not intended to represent a test sequence. In the light of the difficulties presented by big-bang system integration, it is apparent that a strategy is needed that:-

1) Allows system integration to commence early on in the project.

2) Simplifies the process of locating errors.

3) Permits greater control over the conditions under which tests are run.

15.7.2.2 The strategy. The solution is to be found in a combination of bottom-up and top-down testing, as follows:-

1) A skeleton system is first constructed. This consists initially of the operating system and possibly also stub programs (analogous to stub modules) standing in for the programs that will subsequently be integrated into the system.

   Some program stubs may need simply to print messages to indicate entry. Others may be required to generate simulated responses, and to call (via the scheduler) other programs.

The advantage of this scheme is that system structure can be explored from an early stage in the project, in parallel with the development of the system programs.

2) The programs are added into the skeleton system in a pre-planned sequence, replacing stubs in the process. This sequence should be used to plan the sequence of program development rather than the reverse. (The factors relevant to determining the integration sequence are outlined below).

The system is thus gradually expanded, and with each expansion new tests are performed and earlier tests rerun (tests that ran successfully in an earlier version of the system may not run with the latest version). Since the expansion is gradual, location of faults is made easier.

15.7.2.3 Factors relevant to the integration sequence. Several factors need to be taken into consideration when planning the integration sequence. The most critical areas of the system should be identified, the related programs being developed early on and integrated early. (Of course, actually identifying the critical areas is not always easy!) It is also desirable to minimize the number of complex stubs that need to be written. Another important consideration is that the relationship between system functions and the programs that achieve those functions should be identified as it is more useful, and easier, to test a complete system function than a lot of part functions.

15.7.2.4 Integrating large systems. In large systems having subsystems as their highest level components, the integration scheme described above needs modification. It is the subsystems, rather than individual programs, that are the units with which the system is expanded. The bottom-up testing continues up to the subsystem level. Subsystems usually contain a small number of programs, so that the programs of a subsystem can usually be bought together in the big-bang manner. Only after a subsystem has been tested in isolation from all other subsystems (thereby facilitating control of test conditions and location of errors), is that subsystem integrated into the expanding system, tests then being performed to examine the interactions between the new subsystem and those that have already been integrated.

15.8 CONCLUSIONS

The discussion in this chapter has necessarily been of a somewhat general nature. Systems vary enormously, and the details of a testing strategy will vary correspondingly. Nevertheless it is apparent that the danger of failing to plan such a strategy and to exercise control over its implementation can hardly be overemphasized. Awareness of the advantages and disadvantages of the several approaches available can reap enormous benefits in terms of higher product quality, cost effectiveness and team morale.

Chapter 16

Project procedures and documentation

J. Gallacher

16.1 INTRODUCTION

Software projects are notoriously difficult to control. The general picture is that they are always over budget, and the software produced is unmaintainable and difficult to modify. Indeed a classic precedent of a two or three fold miscalculation of programming effort is described by Ershov and Shura-Bura(1) as being established in 1960. A system estimated at 15,000 instructions taking 15 manyears actually turned out to be 45,000 instructions which took 30 manyears. Another interesting and readable description of a project which got out of control is given by Brooks(2).

However the foregoing situation, common although it is, need not be so. A major cause of the problem is inadequate procedures and documentation. This paper will discuss how to set up the required procedures and produce the documents which are necessary. Possible forms these documents may take will also be discussed. Estimation of resources and the setting out of clearly defined milestones to enable the monitoring and control of project progress require good documentation. The documents required include:

Project manual
User requirement specification
Functional specification
High level design specification
Low level design specification
Implementation and coding documentation
Acceptance test schedules

It is important that each stage of the documentation is adequately completed before proceeding to the next. However the production of these documents is an interactive and iterative process. The main task in designing software is the production of a set of documents from which the implementation, testing, and maintenance of a software system may be carried out. Software maintenance is all work which is done on a software system after it has been tested and taken into service.

The procedure starts with the appointment of a Project Leader and the delegation of the responsibilities for the specification and implementation of the system to him.

16.2 FUNCTIONS OF A PROJECT LEADER

16.2.1 Establish the project's technical objectives, time-table, quality standards and any staff objectives.

16.2.2 Establish levels of authority and routes and methods of reporting.

16.2.3 Maintain a project log on a regular time basis, preferably daily but certainly not less than weekly.

16.2.4 Study and be fully familiar with work and documentation relevant to the project, which exists at commencement.

16.2.5 Establish the project files and documentation structure.

16.2.6 Draw up plans for the execution of the project, monitor progress against the plan, and submit a written report to management on a regular basis.

16.2.7 Control the project so as to maintain progress according to plan, ensuring external dependencies materialise on time.

16.2.8 Determine project organisation and delegate work activities to the team. Monitor these activities to ensure completion according to the project standards and planning.

16.2.9 Report to management on the performance of team staff.

16.2.10 Responsibility for all project related communications with the customer and any subcontractors or suppliers.

16.2.11 Responsibility for all project final documentation and software source files and listings. Ensure that there is an evenness of quality.

16.2.12 Set up a formal mechanism for the discussion, agreement and recording of changes to the specification.

16.3 USE OF THE PROJECT LOG

16.3.1 Recording the date of meetings where important decisions were made.

16.3.2 Recording telephone conversations where verbal commitments have been given.

16.3.3 Recording important decisions made by the project team.

16.3.4 Recording hardware and software failures.

16.3.5 Recording actions which it may be desirable to set in chronological order when later writing a report.

16.4 PROJECT MANUAL

The project manual may be common to a number of projects but is specific to a particular computer and operating system.

Its function is to provide information and guidance on the particular computer and operating system to all members of the project team and to ensure uniformity of treatment by them of all aspects of the system. The project manual covers such topics as:

- Coding Standards
- Naming Conventions
- Disk and File Naming and Organisation
- General Purpose Macros
- Development Tools
- Common Software Modules
- Building a system from software modules

Some of the more important points which may be included under the above headings will now be discussed in relation to a Z8002 computer with a MSP operating system.

16.4.1 General Coding Standards

16.4.1.1 All subroutines must have only one entry point and one exit point.

16.4.1.2 No use will be made of the instruction for conditional return from a subroutine.

16.4.1.3 All entry and external statements in any module will be made immediately after the module header.

16.4.1.4 All constants and variables which are internal to a module will be defined in statements before any module code.

16.4.1.5 Prolific use will be made of comments, preferably as a block text before a section of code, although also on the same line as code if required. Comments must explain why the code is necessary and do not simply parrot the code itself.

16.4.1.6 Code layout and headers. All software module listings will begin on a new page with the standard module header (Fig.16.1). The second page will begin with the entry and external definitions, followed by local definitions (Fig.16.2).

	DIAC 4ØØØ - TI SUBSYSTEM
TITLE:	SCANNER MODULE
AUTHOR:	NIGEL HAWKINS
VERSION:	1.Ø
DATE:	16.3.82
PRAXIS REF:	CPØ-ØØ9
CUSTOMER REF:	H36-532
COPYRIGHT:	PRAXIS INSTRUMENTS BV

Fig. 16.1 Standard Module Header

All subroutines must begin on a new page and be preceded by a standard header (Fig.16.3)
As a general rule, no single subroutine should spread over more than two or three pages.

16.4.2 Naming Conventions

All names must consist of six alphanumerics and begin with an alpha. This first letter is used to identify the kind of thing being named:

A - spare
B - bit definition
C - equated constant
D - data structure field (longword)
E - subroutine exit
F - data structure field (word)
G - data structure field (byte)
.
.
.
.
Z - variable name (external)

The second position in a name is used to identify the program:

A - alarm
S - scanner
H - highway controller
O - operating system
etc

The third position in a name is used to identify the module within the program. Allocation of these letters is left to the program designer. However the following letters are reserved in all programs:

```
          T       -  table manager module
          B       -  BOSL comms module
          A       -  HDLC comms module
          C       -  comms manager module

 PAGE     SCANNER
*
 ENTRY    STSSCC    STATE CHANGE COORDINATOR
 ENTRY    STSEVH    EVENT HANDLER
 ENTRY    STSCHH    CHARACTER HANDLER
*
*
*
 EXTERNAL STQRCH    READ CHARACTER
 EXTERNAL STQWCH    WRITE CHARACTER
 EXTERNAL STUPID    PROCESS INDICATOR
 EXTERNAL SMAGMD    GET MESSAGE BLOCK
 EXTERNAL SMAPMD    PUT MESSAGE BLOCK
*
*
*
 INCLUDE  XX.CONFG.EQU  SYSTEM CONFIGURATION CONSTANTS
 INCLUDE  XC.CONFG.EQU  COMMS CONFIGURATION CONSTANTS
 INCLUDE  XX.SYSTM.MAC  GENERAL PURPOSE MACROS
*
```

Fig. 16.2 Entry and external definitions

```
TITLE:         STSEVH  -  EVENT HANDLER

FUNCTION:      CHECK VALIDITY OF THE EVENT IN THE CURRENT
               STATE AND CALL THE APPROPRIATE PROCESSING
               SUBROUTINE

INPUT:         RHØ = EVENT CODE

OUTPUT:        RLØ = RESULT STATUS

CHANGED DATA: VTSLRE, LAST RECEIVED EVENT BYTE

CHANGED REGS: RLØ, R1, R2
```

Fig. 16.3 Subroutine standard header

The fourth, fifth and sixth positions in a name are left to the discretion of the module designer. Where possible this three character sub-name should be an acronym.

16.4.3 Disk and File Naming

All files will have names of maximum eight characters followed by a fullstop followed by a three characters extension. The extensions can be the following:

```
    .DEF    -  table definition file
    .ASM    -  assembler source file
    .PAS    -  pascal source file
    .REL    -  object code file
    .BIN    -  binary file
 etc.
```

16.4.4 Standard Equates

As a general rule, the use of numbers as immediate constants in code statements should be avoided, and instead names should be used. The names are then equated to a value, in a group with explanatory comments, at the head of the program module listing.

The following standard equate files are available:

```
XXØARITH.EQU  -  9511 arithmetic commands
XXØOPSYS.EQU  -  operating system constants

etc.
```

16.4.5 Development Tools

These programs can be found as .BIN files. The following are available:

```
DTSECTD.BIN -  dump disk sectors to memory.
DTDUMP.BIN  -  dynamically dumps memory to
               printer.
DTTMNT.BIN  -  table maintenance
DTQMNT.BIN  -  queue maintenance
DTTRACE.BIN -  dynamic program tracing
```

DTTMNT and DTQMNT utilise calls to common software modules via system COMMON.

16.4.6 Common Software

These modules can be found as .REL files. The following are available:

```
XCCOMMS.REL  - communications manager
XBBOSLH.REL  - BOSL protocol handler
XBBOSLD.REL  - BOSL protocol driver
XXTMANG.REL  - table manager
```

16.5 SYMPTONS OF A DOOMED PROJECT

16.5.1 There is a lack of understanding in the contract objectives.

16.5.2 The functional specification is not complete and precise. Thus the high level design is not correct and significant pieces of work may be left out.

16.5.3 Inadequate high level design means that the estimates of time and resources are incorrect, usually underestimates. "More software projects have gone awry for lack of calendar time than for all other causes combined" (2).

16.5.4 Staff requirements are unfulfilled.

16.5.5 Requirements for material resources are not fulfilled on time.

16.5.6 User requests for changes to the system are accepted without being formalised and the effects of the change fully assessed and agreed.

16.6 PROJECT DOCUMENTATION

16.6.1 User Requirements Specification (URS).

This information sets out the user's requirements for the system. It should cover a specification of the system inputs and outputs and the relationships between them. The URS comes in many forms with varying degrees of adequacy. It may come in the form of a single document or a collection of notes, minutes of meetings, etc. In whatever form, it comprises the information currently available from the user on the system requirements. It will not be complete nor will it be final.

16.6.2 Functional Specification (FS).

This document is derived from the URS as a much fuller statement of what the system should do. It will be prepared in a standard way, and in a standard format, by the project leader. The FS presents to the user the designers understanding of the system requirements. It must be presented to the user for discussion, amendment, and formal approval on an agreed timescale. It should be a contract requirement that the user signs the final FS as formal approval of its statements.

From this point in time the FS totally supersedes the URS, and is used as the basis of all design work and for the preparation of the acceptance schedules. It is important that all changes are incorporated into the FS as soon as they are agreed, and the amended FS distributed to all concerned.

There are a number of requirements to which an adequate functional specification must conform. Alford (3) lists the following properties which will be covered by an adequate specification:

Completeness - all functions required by the user must be included.

Consistency - there must be no internal contradictions.

Correctness - this is obvious.

Testability - all statements of functionality must

be directly testable in the final system. If there is a software requirement which cannot be tested it might as well not be included in the specification.

Unambiquity - requirements must be clear, precise and unambiguous. If two interpretations of a statement are possible the wrong one will be followed.

Relevancy - only functions required by the user should be included.

Design freedom - the functional specification should not trespass on design, e.g. it should not make assumptions about the process- and - file constitution of the system as it is the task of system design to deduce these from the functional specification which is itself the result of the URS.

Modularity - it is essential to have a system which is inherently changeable.

An analysis of errors in specifications, Marker (4), categorizes errors into six classes and gives the relative frequencies as follows:

Unclear/unambiguous	10%
Missing/incomplete	20%
Incorrect/untestable/over-restrictive	35%
Untraceable or out of scope	15%
Inconsistent/incompatible	10%
Typing	10%

16.6.3 Project Plan (PP).

This details the effort required, resource utilisation, and the timetable for the whole project. Derived from the FS, this document should be hierarchic in terms of phases, stages, activities and milestones.

16.6.4 High Level Design (HLD).

This details for each deliverable item the software architecture and all external and internal interfaces.

16.6.5 Low Level Design (LLD).

This describes for each deliverable the detailed operation of each of its component modules.

16.6.6 Integration Plan (IP).

This details the procedures to be followed in putting together the hardware and software modules to permit testing to proceed in a controlled way.

16.6.7 Acceptance Test Schedule (ATS).

This details the procedures to be followed in demonstrating satisfactorily to the user that the system satisfies the functions laid down in the FS. The ATS is frequently carried out in two parts, the factory acceptance and the on-site acceptance. The ATS may be written by the customer or the supplier but it must be an agreed document before acceptance testing commences.

16.7 THE HIGH LEVEL DESIGN DOCUMENT

It is in this document that the software architecture is defined. Thus the major components, i.e. modules and data structures, should be identified and their interactions described. The high level design document should include the following standard sections:

16.7.1 Introduction.

A brief statement of the overall functions of the system. It should establish the context of the document within the documentation structure and the system whose design it describes, e.g. user, other systems, hardware, software, etc.

16.7.2 Overview.

A fuller description of the system showing how it operates to provide the defined system functions.

16.7.3 Hardware and Software Environment.

A statement of the hardware and software environment. This includes operating system, programming language, common software and references to other documentation where appropriate. It should list all constraints, options taken, etc.

16.7.4 Data Structures.

Identify and explain all global data structures, message formats, and fixed data. Show relationships between structures where appropriate.

16.7.5 Modules Breakdown.

Describe modular structure and hierarchy. Discuss the operation of each module. Show tasks structure and data flow.

16.7.6 Module Interfaces.

Identify entry points and external interactions of each module. Specify priority and synchronisation for tasks.

16.7.7 Resource Management.

Discuss resource utilisation by the system, i.e. memory, time, disk storage, operating system constructs, etc. Describe how race conditions, deadlocks, and contentions are resolved. Describe any optimisation techniques.

16.7.8 Failure and Recovery.

Where relevant, discuss the philosophy adopted regarding the failure of hardware and software components; specify actions taken by the system on failure and the status after recovery.

16.7.9 System Directory.

A directory of all modules filenames, their declared entry points names, and task names. List all equate files and macro definitions.

16.7.10 System Generation.

Describe how components of the system are generated and linked together to form a whole. Describe configuration options.

16.8 THE LOW LEVEL DESIGN DOCUMENT

Such a design document is required for each module which has been identified in the High Level Design. The document should include the following sections:

- List of subroutines
- List of data structures
- Outline design
- Subroutines design
- Data structure design

16.8.1 List of Subroutines.

This is simply a numbered list of the subroutines which are to be described in detail in the section on subroutines design. Each line of the list is a subroutine name followed by a very short description.

16.8.2 List of Data Structures.

This is a numbered list of the data structures to be described in detail in the section on data structure design.

16.8.3 Outline Design.

This is an overview description of the operation of the module. It should include a short discussion of the design philosophy and how the module performs its required function. A presentation should be made of the relationship between the module's subroutines and data structures.

16.8.4 Subroutines Design.

Each subroutine which is internal to the module is described under standard headings given in this section. The headings must always be shown and 'not applicable' or 'none' entered if appropriate. Each subroutine description should start on a new page:

16.8.4.1 Title. The subroutine mnemonic followed by a one line short description exactly as it appears in the list of subroutines.

16.8.4.2 Objectives. A complete statement of the functions of the subroutine within the context of the module.

16.8.4.3 Assumptions and Restrictions. A specification of any constraints on the subroutine functions, including any design assumptions made about hardware or other software.

16.8.4.4 Inputs. A list of the required inputs which must be established before calling the subroutine.

16.8.4.5 Outputs. A list of the outputs generated by the subroutine.

16.8.4.6 Affected Data. A specification of which data structures are changed as a result of calling this subroutine.

16.8.4.7 Design Description. A very detailed description of the subroutine design. This must be sufficiently detailed that coding from the description is a simple process. The method by which this description is written may be left to the designer. However the methodology should be consistent throughout the document. Diagrammatic representations is to be discouraged for production reasons. A Pascal-like pseudo code is to be preferred.

An example of a subroutine design is given in Appendix 1.

16.8.5 Data Structures Design.

Each data structure, no matter how small, which is internal to the module is described under standard headings given in this section. The headings must always be shown and 'not applicable' or 'none' entered if appropriate. Some data structures will be designed to contain fixed data, or there may be several fixed data implementations with the same structure. In these cases, the fixed data content of the structure should be included in the structure description sub-section. Each data structure description should start on a new page.

16.8.5.1 Title. The data structure mnemonic followed by a one line short description exactly as it appears in the list of data structures.

16.8.5.2 Objectives. A statement of the intended function of the data structure within the context of the module

16.8.5.3 Assumptions and Restrictions. A specification of any constraints imposed, or assumptions made, on the generation, updating, accessibility, structure, or content of the data structure.

16.8.5.4 Structure Description. A full description of the logical organisation of the structure under the mnemonic headings of its component fields. Their use, and content or value in the case of fixed data implementations, should be detailed.

Fields which have a complex structure, such as records should be defined by means of separate data structure descriptions suitably cross referenced.

16.8.5.5 Access Description. A precise description of the methods of access to the data structure, specifying any special procedures and identifying any macros or common software.

16.8.5.6 Storage Utilisation. A calculation of the physical storage space occupied by the structure.

16.8.5.7 Layout. A presentation of the physical organisation of the data structure showing the packing arrangements, etc. Mnemonic field names should be included.

An example of a data structure description is given in Appendix 2.

16.9 PROJECT PLANNING

A number of aspects of software management practice, including project planning, are covered by Sommerville (5) and Tsichritzis (6).

Effective management of a software project depends on thorough planning, anticipating problems which might arise and preparing tentative solutions in advance. As stated earlier the project leader is responsible for planning from the functional specification to delivery of the complete system.

The planning discussed here is that required for larger systems which require a team to complete them in the given time.

Metzger (7) defines a project plan to be made up of eleven distinct sections. These are:

16.9.1 Overview

This describes the plan organisation in general and summarises the remainder of the document.

16.9.2 Phase Plan

This describes the project development cycle, high level design phase, low level design phase, etc. Associated with each phase should be a date specifying when that phase should be complete and an indication of how different phases of the project may overlap.

16.9.3 Organisation Plan

This defines the specific responsibilities of each group involved in the project.

16.9.4 Test Plan

This outlines the testing required and the tools, procedures and responsibilities for carrying out the system test.

16.9.5 Change Control Plan

This sets out a mechanism for implementing changes which are requested as the system is being developed.

16.9.6 Documentation Plan

This is intended to define and control the documentation associated with a project.

16.9.7 Training Plan

This describes training of the programmers involved in the project and training users in the use of the delivered system.

16.9.8 Review and Reporting Plan

This discusses how the project status is reported. The formal reviews associated with the progress of the project are defined here.

16.9.9 Installation and Operation Plan

This describes the procedure for installing the system at the user's site.

16.9.10 Resources and Deliverables Plan

This summarises the critical plan details such as schedules, milestones and all items to be delivered under contract.

16.9.11 Index

This shows where to find things in the plan.

16.10 PROJECT REPORTING

Information about the progress of a project must be presented to management at regular intervals in order that control of the project be maintained and cost estimates and schedules updated. When planning a project, a series of milestones should be established. At each milestone a formal progress report should be presented to management.

These milestones should be distinct, clearly defined and measurable, e.g 'High level design complete'. Milestones should be chosen with discretion in order to make the most effective use of project team and management time.

16.11 PROJECT SCHEDULING

Project scheduling is one of the most difficult tasks of software management. Typically projects break new ground with the consequence that previous estimates have limited relevance.

Different projects may use different programming languages and operating systems. These uncertainties make scheduling an iterative process. An initial schedule must be prepared. It is based on experience and intuition and is typically optimistic. Project scheduling is very dependent upon how well the project documents, i.e. user requirement specification, functional specification, high level design, low level design, etc are prepared. Scheduling is difficult with good documents, without them it is guesswork.

16.12 DOCUMENTATION PRODUCTION AND MAINTENANCE

The production of the documentation for software projects is a time consuming and expensive operation. However the cost of not doing it properly is even greater. It must also be clearly recognised that the various documents will be subject to continuous revision. A change to one document may mean changes to many others. The subject is discussed by Sommerville (5) and Goos (8).

Project documentation has been discussed earlier. It is essential that this documentation is produced to a uniform and high standard. A standard procedure for producing, checking, laying out documentation is essential to document quality control. Document inspections may be used to check and improve documents. Document standards should describe exactly what the documentation should include. They should cover notations and numbering conventions. The numbering of headings and sub-headings may appear to be a trivial matter but its proper organisation is of great importance to reference procedures. In order to produce the documentation it is necessary to have documentation tools the most important of which is a powerful text editing system.

16.13 CONCLUSION

In order to ensure the success of a software project it is necessary firstly to select an experienced and able project leader and clearly define his duties and reporting route, and secondly produce good and timely documentation. and maintain it well.

REFERENCES

1. Ershov, A.P. and Shura-Bura, M.R., 1980, 'The Early Development of Programming in the USSR', 'A History of Computing in the Twentieth Century', Ed. Metropolis et al, Academic Press, New York,USA.

2. Brooks, F.P., 1975, 'The Mythical Man-month', Addison-Wesley, Reading, MA, USA.

3. Alford, M., 1977, 'A Requirements Methodology for Real-time Processing Requirements', 'Software Engineering Techniques. State of the 'Art Report', Infotech, Maidenhead, England.

4. Marker, L.R., 1976, 'Structured Design'. 'Infotech State of the Art Conference'. Amsterdam.

5. Sommerville, I., 1982, 'Software Engineering', Addison-Wesley, Reading, MA, USA.

6. Tsichritzis, D., 1973, 'Project Management', 'Software Engineering', Ed. Bauer, Springer Verlag, Berlin, Germany.

7. Metzger, P.W., 1973, 'Managing a Programming Project', Prentice-Hall, New Jersey, USA.

8. Goos, G., 1973, 'Documentation', 'Software Engineering', Ed. Bauer, Springer Verlag, Berlin, Germany.

Appendix 1

SUBROUTINES DESIGN EXAMPLE

TITLE

STADEL - delay if idle

OBJECTIVES

This routine checks if activation requests have been received. If not the task is delayed. If yes no action is taken.

ASSUMPTIONS & RESTRICTIONS

This is a monitor routine in order to ensure synchronisation.

INPUTS

none

OUTPUTS

none

AFFECTED DATA

TTXPTR - point ready 2-Ø1.48
VTADVS - local device status

DESIGN DESCRIPTION

```
BEGIN  STADEL
ENTERMON
IF all bytes in TTXPTR = Ø
  AND all bytes in TTXDVS = Ø
    THEN * system idle *
      SC DELAY RR6 = -1 *max delay*
EXITMON
END
```

Appendix 2

DATA STRUCTURE EXAMPLE

TITLE

VTXTAB - example table

OBJECTIVES

This structure is an example of how data structures should be documented.

ASSUMPTIONS & RESTRICTIONS

This structure is not used.

STRUCTURE DESCRIPTION

This structure consists of a number of records (CTXNRC). Each record contains the following fields.

```
longword - used for
byte 1   - used for
byte 2   - used for
text     - used for
```

ACCESS DESCRIPTION

This structure is accessed by the table manager on a per record basis.

STORAGE USE

1024 bytes

```
LAYOUT

     VTXTAB:

          Record Ø
          RTXREC

            .
            .
            .
            .
            .

          Record n



          Record Structure RTXREC
 Ø
          Longword
          DTXLNG
 4   byte 1              byte 2
     GTXBT1              GTXBT2
 6

          Text (16 bytes)
          HTXTXT
```

Notes

This structure uses defined offsets:

e.g GTXBT2 = 5 - offset to byte 2

and defined lengths:

e.g HTXTXT = 16 - length of text

```
     NTXREC = NTXLNG + NTXBT1 + NTXBT2
            = length of a record
```

These values may be used to access elements from the structure, e.g

```
     If R3 = address of table = VTXTAB
        R2 = destination
```

The following can be used to move the text field from record N:

```
LDIRB(R2),(N*NTXREC)+ HTXTXT(R3), NTXTXT
```

Chapter 17

Performance analysis in system design

J.M. Porteous

17.1 INTRODUCTION

"There is no need for performance analysis in the design of modern micro-computers. If you think you have a problem then just add in more processing power or more memory and the problem will disappear. If you throw in enough to start with you will never get the problems!"

17.1.1 So Why Analyse?

The misconception quoted above is a popular belief amongst system designers, project leaders and senior managers, especially those not directly connected with the micro-computer industry. It is one of the main reasons why performance analysis is not done, the others are all that the mathematics can get very hard!

If you follow the arguement in a competative market and your product costs even 5% more than that of your competitors you will loose more sales than the analysis would have cost. Indeed getting your production or installation costs down is one of the major reasons for doing performance analysis. Even in the low volume or specialist market you can be sure that in a year or two someone will have the bright idea of using all this 'spare' capacity to implement a few extra facilities. The result is that the problems you hadn't identified rise like a pheonix from the embers of the code you forgot to document - and you have to start all over!

The other principle reasons for doing performance analysis are proving to your customer that your system will work under all of the conditions he has specified or, if you are the customer, proving to the supplier that it will not.

17.1.2 What is Performance Analysis?

"Performance analysis is the application of highly complex mathematical techniques to analyse over simplified problems giving results of questionable accuracy and dubious validity".

To be more precise the value of performance analysis is determined not by the parts of the system that you choose to analyse but by those you choose not to analyse. Inevitably, if the analysis is done to assist the design you will be forced to approximate (or guess) the values of system parameters; if the system is complex you will be forced to make simplying assumptions so that you can complete the analysis. (Note that you should continually review your assumptions and approximations as the design evolves).

There are three basic methods employed in performance analysis.

17.1.2.1 Mathematical analysis The use of mathematical analysis (probability theory, queuing theory, etc.) is only suitable for detailed analysis of small systems or small elements of larger systems. Alternatively, by carefully over-simplifying larger problems, it can be used to provide approximations (to validated a simulation perhaps) or to define the best possible or worst case boundary values. The importance of such an analysis is not only the detailed results that are obtained but also the insight that it can provide on the way in which the systems' parameters affect its performance. An exact mathematical analysis of large practical systems will invariably be impossible.

Mathematical analysis is often done based on the careful application of solutions to 'standard' problems, particularly to queuing systems. The remaining sections of this chapter detail some of the results that can be usefully applied by most designers, often for very little effort. However, it is of the utmost importance that you understand both the effects of the assumptions that you make and the assumptions made by the author whose work you are using. The literature is full of papers describing the analysis of micro-computer systems where the assumptions made are so specialised that the results are invalid for even the slightest variants of that authors system.

17.1.2.2 Simulation The second method employed is simulation. This is not necessarily any less complex than the mathematical analysis but for large systems it is usually the only possible solution. It is also valuable because of the amount of detailed information that can be obtained. Simulation can, however, be very Time consuming and is as prone to undetected software bugs as any other large program. There are a number of simulation packages available for both bureau and in-house computers. Modern simulation packages, notably SIMULA (1) and the SEE-WHY package (2), are process oriented and the simulation can be constructed by a fairly simple translation of the system flow charts.

17.1.2.3 Direct measurement The third method, building the system and then measuring its performance under a range of operating conditions, should only be done to confirm the results obtained in earlier mathematical analysis or simulation. Any detailed analysis based on this technique is likely to be extremely expensive (especially in terms of the equipment required to generate a load and measure the response) and if the results obtained are not those you expect then you are not likely to have many clues as to the reasons why. Experiments may not be repeatable (to confirm either good or poor results) and it may be difficult to obtain results that have sufficient statistical validity. This is especially true when performing measurements near the limit of the systems capacity. Nevertheless it is important that you design into your system the ability to continually monitor its performance (ie recording queue overflows, excessive system delays, etc.).

17.1.3 How Much Will It Cost?

Performance analysis is not cheap, and can be very difficult to justify as a separate item. In firms that have 'got by' without analysis in the past proving that you should start now can be almost as difficult as the analysis; done properly on a few projects it's value becomes established and its use on future projects becomes automatic.

Whilst the result of performance analysis should result in hardware savings - less of these, slower (and therefore cheaper) ones of those - the cost of analysis is usually related to the software development costs. This is because in only relatively few systems is the hardware itself analysed (the most common exception is in shared bus design).

To a first order, analysis will cost some 5% - 15% of the development costs for a micro-computer based project. Much will depend on the size of the system and the level of detail in the analysis. In deciding how much analysis to do you should keep an eye on the possible savings - remembering that in one system, not using a few hundred bytes of memory may not save you anything (if you have to provide the chip anyway) whereas in another, saving a few bytes can save a complete memory chip and therefore several pounds per system.

17.2 WORKLOAD AND PERFORMANCE MEASURES

Before you begin to analyse your system, it is important that you have a proper understanding of the workload that it is to be subjected to, and of the performance critereon that are important. If, for example, you are designing a computer to undertake a traffic census it is not sufficient to know that the mean rate is

60 cars/hour in the day and 10 cars/hour in the evening. There are unlikely to be exactly 60 seconds in between the arrival of each car; it is the distribution of these inter-arrival times that is important since this gives an idea of the likely minimum time between the arrival of successive cars (which could be very small on a multiple lane road) and of the way in which they might be grouped (just past some traffic lights, for example).

In this simple counting system the time required to process each car (it's service time) is unlikely to vary significantly and a constant service time value can be used. If however the performance of a computer used for program development were being considered then, because the service time of a compiler varies considerably (depending upon the source file length, the number and type of errors found, etc.), it would be essential to represent its service time by some form of distribution.

There are a number of possible measures of the performance of a system. In systems where short term overloads results in loss of the input data (eg. you don't re-read your input ports quickly enough) then a common performance measure is the throughput carried. Typically this takes the form shown in figure 17.6.

In systems which involve delay the performance measures are usually the actual delay (which may include the service time) and the queue lengths (which may include the items currently being processed and not just those in the queue).

It is important to remember that if any one of the input parameters is a distribution then the performance measures will invariably not be constant values but distributions. For example, a queueing system with a negative exponential inter-arrival rate (see 17.2.1) will invariably produce a similarly shaped distribution for both queue length and delay. Whilst it is usual to consider the mean values of the distributions it may be equally important to consider the 95 or 99 percentile values.

17.2.1 Poisson Distribution

The Poisson distribution is one of a number of names used to describe a collection of events that occur AT RANDOM. Consider a simple computer system where a message is sent to the computer each time a customer picks up a telephone. During the afternoon customers pick up their telephones at random. That is to say an individual customer is equally likely (probable) to pick up the telephone in any particular second during the afternoon. Stated like this it is called a UNIFORM DISTRIBUTION since the probability that a particular customer will pick up his telephone in any one second is a very low but constant value.

The computer system is likely to have several thousand telephones connected to it, so that an alternative description of the arrival rate of messages is the number of messages that arrive (telephones that are picked up) during each minute of the afternoon. This can be shown to be a limiting case of the binomial distribution known as the POISSON DISTRIBUTION and is given by:

$$P(n) = e^{-E(n)} \frac{[E_{(n)}]^n}{n!} \qquad (17.1)$$

$E_{(n)}$ is the expected (mean or average) number of arrivals per unit time (minute). The distribution can be drawn as shown in figure 17.1.

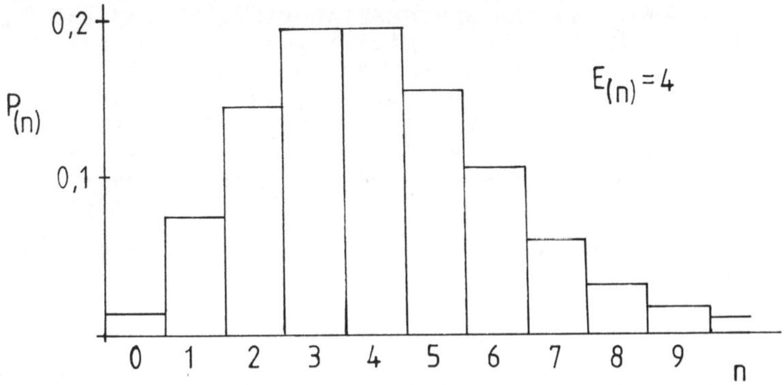

Fig 17.1 Poisson Distribution

Another common alternative is to consider the time between successive messages (the inter-arrival time). In this case the probability that the time between two successive messages is less than or equal to a value T is given by:

$$P_{(ta \leq T)} = 1 - e^{-T/E(ta)} \qquad (17.2)$$

$E_{(ta)}$ is the expected (mean or average) inter-arrival time and is equal to $1/E_{(n)}$.

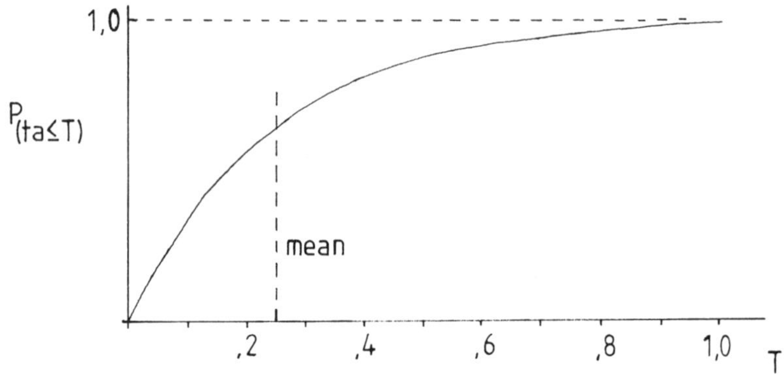

Fig 17.2 Exponential Distribution

This is known as the EXPONENTIAL DISTRIBUTION and is shown in figure 17.2. The probability that the actual inter-arrival interval is less than the value T is considered because, for inter-arrival times, smaller values are more critical. If, however, random service times are considered then larger values are more critical and it is more usual to consider the probability that a particular value has been exceeded.

ie $P_{(ts \geq T)} = e^{-T/E(ts)}$ (17.3)

$E_{(ts)}$ is the expected (mean or average) service time. The resultant curve is usually described as a NEGATIVE EXPONENTIAL DISTRIBUTION.

It should be stressed that all of these curves are different methods of describing what is essentially the same distribution and the terms can, and are, used interchangeably.

17.2.2 Erlangian (Gamma) Distribution

If a processing node has it's own queue of tasks waiting to be executed then it's outstanding work at the point in time where it is about to take the next task (however chosen) from the queue is the sum of the service time of the (k) tasks in the queue. If the service times distribiton is Poissonian then this is the sum of k mutually independent, identically distributed exponential random variables.

The resultant distribution can be described by the following formulae, which gives the probability that the total service time (t) of the tasks in the queue is less than or equal to some value (T).

$$P_{(t \leq T)} = 1 - e^{-\mu t} \sum_{j=0}^{k-1} \frac{(\mu t)^j}{j!} \qquad (17.4)$$

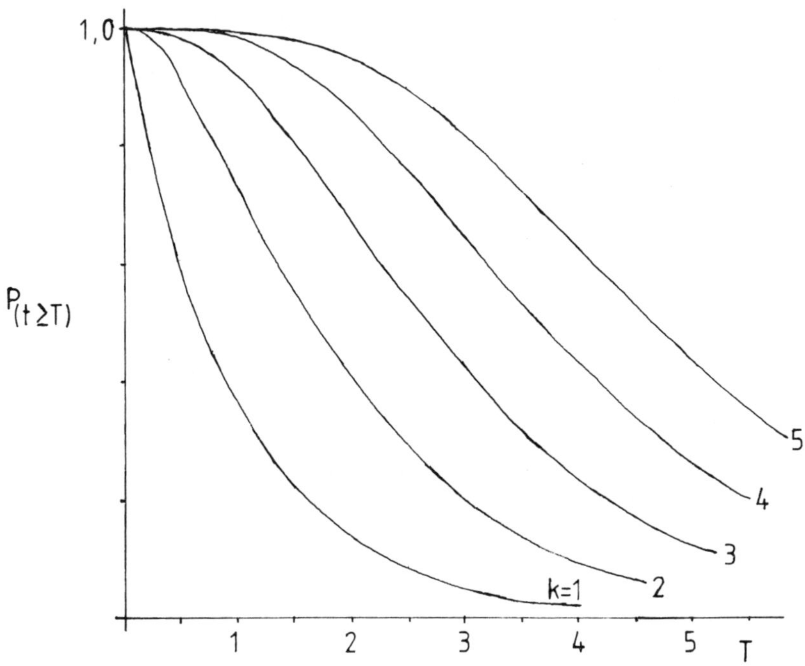

Fig 17.3 Erlangian Distribution

Where μ is $1/E_{(ts)}$. This is known as the Erlangian Distribution of order k, or more simply the Erlang-k Distribution. For service times it is more common to want the probability that the sum of the service times of successive tasks exceeds a particular value and this is given by:

$$P_{(t \geq T)} = e^{-\mu t} \sum_{j=0}^{K-1} \frac{(\mu t)^j}{j!} \qquad (17.5)$$

This function is plotted in figure 17.3 for values of k of 1, 2, 3, 4 and 5. For k=1 the formulae reduces to the Poisson distribution (hence that is sometimes referred to as the Erlang-1 distribution). The curves in figure 17.4 have been normalised to the mean service time by equating μ=1.

17.3 QUEUEING THEORY

The size of projects, for which micro-computers are used, is continually growing (as measured by the software volume per unit). Teams of programmers, rather than a few individuals, are employed to write the software for single projects. To make the software manageable it is written in independently schedulable modules or processes which interface to each other via message queues or buffers. Queues are also used for more sophisticated forms of scheduling and for interfacing to other parts of the system which may operate at a different, or unpredictable speed.

Only a few, simple results are presented here, though they are sufficiently general to enable a sensible, first order analysis to be done on many systems. More detailed results can be found in references (3) - (6) or in any modern queuing theory books.

17.3.1 Single Server Queues

The expected (mean) number of items waiting ($E_{(W)}$) in a single server queue with exponential inter-arrival times is given by the Pollaczek-Khintchine Formulae:

$$E_{(w)} = \frac{\rho^2}{2(1-\rho)} \times \left(1 + \frac{\sigma_{ts}^2}{E_{(ts)}^2}\right) \qquad (17.6)$$

Where ρ is the mean throughput (expressed as a proportion of the maximum) and σ_{ts} is the standard desiation of the service time distribution. (This is, in fact, a derivation from the original formulae but is the one most widely quoted). The formulae applies for any service time distribution and for any dispatching discipline where the selection of the next item to be served does not depend on the service time of the items in the queue (eg LIFO, FIFO). For an exponential service time distribution it's mean and standard deviations will be equal giving

$$E_{(w)} = \frac{\rho^2}{(1-\rho)} \tag{17.7}$$

Little's Theorem gives the expected number of items present ($E_{(q)}$), including one being served where present, as:

$$E_{(q)} = E_{(n)}\, E_{(tq)} \tag{17.8}$$

However, since ρ is also the probability that the server is busy

$$E_{(q)} = \rho + E_{(w)} \tag{17.9}$$

The expected (mean) time in the system is the expected (mean) service time plus the expected (mean) time in the queue, ie:

$$E_{(tq)} = E_{(ts)} + E_{(tw)} \tag{17.10}$$

The number of items in the queue can be obtained by substitution of the above formulae.

$$E_{(q)} = \rho + E_{(w)} = E_{(n)}\, (E_{(ts)} + E_{(tw)}) \tag{17.11}$$

$$\rho + \frac{\rho^2}{(1-\rho)} = E_{(n)}\, E_{(ts)} + E_{(n)}\, E_{(tw)} \tag{17.12}$$

But $\rho = E_{(n)}\, E_{(ts)}$ (17.13)

giving $E_{(tw)} = \rho \dfrac{E_{(ts)}}{(1-\rho)}$ (17.14)

The functions $E_{(tw)}$ and $E_{(w)}$ are plotted on figures 17.4 and 17.5 as the curves for M=1.

17.3.2 Multi-Server Queues

If the tasks arriving at a single queue in a computing system have Poissonian inter-arrival and service times and can be served by any of a number (M) of identical processing nodes then the mean occupancy (throughput) of the system is given by

$$\rho = E_{(ts)}/[M \times E_{(ta)}] \quad \text{for } \rho < 1 \tag{17.15}$$

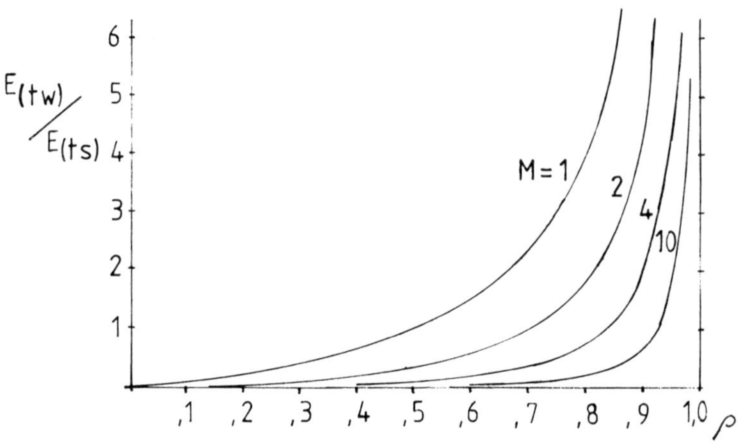

Fig 17.4 Mean Queue Delay

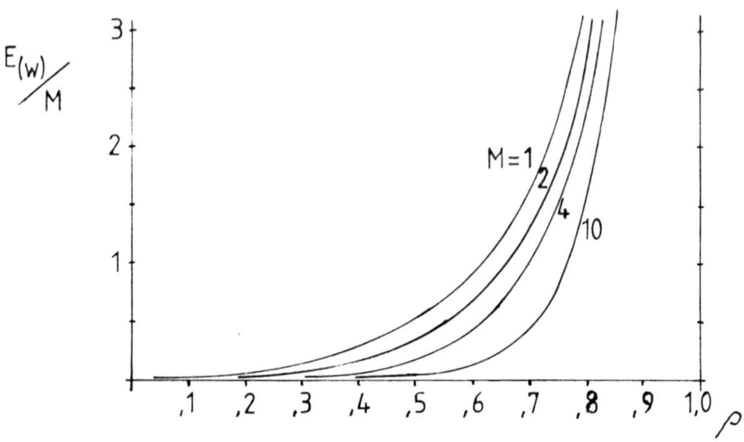

Fig 17.5 Mean Queue Length

The probability that an arriving task will have to wait is the probability (B) that all of the servers are busy. This is given by

$$B = \frac{1 - (X/Y)}{1 - \rho\,(X/Y)} \tag{17.16}$$

$$\text{where} \quad X = \sum_{N=0}^{M-1} \frac{(M\rho)^N}{N!} \tag{17.17}$$

$$\text{and} \quad Y = \sum_{N=0}^{M} \frac{(M\rho)^N}{N!} \tag{17.18}$$

Note that this condenses to $B=\rho$ when there is a single server (M=1). The mean waiting time is given by

$$E_{(tw)} = E_{(ts)} \times \frac{B}{M} \times \frac{1}{(1-\rho)} \tag{17.19}$$

and the mean queue length is

$$E_{(w)} = B \times \frac{\rho}{1-\rho} \tag{17.20}$$

These two functions are plotted in figures 17.4 and 17.5 respectively. The curves for M=1 represent single server queues. Both sets of curves are normalised.

17.3.3 Loss Systems

The above formulae relate to pure delay systems; that is, systems where short term variations in the input rate or service times are catered for by delaying some of the inputs until they can be served. The alternative is to discard inputs that cannot be served. It is extremely rare for processor controlled systems to rely on discarding inputs as their only method of overload control and such systems (ie pure loss systems) will not be considered further here.

Processor controlled systems are invariably combined loss and delay systems. The balance between the two parts being determined by the queue space available and the maximum delay that can be tolerated. A simple analysis will ignore the loss to obtain estimates of the queue length and delay distributions. The estimates obtained in this way will give longer delays and large queue lengths than those that will apply when the loss is considered. For many systems mathematical analysis of the combined loss and delay effects are likely to be impossible and simulation will be required.

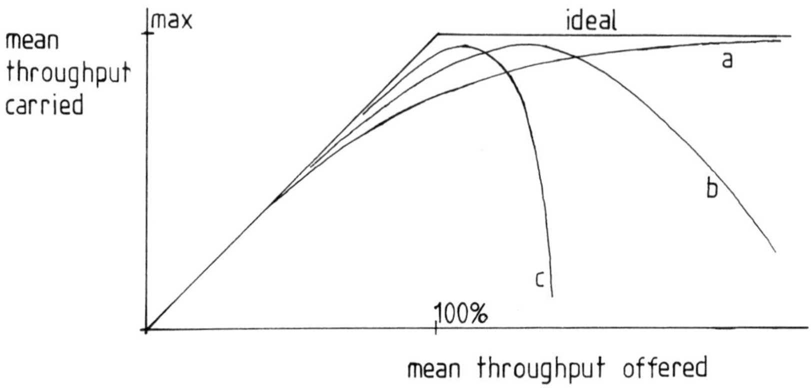

Fig 17.6 Typical Throughput Characteristic

Ideally, the throughput carried (load processed) should be equal to that offered until the maximum capacity of the system is achieved, whereafter the excess load is discarded. In practice, especially with real time systems, it is usually necessary to start discarding some of the input offered before the overall (long term) maximum capacity has been reached (eg because for short periods the input rate may exceed the overall maximum).

Curve (a) represents a very conservative policy. Whilst it is safe (ie it's slope does not become negative) the benefit gained from operating with an offered load of more than 100% is limited, reducing the system's practical capacity to a throughput carried of about 70%.

Curve (c) represents the other extreme and is unsafe. Whilst it's performance up to 100% offered throughput is good with very little being discarded, any excess load will cause the system to collapse catastrophically. This is typical of 'overtuned' systems and of systems involving poorly chosen timeouts.

Curve (b) is a typically well designed system, with the rise and decay portions of the curve being approximately equal.

Two rules need to be observed in order to produce a well designed system.

a) The cost of deciding which input data to reject must be small. Sophisticated algorithms may, on paper, produce excellent results, however the time taken to compute them is often such that very simple algorithms will be better.

b) The cost of a rejected item should be small. This implies both that you should avoid rejecting items in which you have already expended a lot of processing, and that the effort required to reject the item should be small (eg sending a 'rejected' message back to the source, clearing data tables, setting flags so that any 'follow on' data is also rejected).

REFERENCES

1 Birtwistle, G M, et., al., 1979, 'Simula Begin', Chartwell-Bratt Ltd, Bromley, England.

2 Fiddy, E., Bright, J G., and Hurrion, R D., 1981, 'SEE WHY - Interactive Simulation on the Screen', Paper No C293/81, I Mech. E., England.

3 Beizer, B, 1978, 'Micro-Analysis of Computer System Performance', Van Nostrand Reinhold.

4 Cooper, R B, 1981, 'Introduction to Queueing Theory' (Second edition), Edward Arnold (Publishers) Ltd, London, England.

5 Kleinrock, L, 1976, 'Queuing Systems', John Wiley and Sons, New York.

6 Martin, J, 1981, 'Computer Networks and Distributed Processing', Prentice-Hall.

Chapter 18

Project estimation and control

J. Gallacher

18.1 INTRODUCTION

Project management and control depend upon realistic estimation to provide the data from which a project may be costed and progress monitored. The history of software development has not been a happy one with typical 200- 300 per cent cost overruns and up to 100 per cent schedule slippages. This is not tolerable. Manpower costs and time schedules have to be predictable within reasonable engineering limits before investment decisions are made. As Sommerville (1) states, the most commonly used technique for estimating software costs is to estimate the size of the system and hence calculate the programmer man-months required to produce the system. This simplistic approach arose from the standard industrial practice of measuring average productivity rates for workers. The usual assumption, which gave rise to the concept of the 'man - month', was that the work to be done was the simple product of constant manpower times schedule time and that these factors could be manipulated.

Brooks (2) has shown that this is not so. Manpower and time are not interchangeable, programmer productivity rates vary greatly, and system size and complexity have a great influence on the time required to carry out a project. The understanding of the software development process is improving and data is becoming available which permits an empirical approach to the problem. However it is also necessary to understand the importance of an adequate input to the estimation process. This input consists of the specifications available at the various phases of the project.

These specifications must be formalised and should include:

User requirement specification
Functional specification
High level design specification
Low level design specification

Estimation is an interactive and iterative process, it achieves a progressively better foundation as the specification process proceeds through its various phases. It is therefore necessary to check the estimates at each defined stage. An estimate formed at a preliminary stage of an user requirement specification can be subject to ± 75% error. At this early stage answers to the following questions are being sought:

Is it feasible?
What will it cost?
How long will it take?
Manpower loading?
Risks?

Having achieved adequate documentation and estimation it is necessary to set clearly defined milestones to monitor the progress of the project. These may be such as 'High Level Design complete', 'Low Level Design: Module A complete','Coding Module A complete', etc. Percentage completion is a meaningless term in software engineering.

The time sensitivity of software projects must be emphasized. A software project which has been under-estimated can only be rescued at great cost, if indeed it can be rescued at all. Brooks (2) states 'more software projects have gone awry for lack of calender time than for all other causes combined'. He also discourses about 'gutless estimating', and its causes and effects. In a case of considerable schedule slippage it is best to re-schedule the project and accept the consequences. This way, at least the extra costs can be optimised.

Software estimating is still an art to which some science can be applied. The work being carried out in this field is aimed at increasing the proportion of science. Certain equations have been evolved, with some quantitative back-up, which assist with macro and micro estimating. The main areas of uncertainly are in sizing the system and modules, and in assessing an appropriate productivity for a particular activity.

18.2 SOFTWARE ESTIMATING

Brook's (2) law states 'adding manpower to a late software project makes it later'. This together with his other law 'men and months are not freely interchangeable' and observations from other sources seem to mean that if an appropriate development schedule could be established initially, work of satisfactory quality could be accomplished within the allotted time by the assigned programmers at a high rate of productivity, at a minimum total cost. Many software schedules are established not on the basis of the work to be done, but by external factors. In the absence of good methods of estimating development time, software managers have been in a weak position to argue against imposed schedules.

There are two fundamental ways of approaching the task of software estimating. One is to work at the detail level and may be called micro - estimating. The other attempts to forecast manpower and schedule time at the start of the design, and may be called macro-estimating.

18.2.1 Micro-estimating

This conventional technique starts with fixing the size, start date, and duration of each activity. Adjustments are made for calibre of personnel, complexity, and other factors. Over 100 factors are identified by Doty (3). Of these, 42 were judged to be significant, and data were found enabling 29 to be quantified. Some traditional methods of estimating are:

- Experience method
- Constraint method
- Top-down estimating
- Similarities and differences estimating
- Analogy method
- Ratio estimating
- Standards estimating
- Bottom-up estimating
- Percent of hardware estimating

However, the traditional methods have often led to unsatisfactory results. Doty (3) reported that most of the errors result from underestimates of size, sometimes by an factor of three. It was further reported that size errors could be greater than 200 percent at the user requirement specification, 100 percent at the functional specification, 75 percent at the high level design, and 50 percent through the remainder of the development.

18.2.2 Macro-estimating

The traditional methods were based on the assumptions that the development process is linear and static. Norden (4) and Putnam (5) put forward that the software development process is curvilinear in its fundamental relationships and also possesses a random character. Thus probability theory and statistical laws may be used. It means that rates, effort, time, and product cannot be measured with great precision because these quantities are always fluctuating about some average which may be changing with time. So it is necessary to work with averages of the quantities and a measure of the variability of the quantities, i.e. standard deviation.

Norden(4) and Putnam (5) use a dynamic life cycle pattern based on the Rayleigh curve. Each has found the patterns from many projects fitted the Rayleigh curve within the 'noise' of the process. These patterns were mainly for large software projects. As is to be expected from a statistical approach the correlation reduces as the system size reduces which means that a certain amount of interpretation is necessary when applying these techniques in a quantitative manner to microprocessor systems.

However they can certainly be used in a qualitative way to highlight certain important relationships. The life cycle approach is a macroscopic, strategic methodology dealing with the aggregate behaviour of systems. It is not designed to estimate the parameters of individual small programs or the work of individual programmers. As a general guide the life cycle approach may be used whenever two or more of the following criteria apply:

18.2.2.1 The system size is 5000 instructions or more.

18.2.2.2 The project duration is six months or longer.

18.2.2.3 Three or more people will be used concurrently on the project.

18.3 LIFECYCLE

Norden (4) established from a large body of empirical evidence that there are regular patterns of manpower build-up and phase-out in complex projects. This life cycle pattern follows the distribution formulated by Lord Rayleigh to describe other phenomena. Norden uses the model to describe the quantitative behaviour of complex projects. Putnam's (5) contribution was to apply this model, which he refers to as the Norden/Rayleigh model, to software development. Putnam examined data from a large number of systems and found a good correlation with the model, in many cases 0.95 or better. Fig.18.1 shows both the integral and derivative forms of the normalized (K=1) Norden/Rayleigh model.

The derivative form, which is the current manpower utilization is represented by

$$dy/dt = 2\,Kate^{-at^2} \quad \text{percent effort/time}$$

where dy/dt = manpower utilized each time period
K = total cumulative manpower utilized by the end of the project
a = shape parameter
t = elapsed time from start

As each of the parameters K and a can have a range of values, the Norden/Rayleigh equation may have a wide variety of shapes and magnitudes. These are shown in Fig. 18.2.
The shape parameter $a = 1/2t_d^{\,2}$, where t_d is the time at which the curve reaches a maximum, governs the time taken to the project and can be thought of as a measure of the importance of the project. Some interesting conclusions may be drawn from this curve. Firstly it shows that a project does not start fullblown. The manpower builds up at a rate determined by the shape parameter a.

A high value of a giving a sharply peaked curve corresponds to a crash project. Smaller values of a giving shallower curves are associated with stretched-out projects.

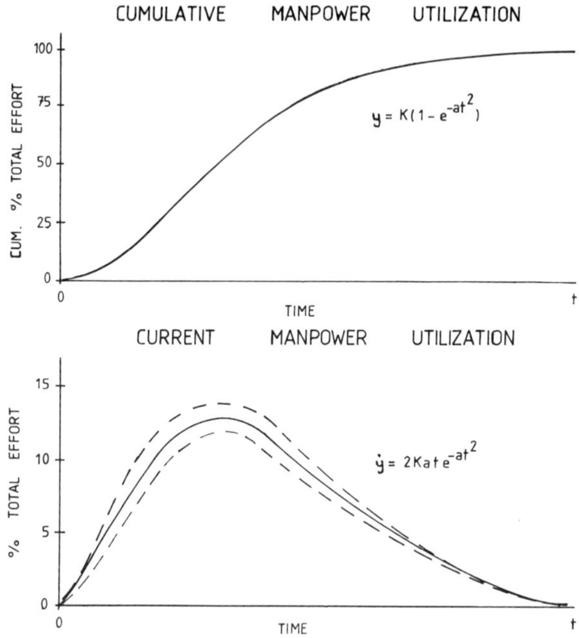

Fig. 18.1 Manpower Utilization

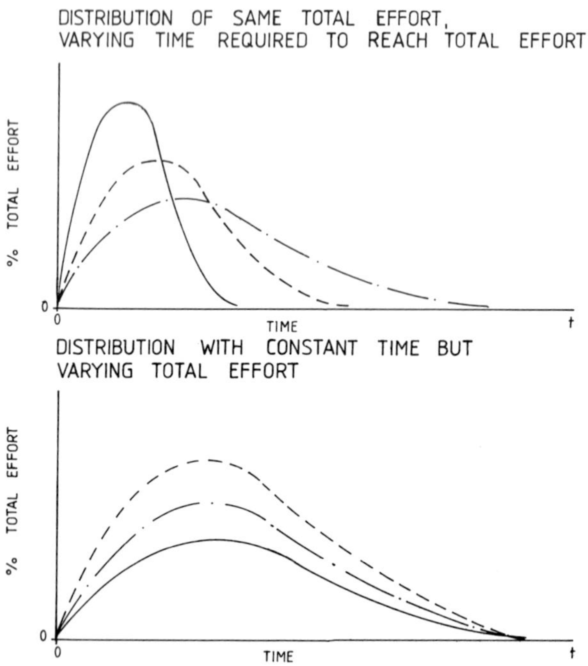

Fig. 18.2 Manpower Utilization Distribution Curves

The curve of Fig. 18.1, where a = 0.02, represents a buildup rate to peak manpower averaging about 20% per annum. If a is increased to approx 0.05 the buildup rate now averages about 30% per annum. There is a limit to the rate of manpower buildup beyond which the evolution of the project structure and communication pathways will be inhibited and thus limit the magnitude of the shape parameter. Myers (6) sets this limit at about 30% per annum.

The second point is the long tail to the curve which supports the view that percentage completion is a meaningless concept in software projects, i.e a project remains nearly complete for a very long time.

The integral form of the Norden/Rayleigh equation, which is the cumulative manpower utilization, is represented by

$$y = K(1-e^{-at^2})$$

From this equation it will be seen that about 90% of the work is accomplished in about two-thirds of the development time. This is why software work tends to perch at about 90% complete for an interminable time. In the real world where requirements are never finaly fixed and changes to specifications are occurring, K and t_d are not completely fixed or deterministic. Also management may not be responding perfectly to cues from the project for personnel, time, or technical support. Thus the system has random or stochastic components superimposed on the deterministic behaviour.

This could be described as 'noise' and is illustrated by the dotted lines in Fig. 18.1.

18.4 DIFFICULTY AND FEASIBILITY

The Norden/Rayleigh equation may be rewritten substituting $1/2t_d^2$ for a which gives

$$dy/dt = \frac{K}{t_d^2}.t.e^{-t^2/2t_d^2}$$

The factor modifying the variable t is K/t_d^2, which on any given project is constant.

It may be seen as an expression for difficulty D and supports the intuitive feeling that the larger a project the more difficult it will be to accomplish. Increasing project size involves more levels of management, greater problems of communication, and geometrically increasing communications relationships. Brooks (2) points out that n workers generate n(n-1)/2 interfaces.

It also seems reasonable that the shorter the development time, the greater the difficulty. More work, relationships, and communications have to be packed into less time.

Data examined by Myers (6) and Putnam (5) show that if programming rate, i.e. productivity, is plotted against difficulty D on a log-log plot, there is a straight line relationship.

Additional evidence indicated that the situation is more complex and that there is a family of parallel straight lines as shown in Fig. 18.3. The difference in constants is caused by different environments and standards, and the number of systems which would be installed.

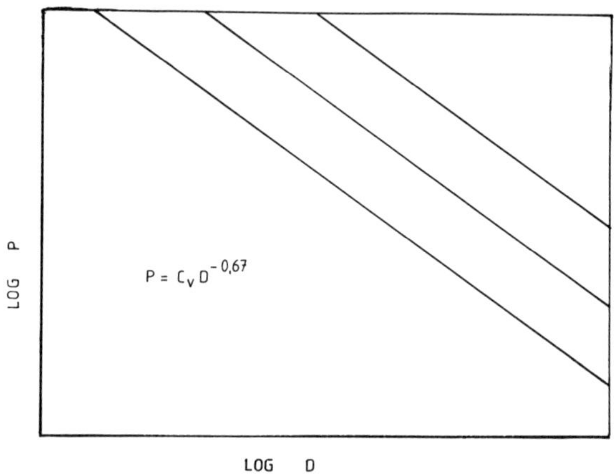

Fig.18.3 Productivity vs. Difficulty (Log-Log Plot)

Development feasibility depends upon the interaction of the three parameters, difficulty D, development time t_d, and size K.

In practice there is not an indefinite range of these parameters. The time region is constrained at the minimum end by the maximum buildup rate which is possible, and at the other end by the economic viewpoint. There is a development time beyond which a system is no longer of interest. When the feasible region is portrayed in three dimensions by introducing the difficulty $D = K/t_d^2$ as a third dimension, it can be represented as a difficulty surface, see Fig. 18.4. It will be seen that the difficulty increases dramatically as the development time is shortened. Systems tend to fall on a set of lines which are the trace of a constant magnitude of difficulty gradient.

Each line is a characteristic of skill to do a certain class of work.

The rate of change of difficulty can be studied by taking the gradient of D. The unit vector i points in the t_d direction. The unit vector j points in the K direction. Grad D points almost completely in the $-i(-t_d)$ direction. The significance of this fact is that shortening the development time, e.g. by management edict, dramatically increases the difficulty, usually to an impossible level.

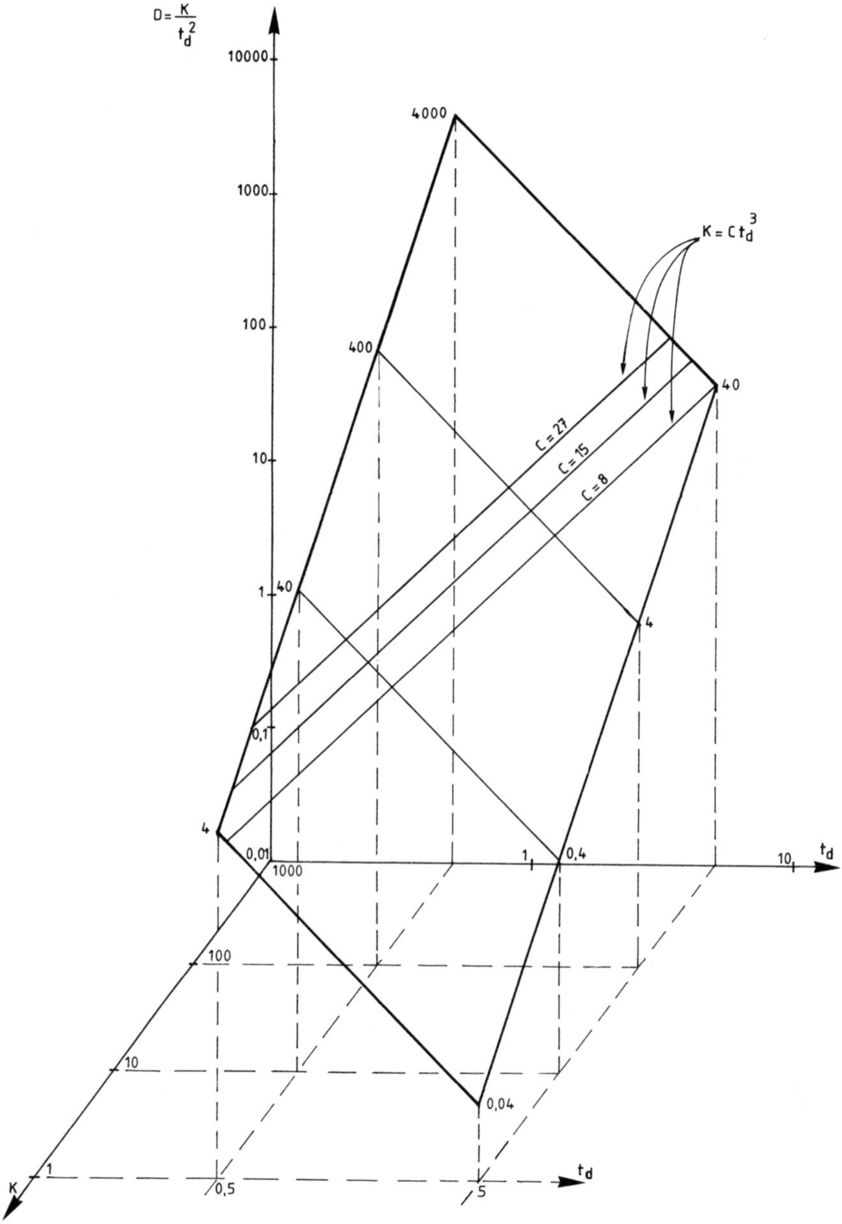

Fig.18.4 Difficulty surface

The expression for grad D is

$$\text{grad } D = \frac{-2K}{t_d^3}.i + \frac{1}{t_d^2}.j$$

The magnitude of the i component is of the form K/t_d^3. This is the major component and points in the negative $i(t_d)$ direction. The trace of all such points is a line $K = Ct_d^3$. Such a line appears to be measure of skill and seems to be the maximum difficulty gradient that a software organisation is capable of accomplishing. As the system size is increased, the development time will also increase so as to remain on a line of constant magnitude of gradient defined by $K/t_d^3 = C$.

A study of all US Army Computer Command systems by Putnam (5) gave the following:

18.4.1 If the system is entirely new, and has many interfaces with other systems, then C is approximately = 8.

18.4.2 If the system is a new stand-alone system then C is approximately = 15.

18.4.3 If the system is a rebuild, or a composite built up from large parts of existing logic and code, then C is approximately = 27.

Two aspects of software development difficulty have been separated out and expressed in terms of Rayleigh parameters. One is the difficulty of the work itself, $D = K/t_d^2$.
The other characterizes the skill level of the software organisation in doing the class of work for which the constant was derived, $C = K/t_d^3$.

18.5 THE SOFTWARE EQUATION

Using the Norden/Rayleigh equation, a relationship has been established between the management parameters K and t_d and the instantaneous and cumulative effort at any time t.

However it is necessary to have a relationship between K, t_d and the product, i.e. the total quantity of source code. This may be achieved by using the empirical relation between productivity P and difficulty D already discussed and shown in Fig.18.3.

Let S = product = total number of statements

$S = \int \dot{S}.dt$

where S = source statements per unit time

$S = \int P.\dot{y}_1.dt$

where p = source statements per unit man-time, e.g. man-month

$\dot{y}$ = men at time t

$$= \frac{K}{t_d^2}.t.e^{-3t^2/t_d^2}$$

the equation for $\dot{y}$ is derived from the Norden/Rayleigh system equation and represents the design and coding part of the work modified to take into account overheads. It is achieved by substituting a term $t_o = t_d/\sqrt{6}$.

Continuing the main development

$$S = P\int \dot{y}_1.dt$$
$$= P.\frac{K}{6}$$

The empirical relationship between P and D has been discussed and shown in Fig.18.3.

It is expressed as

$$P = C_n D^{-2/3}$$

$$\text{therefore } S = C_n \left(\frac{K}{t_d^2}\right)^{-2/3} .\frac{K}{6}$$

$$= C_n K^{1/3} t_d^{4/3}$$

A reasonable relation linking the output (S) to the input (K, t_d) and a constant (C_n) has now been found.

The constant C_n may be seen as a technology constant and is a measure of a number of conditions including:

The state of the technology being applied to the software development.

The environment in which the development takes place.

The development equipment available.

The methodology and programming practices applied.

18.6 PRODUCTIVITY

18.6.1 The Effort-Time Tradeoff Law

The software equation may be transformed into an

expression for productivity.

$S = C_n K^{1/3} t_d^{4/3}$, the software equation transforms into the productivity definition

$$P = \frac{S}{E} = \frac{C_n K^{1/3} t_d^{4/3}}{E}$$

where E is an empirical factor equal to 0.4K

$$\text{therefore } P = \frac{C_n \; (E/0.4)^{1/3} t_d^{4/3}}{E}$$

$$= 1.36 C_n \frac{t_d^{4/3}}{E^{2/3}}$$

This means that to increase productivity it is necessary to:

increase the state of technology

increase the development time

decrease the development effort

Another way of looking at this is that a system size of a certain number of source statements implies $K.t_d^4$ constant. The high power of t_d emphasizes the time sensitivity of projects.

It should be remembered that the development time is only compressible down to a value corresponding to the maximum buildup rate. From the foregoing the effort-time tradeoff law is:

development effort = constant/t_d^4

18.6.2 Effect of Constant Productivity

Another relation worth considering is where average productivity remains constant.

$P = C_n D^{-2/3}$ = constant implies that

D = constant.

So the productivity for different projects will be the same only if the difficulty is the same.

It is not reasonable to expect this very often as the difficulty is a measure of the software work to be done, i.e. a function of the number of files, the number of reports and the number of programs. Thus, planning a new project based on using the same productivity as a previous project is fallacious unless the difficulty is the same.

The significance for an individual system is that the difficulty is a function of the system characteristics. If these are changed during development, e.g. the number of files, reports and sub-programs, then the difficulty will change and so will the average productivity.

This in turn will affect the instaneous rate of code production ($\dot{S}$) which has both parameter terms and time-varying terms.

18.6.3 Communication Channel Analogy

Software development may be viewed as a communication process. As such it should be subject to Shannon's expression for the capacity of a communication channel. The derivation summarized here shows that the signal-to-noise ratio of the software development channel varies exponentially with t_d.

The Shannon expression is

$$\bar{\dot{C}} = B \log_2(1+S/N) \text{ bits/second.}$$

The bandwidth for a software system is

$$B = 0.6/t_d \quad \text{where } t_d \text{ is in seconds.}$$

therefore

$$S/N = 2^{1.6\, \bar{\dot{C}}\, t_d} - 1$$

For a given system, $\bar{\dot{C}}$ is fixed, therefore

$$S/N \sim 2^{t_d}, \quad N/S \sim 2^{-t_d}$$

In the Shannon expression:

C is the maximum information transfer rate (maximum flow rate or entropy rate) measured in bits/second.

B is the system bandwidth

S/N is the signal-to-noise power ratio.

Thus, increasing the channel bandwidth increases the channel capacity, as does reducing the noise. In software development, the average flow rate over the development period may be expressed as source statements over development time: S/t_d.

The instantaneous flow rate is expressed as dS/dt and is proportional to the analyst-programmer manpower curve, represented by $\dot{y}_1$.

These relationships may be summarized as follows:

$$\dot{S} = dS/dt = P.\dot{y}_1 = P\ (K/t_d^{\,2}.t.e^{-3t^2/t_d^{\,2}})$$

source statements per unit time.

This instaneous flow rate reaches its maximum at $t_d / \sqrt{6}$, or at approximately 42% of the development time.

In terms of the parameter variations, the greatest average flow rate, (S/t_d) max, occurs at the minimum development time for the class of systems under consideration. A class is defined by its difficulty gradient.

Operating at the minimum development time requires the greatest effective expenditure of effort. At this point the signal-to-noise ratio is at the cutoff threshold, it is as low as it can be and still allow progress. If the development time is arbitrarily shortened below this minimum, then progress can no longer be made. A below threshold signal-to-noise ratio generates more 'noise' than the system can tolerate. In a communications system, the message no longer gets through. In a software system, the 'noise' takes the form of human intercommunication problems, and the work no longer gets done at the rate necessary to finish the development in the 'minimum' development time.

On the other hand, taking a little longer reduces the average flow rate a little, but the signal-to-noise ratio improves exponentially. The software difficulty gradient is analogous to the bandwidth limitation in communications theory. Where in software development the gradient acted as a data limitation, by analogy it appears to be a theoretical limitation that is well understood in other contexts.

The signal-to-noise power ratio is analogous in software development to the quality and efficiency of the software building process. Bandwidth is by definition the inverse of the applicable time metric, in this case t_d. Mathematical derivation gives a software bandwidth of $1/1.6t_d$.

In this concept modern software engineering techniques may be seen as noise reduction techniques.

18.7 SIZING

During the early user requirement specification phase, a broad estimate of system size is required to establish economic feasibility.

At this point no hard data is available regarding the system as no design has been done. Therefore all that can be done is to make an intelligent guess as to the range of size of the system, based on past experience and what little is known about it.

Letting a equal the lowest possible number of source statements, and b equal the highest possible number of source statements, the expected size and standard deviation may be determined.

Putnam and Fitzsimmons (7) give an example of the successively improving estimation of a project as its design progresses.

At the beginning of user requirement specification the size is broadly estimated to be between 50,000 and 140,000 statements.
The size is S = (a+b)/2 = 190,000/2 = 95,000
and the standard deviation is:

$$\sigma S = (b-a)/6 = 15,000$$

The expected size is:

$$95,000 \pm 15,000$$

Towards the beginning of the high level design the major subsystems will be known. At this point a Delphi polling of the members of the project team who have worked on the functional specification should be carried out. To a and b is added m, the most likely size. Averages of these values are used to calculate the expected size and standard deviation. An estimate of the expected value is given by:

$$S = (a+4m+b)/6$$

The results at this stage is given by Table 1.

Function	Smallest	Most likely	Largest	S	Std.Dev.
File handlers	25000	40000	70000	42500	7500
Utilities	5000	15000	26000	15200	3500
System Procs.	12000	36000	50000	34300	6300
				92000	10300

Table 1.

At the end of the high level design the system is reasonably well defined, and the statistical process is repeated. See Table 2.

Function	Smallest	Most likely	Largest	S	Std.Dev.
Maint	8675	13375	18625	13467	1658
Search	5577	8988	13125	9109	1258
Route	3160	3892	8800	4588	940
Status	850	1425	2925	1579	346
Browse	1875	4052	8250	4389	1063
Print	1437	2455	6125	2897	781
Aids	6875	10625	16250	10938	1563
Inc Msg	5830	8962	17750	9905	1987
Sys Mon	9375	14625	28000	15979	3104
Sys Mgr	6300	13700	36250	16225	4992
Com Proc.	5875	8975	14625	9400	1458
				98475	7081

Table 2.

18.8 CONCLUSION

The conclusion to be drawn from this empirical treatment of a very difficult and important subject may be condensed into the following axioms:

18.8.1 Software development has a characteristic behaviour.

18.8.2 Software development is dynamic, not static.

18.8.3 Productivity and coding rates are continuously varying, not constant.

18.8.4 Productivity rates are a function of system difficulty. They cannot be arbitrarily increased. They can be favourably influenced by providing sufficient time.

18.8.5 Software development is very time-sensitive. There is a minimum time to do any software job and it cannot be violated.

18.8.6 Time and manpower are not freely interchangeable.

18.8.7 Keep a record of what happened. It will help with future projects.

REFERENCES

1. Sommerville, I., 1982,
'Software Engineering', Addison-Wesley,
Reading, MA, USA.

2. Brooks, F.P., 1975,
'The Mythical Man-month', Addison-Wesley,
Reading, MA, USA.

3. Doty, D.L., et al, 1977,
'Software Cost Estimation Study',
Doty Associates Inc., Rome Air Development Centre,
Italy.

4. Norden, P.V., 1963,
'Operations Research in Research and Development',
John Wiley & Sons, Inc., New York, USA.

5. Putnam, L.H., 1978,
IEEE Trans. Software Eng., 7, 141 - 157.

6. Myers, W., 1978, Computer, 12, 128-140.

7. Putnam, L.H., and Fitzsimmons, A.,
Datamation, 9, 312-315.

Index